W. Dilthey
Selected Writings

W. Dilthey
Selected Writings

edited, translated and introduced by
H. P. RICKMAN
Reader in Philosophy
The City University, London

CAMBRIDGE UNIVERSITY PRESS

CAMBRIDGE

LONDON · NEW YORK · MELBOURNE

Published by the Syndics of the Cambridge University Press
The Pitt Building, Trumpington Street, Cambridge CB2 1RP
Bentley House, 200 Euston Road, London NW1 2DB
32 East 57th Street, New York, NY10022, USA
296 Beaconsfield Parade, Middle Park, Melbourne 3206, Australia

Library of Congress catalogue card number: 75–23530

ISBN: 0 521 20966 8

First published 1976

Printed in Great Britain
at the
University Printing House, Cambridge
(Euan Phillips, University Printer)

Contents

Introduction

The aim of this book is to present a more comprehensive and representative selection of Dilthey's work than has been available in English so far.[1] It should be of interest not only to philosophers but also to students of literature, history, psychology and sociology; indeed, to all those who are concerned with the wider implications of their disciplines. They will find that Dilthey's epistemology and methodology of the human studies and the philosophy of life in which they are embedded have a direct bearing on contemporary debates about the theories and methods of all the studies concerned with man. In this introduction I have, therefore, outlined Dilthey's main theories, for the benefit of those who have not read him before, and tried to stress their contemporary relevance.

1. *The importance of Dilthey*

Dilthey's role as a major German philosopher who exercised a powerful influence on intellectual life should be studied by students of the history of ideas. In the English-speaking world he has received less than his due because – ironically – what makes him important, namely the large body of his writings and the width of his interests,[2] is an obstacle to presenting his main ideas concisely. Many of Germany's most influential thinkers were themselves influenced by him – Husserl, the founder of Phenomenology, Heidegger and Jaspers, the originators of modern Existentialism, the philosopher and psychologist E. Spranger[3] and, last but not least, Max Weber.[4] So reference to Dilthey's work can help us to understand many ideas we encounter in contemporary philosophy, psychology or sociology.

The reputation Dilthey enjoyed in his lifetime was consolidated and greatly increased after his death when a group of his most devoted disciples – men such as G. Misch,[5] H. Nohl and B. Groethuysen – published his collected works. This edition began to appear in the twenties and originally consisted of eleven large volumes which included previously published writings and manuscripts, particularly from his last years. In the 1930s and early 1940s the success of

[1] See Bibliography, 'Dilthey's work in translation'.
[2] See Bibliography, 'Dilthey's writings'.
[3] See Bibliography, 'Secondary literature'.
[4] See Bibliography, 'Secondary literature'.
[5] See Bibliography, 'Secondary literature'.

Introduction

Heidegger's more flamboyant philosophy and National Socialism's lack of sympathy for so liberal and internationally minded a thinker, overshadowed interest in Dilthey's work; it revived powerfully after the war. As the grimly melodramatic and oracularly phrased philosophy of Existentialism lost its appeal Dilthey's tolerant humanism, his urbane, undogmatic and even tentative approach re-emerged as an attractive alternative. A spate of new monographs about his work has appeared and his collected works – long out of print – have not only been re-issued but augmented – a significant testimony to his renewed importance. Twenty volumes have now appeared and a group of German scholars is still working on unpublished lecture notes, letters and manuscripts.

2. Dilthey's life

Dilthey's life was that of a respectable and successful academic and there is nothing spectacular about it except his single-minded devotion to scholarship. He was born in 1831 in the village of Biebrich (in the Rhineland), grew up there and went to secondary school in Wiesbaden. His father, like several other members of his family, was a protestant clergyman and when the young Dilthey went to Heidelberg University in 1852 it was with the intention of studying theology. When, a year later, he moved to Berlin he gradually became more interested in history and philosophy and decided on an academic career. Because of the width of his interests and his painstaking thoroughness he was in his early thirties before he qualified for his doctorate and, almost simultaneously, for the right to teach at a university (the latter is called habilitation and is based on the submission of a thesis). Though he had supplemented his income by school teaching – which he disliked – and by journalism, he had remained in rather straitened circumstances and was partly dependent on help from his parents. But he had already achieved a scholarly reputation and was appointed to a chair of philosophy at Basle in 1867. Professorships at Kiel and Breslau followed until he went to Berlin in 1882 to occupy – until 1905 – the chair which Hegel had once held. He married late in life and had a son and a daughter who married his disciple, the distinguished philosopher, G. Misch. Berlin remained Dilthey's home though he actually died on a holiday to the Tyrol in 1911.

We are given a lively picture of his early years in a selection of his letters and diaries made by his daughter Clara Misch.[6] We see him there as an extremely serious young man who spent endless hours over

[6] *Der junge Dilthey* (Göttingen, 1933).

his books and wrote affectionately and at length to his parents. He wrote equally affectionately but sometimes didactically to his brother and also corresponded with other members of his family and a large circle of friends, revealing the development of his interests and his struggles to establish himself in his chosen career. Even his relaxation was not exactly frivolous; for example he might join a party which read Greek plays.

Few personal details of his later life are available in print but the picture may be filled in by the continuing work on the Dilthey archives which is likely to produce further selections from his letters.

3. *Cultural and intellectual background*

The fifty or sixty years before Dilthey's birth had been one of the most exciting and formative periods of German intellectual life. Kant's Critiques had appeared during the last decades of the eighteenth century and had been followed by the works of Fichte, Schelling, Hegel, Schleiermacher and Schopenhauer. Lessing, Goethe and Schiller had established what came to be known as the classic tradition of German literature and been succeeded by the Romantic movement led by the Schlegels, Tieck and Novalis.

Dilthey grew up in and was influenced by this intellectual climate. All his life he examined and evaluated its varied ingredients and tried to combine them into a philosophy of his own. He was asked to edit some of Schleiermacher's papers[7] and developed an abiding interest in his work. From him Dilthey derived the hermeneutic method and the emphasis on personal experience by means of which Schleiermacher had revolutionized theology. He admired and examined Goethe's receptiveness to experience and intuitive method. From Kant he derived the model for his epistemology and from Hegel the concept of reality as a process of historical change and the idea of *Geist* (spirit or mind) which, as we shall see, he adapted to his own use. He shared with the Romantics an interest in the past, and the creative imagination, and a belief in the uniqueness of individuals.

To these influences must be added that of Spinoza, whom he studied thoroughly when he found that his work had affected the thinking of Schleiermacher as well as that of Goethe, Hegel and the Romantics. His original interest in theology led Dilthey to a study of the Christian thinkers of late antiquity and he drew on this knowledge in his account of the history of hermeneutics. Indeed the difficulties he encountered in grappling with these thinkers, who were not congenial to him,

[7] See p. 45.

prompted him to think about the problems of historical understanding.

The period before Dilthey's birth had been decisive for Germany
politically as well as culturally. After the Napoleonic wars, in which a
fragmented Germany had been humiliated, a reformed and dynamic
Prussia emerged as the most powerful of the German states and
eventually – in Dilthey's lifetime – unified Germany. Dilthey was
greatly interested in this development and applied his energies to
exploring the rise of Prussia and the Prussian spirit. He wrote about
Frederick II, the original architect of Prussia's greatness, the founding
of the Prussian Academy of Science, Prussian law and men like Stein
and Gneisenau, who inspired Prussia's regeneration.[8] It was to the
Prussian, Bismarck, that he referred whenever he wanted to discuss
statesmanship and the use of political power.

Dilthey also responded to contemporary intellectual developments.
He was particularly sympathetic towards the so-called historical school
of which Ranke is the most famous representative (other names will be
found in the texts) and considered it part of his mission to provide it
with philosophic foundations.[9] At that time psychology and sociology
were gradually becoming independent disciplines which attracted his
interest; he studied and commented on the works of Fechner and
Wundt, Comte and Spencer. He took issue with Nietzsche[10] and
philosophically orientated writers like Maeterlinck[11] and engaged in
polemics with Neo-Kantians like Windelband and Rickert[12] who
shared his interest in the epistemology and methodology of the human
studies. In his last writings he was influenced by Husserl whom he, in
turn, affected.

Though it was natural that his outlook should have been shaped
mainly by the intellectual traditions of his own country and that he
should be particularly interested in its history, his astonishingly broad
scholarship was not confined to the German world. Besides German
historians like Ranke, Niebuhr and Mommsen he also discussed
Herodotus, Thucydides and Polybius, Machiavelli, Voltaire, Macaulay
and Carlyle. Not only did he write about Goethe,[13] Schiller[14] and the
German Romantics,[14] he was also interested in Calderon and
Cervantes,[15] Corneille and Molière,[15] Marlowe,[15] Shakespeare[15] and

---

[8] See Bibliography, 'Dilthey's writings', esp. Vol. xii.   [9] See p. 160.
[10] See pp. 116–18ff.   [11] See pp. 116ff.
[12] W. Windelband's *Geschichte und Naturwissenschaft* (Strassburg, 1894) and
H. Rickert's *Die Grenzen der naturwissenschaftlichen Begriffsbildung* (Tübingen, 1896)
present a distinction between the sciences and the human studies which differs from
Dilthey's.   [13] See pp. 54–64 and 99–103.
[14] See Bibliography, 'Dilthey's writings'.   [15] See pp. 79–84.

Dickens.[16] He was familiar with the British tradition of philosophy and considered J. S. Mill's approach to the moral sciences critically, though not without sympathy.

His philosophy is thus made up of many threads, but is not eclectic. He tried to preserve, develop and combine into a coherent whole what he considered worthwhile in a rich and varied tradition. From his struggles to come to terms with, and assess, the disparate ideas he encountered there emerged a distinctive point of view.

4. *The study of man*

The central aim of Dilthey's long working life was to gain knowledge of the human world, the social-historical reality, as he often called it. All his particular undertakings – his massive Schleiermacher biography and shorter biographical sketches, his literary and historical studies, his work on education, music and law – were intended to be parts of more comprehensive studies of German culture, of the basis of individuality or of the history of the human studies. Ultimately they were all to contribute to a general understanding of man. But while he pursued knowledge about, for example, the influence of Hegel's theological background on his philosophy[17] or the development of choral music in protestant church services[18] he also reflected on the methods required for gaining such knowledge and the principles which justify them. The remarkable and important thing about Dilthey is that he was both a practising historian of ideas and a philosopher.

Dilthey's attempt to construct a broad theoretical framework for the objective study of man is his most original achievement. Like other nineteenth-century thinkers he turned his attention to the social sciences because disciplines like psychology, sociology, economics and social anthropology had just begun to develop into independent fields of study with methods of their own. Clarification of their scope and status was needed. Could they use the successful methods of the physical sciences in spite of the difference between physical and social processes or were different methods necessary? Could bias be avoided when dealing with human ideals and beliefs? What conditions were important for valid and objective knowledge of the human world?

Problems such as these are still very much with us, and we still lack a common framework and agreed methods. Some pieces of research are trivial while others are based on unconvincing evidence. There is indeed something to the often heard criticism that what is known with

[16] See Bibliography, 'Dilthey's writings'.
[17] *Der Junge Hegel*; see list of contents of *Collected Works*.
[18] See *Von Deutscher Dichtung und Musik* (Dilthey's Writings).

reasonable certainty in the social sciences is not interesting and what is interesting not known with reasonable certainty. This is why Dilthey's more comprehensive approach is relevant today.

His theories are based on his recognition that the human world, with which the social sciences deal, differs significantly from the physical world which is the subject-matter of such sciences as physics, chemistry or biology. Human beings, unlike stones and trees, or even insects and guinea-pigs, reflect on what they do. They interpret the situations they are in, set themselves deliberate aims and plan for the future, communicate with each other, adopt conventions and follow traditions; we cannot study man without taking these into account. To this we must add that in the human disciplines men study themselves and their fellows. They bring an immediacy of insight to the study of the human world but are also exposed to the danger of prejudice.

All this is resoundingly obvious and only needs saying because certain social scientists, for example the behaviourists, have sought scientific respectability by deliberately denying or absent-mindedly ignoring these palpable facts. As a result they distort their subject-matter and are unable to take advantage of the opportunities it offers or avoid its pitfalls.

5. *Dilthey's methodology*

Dilthey believed that to be scientific – by which he meant working towards objective, well-tested knowledge – one must adjust one's methods to the subject-matter.[19] So his methodology – not to be confused with the research techniques which may follow from it – maps out the fundamental approach he thought necessary for the comprehension of the human world. It is implied in all his work and often referred to explicitly. Here are its salient features.

1. We must start our investigations with painstaking descriptions and careful analyses of the most complex phenomena we encounter; these include the mental processes of mature, cultured personalities, the imagination of poetic geniuses, the strong will of great statesmen, the functioning of elaborate cultural systems or sophisticated social organizations, the structure of rich languages and systematic philosophies.[20]

Dilthey thus rejected the analytical or brick-and-mortar approach which starts from simple elements and attempts to reconstruct more complex entities from them. He believed that human life as we know it cannot be accounted for by a hypothetical combination of elementary

[19] See below, p. 89.   [20] See pp. 91, 93, 227.

responses, instincts observed in animals or children, and artificially elicited laboratory responses.

Complex structures can, and should, be analysed so as to reveal the elements they consist of but, if we begin with these, we cannot easily recapture the richness of experience which gives human life its distinctive qualities. For this reason Dilthey advocated and illustrated in his own work the use of autobiographies, literary works, letters and diaries as suitable material for research.

2. Social-historical reality consists of individual human beings for they alone think, feel and act and so produce languages, religions and institutions.[21] Dilthey was convinced that such mysterious entities as the collective mind, the common will or a national spirit have no real, independent existence. This conviction did not convert him to methodological individualism (i.e. he did not believe that the individual was the only subject-matter of the social sciences).[22] He considered that to reduce all social and cultural phenomena to the activities of individuals was methodologically impossible and believed that the *use* of various impersonal, theoretical entities was both necessary and justifiable. When people share beliefs and attitudes or act together to produce particular results and achieve a common purpose we can attribute ideas, policies or actions to classes, nations and associations. We can speak of the decisions of committees and the spirit of an age.

Particularly important in this context are the entities which make up the cultural and intellectual heritage of mankind – languages, religions, works of literature, ideologies and codes of law. Though these are the products of individual minds working together they can and sometimes have to be studied without reference to individual authors. There are innumerable cases where it is best to think of these entities as independent forces confronting and influencing individuals so that – and this is the crucial point – the individual's behaviour can only be explained in terms of these entities. 'X. is the product of the English educational system', 'Y's activity was influenced by Marxist ideology' are obvious examples. Dilthey insisted that this sphere, which he called the world of mind, or objectified mind, can be studied directly and is vital to the understanding of human behaviour.[23]

3. The different human disciplines deal with the various aspects of the human world which are singled out by the questions each discipline asks and the methods it uses. This means that the disciplines are

[21] See below, pp. 197, 201–2, 224.
[22] A detailed discussion of methodological individualism is to be found in *Modes of Individualism and Collectivism*, ed. J. O'Neil, London, 1974.
[23] See below, pp. 191–3 and 224.

interdependent and once we understand the nature of this interdependence a strategy of inter-disciplinary co-operation becomes possible. This, in turn, can promote a fuller understanding of man and the solution of particular practical problems. Delinquency, for example, is not just an economic, psychological or sociological problem but has economic, psychological and sociological ramifications which must be co-ordinated.

This interdependence has many aspects. For instance, historial material is needed by sociologists and economists and, in the form of case studies, by the psychologist, while the historian, in turn, can only understand the connection between particular events in terms of the psychologist's or sociologist's generalizations.[24] This point is well worth making at a time of extreme specialization. Dilthey would have considered it a scandal that there should be psychological theories which have nothing whatsoever to offer to a historian or economist.[25]

4. To think of the subject-matter of the human studies as 'behaviour' and call the disciplines concerned with man 'behavioural studies' is misleading, because it suggests that psychology or sociology should be content to deal with the observable movements of human bodies in just the same way as physics may be said to deal with the behaviour of gases and metals. It is more illuminating, as Dilthey urged, to treat human activity as meaningful and capable of communicating meaning.[26] Human beings are unique in their tendency to reflect and comment on their actions. They also convey meaning – i.e. what they think or feel or want – by gestures and actions. A proper study of mankind must emphasize, not obliterate, these features.

Dilthey called the whole range of 'behaviour', which manifests mental states, 'expressions'. These – ranging from smiles to pamphlets, from doodles to purposive actions – are the material the human studies must deal with. So it is especially necessary to classify expressions and assess the value and drawbacks of different types – such as facial expressions, posture, literary works or questionnaire responses. The methods most appropriate for studying each type must also be discussed.[27]

There have been many developments in the systematic use and evaluation of expressions in such spheres as personality assessment and psychiatric diagnosis, for example the Rorschach or Thematic

---

[24] See pp. 171, 187–90, 202, 205.

[25] See below, pp. 89–90.

[26] Compare with M. Weber's approach and the schools of sociology which focus on 'action'.

[27] See below, pp. 219–20.

Apperception tests,[28] psycho-drama[29] and Goffman's dramaturgical approach.[30] Freud's work provides a particularly good illustration because psycho-analysis is based on the inspired theory that some human behaviour not previously considered meaningful – mistakes, slips of memory or of the tongue, doodles, neurotic compulsions and hysterical symptoms – can be treated as expressions through which it is possible to understand the mental life of the people who produced them. At the same time Freud fails to disentangle himself from a conception of knowledge modelled on the physical sciences. Psycho-analytical interpretations, because they are not verifiable or falsifiable like the theories of the physical sciences, therefore seem scientifically disreputable. They may be seen in a different light if – as Dilthey suggests – criteria like those used by historians or literary critics are applied to them.

5. Dilthey called the process by which we comprehend the meaning of an expression (i.e. recapture the mental content conveyed by a physical manifestation) 'understanding'. So defined it must be treated as a technical term and the fact that the term, as commonly used, can stand for any type of comprehension, or, in a narrower sense, for sympathetic insight, is completely irrelevant. It has, however, side-tracked some critics.

Dilthey argued that understanding[31] differs significantly from other forms of knowing such as perceptual awareness. Because it is essential to human studies understanding must be assessed criticially and its methodology developed.

Dilthey's case can be succinctly illustrated by pursuing the analogy between understanding and perception. Both processes are taken for granted in everyday life; we perceive houses or cars and understand (as well as perceive) the smiles of friends or the signals of policemen. Both processes are fallible but also fundamental because we cannot correct mistakes by appealing to another form of cognition. We can only *look* again or try, once more, to *understand*. The methodology of the sciences tries to minimize error by indicating how the conditions of perception can be controlled and its results checked. The corresponding requirement of the human studies is a methodology of understanding and this Dilthey attempted.

6. Dilthey called the systematic co-ordination of elementary acts of understanding in order to comprehend the meaning of a complex,

[28] See for example, B. Klopfer and H. H. Davidson, *The Rorschach Technique*, New York, 1962. H. A. Murray: *Thematic Apperception Test* (Cambridge, Mass., 1943).

[29] See J. L. Moreno, *Psycho-drama* (New York, 1946).

[30] E. Goffman's *The Presentation of Self in Everyday Life* (Garden City, New York, 1959).   [31] See below, pp. 172, 176, 186–95, 218, 220–31, 248–9, 260–3.

permanent expression 'interpretation' and its methodology 'hermeneutics'.[32] It follows from his general approach that the methodology of interpretation was a crucial ingredient of the methodology of the human studies. (It must not – as I shall explain presently – be treated as *the* methodology of the human studies.)

When he gave hermeneutics its crucial role in the human studies Dilthey put forward his most original and fruitful methodological thesis, which may be formulated as follows. The study of the human world involves not only the extensive interpretation of texts and verbal utterances but also the treatment of many other social phenomena *as if* they were texts to be interpreted. In other words, investigating the human studies is frequently more like finding the meaning of a poem than like researching in physics or chemistry. Interpretation of literary (or of legal and theological) texts has – he added – as long and respectable a history as experimental science and, like the latter, aims at truth. Hermeneutics, long neglected or even disparaged by philosophy, must be re-established as a paradigm of legitimate cognition.

Dilthey's revival of the disipline of hermeneutics has exercised a considerable influence on the modern intellectual scene. Heidegger explicitly adopted a hermeneutic approach and so did his followers. Probably the most substantial exposition of hermeneutics, as interpreted by the school of Heidegger, is Gadamer's *Truth and Method* (1960). The hermeneutic approach has been adopted by theologians, literary critics and theoreticians of the social sciences, not only in Germany but also in Switzerland, Italy and America.[33]

7. The so-called 'hermeneutic circle'[34] is one important aspect of Dilthey's methodology. It arises in the understanding of complex wholes and their parts, because a whole can only be comprehended in terms of its parts while the latter acquire their proper meaning within the whole. Words and sentences are the most obvious example. We understand 'hand me my clubs' by grasping the meaning of the individual words; but we can only select the appropriate meaning of 'club' or discard the use of 'hand' as a noun when we have an idea of what the whole sentence means. In practice we solve this problem by a to-and-fro, or shuttlecock, movement, though in simple cases we are hardly aware of it. When we are confronted with more complex problems, for example understanding Plato's philosophy in terms of his individual dialogues and, at the same time, understanding the individual dialogues by reference to the over-all context of his thought,

[32] See pp. 228–31, 247–63.
[33] See in particular the works by Betti and Palmer listed in the Bibliography, 'Secondary literature'.   [34] See below, pp. 203, 259, 262.

this shuttlecock movement must become a matter of deliberate method. (This illustration is not chosen at random for it describes Schleiermacher's approach to the interpretation of Plato which Dilthey considered a major advance.)

The hermeneutic circle is so important because the part–whole relationship is, according to Dilthey, pervasive in the human world. Individuals are members of organizations which, in turn, are part of society. Instinctive drives, or mental images, have their place in a mental structure. So, to understand a person, we must consider the role which his imagination or reason plays in the structure of his mental life. Similarly, to interpret a culture we must treat it as a system in which art, literature and science are related to each other and in which each fulfils a function. This is why such concepts as system, structure and function have become key terms in the human studies.

Put negatively this principle means that there are no absolute starting-points, no self-evident, self-contained certainties on which we can build, because we always find ourselves in the middle of complex situations which we try to disentangle by making, then revising, provisional assumptions. This circularity – or perhaps one might call it a spiral approximation towards greater accuracy and knowledge – pervades our whole intellectual life. An outstanding example is the fact – already noted as crucially important for the human studies – that the thinking of individuals can only be understood by reference to the world of mind or the cultural sphere while comprehension of the latter involves knowing about the mental processes of individuals.[35] This is, of course, logically unsatisfactory; but the scientist, concerned mainly with relationships between the general and the particular rather than with the whole and its parts, is involved in an analogous circle. He can only have a general conception of what dogs are like by gaining knowledge of individual dogs, but could never recognize an animal as suitable for his study on dogs unless he had a general ideas of what a dog is.

6. *The human studies and the sciences*[36]

Because Dilthey pioneered and lovingly elaborated an approach to the human studies based on understanding and hermeneutics he has often been misunderstood as advocating this approach as a complete methodology superseding and excluding other methods. To set the record straight one must, first of all, eliminate an ambiguity in Dilthey's

[35] See below, p. 196.
[36] See particularly pp. 61, 164–7, 171–5, 177, 211.

use of the term *Geisteswissenschaften* which makes him responsible for some of these misapprehensions. Dilthey used this term – though with some misgivings as to its adequacy – as a translation of 'moral sciences', i.e. the human disciplines like history, sociology, jurisprudence, linguistics and literary criticism. But he also used *Geisteswissenschaften* – in contrast to the *Naturwissenschaften* which deal with matter – for the disciplines which deal with mind and its products. These are only accessible to understanding and require interpretation. If men were disembodied minds the studies of man would coincide with the studies of mind. Obviously this is not so, a fact which Dilthey recognized and stated emphatically. So *Geisteswissenschaft*, in the sense of the study of mind, can only be a part, though a crucial one, of the *Geisteswissenschaften* in the sense of the studies of man. This ambiguity has, in spite of Dilthey's warnings, led many commentators astray.

Dilthey was concerned with the whole human being who, for him, was a psycho-physical unit, a person. Mind and matter were merely convenient concepts arrived at by abstraction from the rich variety of experience. So, having differentiated the sciences from disciplines which deal with mind in terms of subject-matter, we must put them together again in the study of man. This was Dilthey's programme and he was passionately interested in the development of physiological psychology, man's place in the evolutionary scale and the role of the physical environment, all of which involve the use of scientific methods. This is obscured by the fact that Dilthey made no original contributions to these spheres, but it should be stressed that his theoretical framework can accommodate any kind of approach from ethnomethodology to physiological psychology.

7. *Dilthey's philosophy of science*

Dilthey's conception of understanding has so often been misconceived[37] (as a heuristic device, as an alternative method to science and the like) that a clarification may be useful. Understanding is as little a method or a heuristic device as perception. It is a mental process which is a necessary ingredient of the combination of intellectual operations by which we come to know anything in the world of mind. He did not treat understanding in isolation but in the context of a general theory of how systematic knowledge is acquired through research; this might be called a philosophy of science. Though mainly

---

[37] For discussion of various misunderstandings, see Rickman, *Understanding and the Human Studies*, pp. 24–6.

derived from, and applicable to, the social sciences, it also has a wider relevance.[38] A few points may suggest the outlines of this theory.

1. The acquisition of knowledge in any sphere – in everyday life, in physics, biology, history or psychology – always involves the use of a combination of the same intellectual procedures, comparing, generalizing, abstracting, classifying, arguing from analogy, framing hypotheses, deduction and induction.

2. Different disciplines, or groups of disciplines, have their own methods, intellectual operations and techniques. Quantification plays a crucial role in physics but not in jurisprudence, while understanding is necessary in the human studies but not in astronomy.

3. Some procedures or methods, peculiar to and originally developed in one discipline, can be profitably adopted by others. Dilthey mentions, for example, that the human studies derived the use of the comparative method from the biological sciences. When, in turn, today's biologists speak of a genetic code their approach must, surely, be indebted to linguistics.

4. Dilthey also contributed to the philosophy of science by clarifying the relationship between two forms of explanation. The first, widely considered to be the main job of science, is to account for the particular in terms of the general, i.e. as a case falling under a general law. The second form of explanation is that of hermeneutics which focuses on the relation between part and whole and deals only with particular, more or less complex entities.

But if one defines science and hermeneutics in this way one must add, as Dilthey did, that physics and chemistry are scientific and the social sciences hermeneutic according to the degree in which one approach or the other predominates. To study the relationships between parts of a whole, even within the human studies, we must refer to generalizations and laws. In astronomy, field theory and the new types of systems approach, science must deal with particular configurations and use, if not actual hermeneutics, at least the hermeneutic technique of relating parts within a whole. So here, too, we are not speaking of the different methods of different disciplines but of complementary intellectual *approaches* which vary in proportion according to the problems to be solved.

5. The abandonment of absolute starting-points and basic certainties implied by the theory of the hermeneutic circle applies to all knowledge. The simplest positivist distinction between sacred facts and the tentative theories based on them must be abandoned. We must decide what the facts are in terms of our theoretical frame of reference

---

[38] See P. Krausser, *Kritik der endlichen Vernunft*, Frankfurt, 1968.

just as we modify our theories in the light of the facts. The whole process of coming to know reality, whether in the sciences or the human studies, becomes more and more a question of accommodation between putative facts and hypothetical theories. So the limited intellect gains more insight but never reaches the goal of absolute knowledge.

In attributing this theory to Dilthey I am interpreting the tendency of his arguments. He was not entirely consistent and clear on this (which is not surprising when one remembers the thousands of pages he wrote over many decades) and, at times, spoke of the certainty of introspective knowledge[39] about our own mental processes and also of the 'incontestable' results of science.[40] No doubt we must treat some findings as true if we want to construct a body of knowledge. But if he had meant this certainty and incontestability quite literally his whole philosophy would have had to be different from what it is. In the light of his maturest reflection he must have considered these 'truths' as fragmentary, one-sided and provisional.

What I have here called Dilthey's philosophy of science has not been sufficiently appreciated because there is, to my knowledge, no sustained discussion of it in his works; it has to be extrapolated from interspersed remarks and from the style of analyses which he makes. Yet we cannot properly understand Dilthey's approach to the human studies unless we see it in the context of this general theory.

8. *Dilthey's epistemology*

Dilthey's methodology and philosophy of science is rooted in his epistemology, his enquiry into the conditions under which successful cognition can take place. This part of Dilthey's work has, I believe, important and far-reaching implications but, as Dilthey formulated his most incisive ideas on this subject in the last years of his life, he never shaped it into a coherent theory. Vol. VII of the collected works, which contains the bulk of Dilthey's epistemology, consists of fragments some of which are obscure or reflect different, inconsistent stages in his thought. A measure of reconstruction and interpretation is, therefore, necessary in presenting his theory of knowledge.

Following the epistemological point of view predominant in Western philosophy from Descartes to Kant, Dilthey starts with the knowing subject and asks what makes him capable of understanding. But he departs from this epistemological tradition when he criticizes its intellectual bias and argues that, by starting from a pure thinking

[39] See below, p. 160.   [40] See below, p. 164.

Introduction

consciousness, epistemology has substituted bloodless shadows for living men.[41] He assumes that we know the world through our feelings and strivings as well as through our sense impressions and thinking. The real cognitive subject is the whole human being, conditioned by the functioning of his body and by social and historical conditions, who not only perceives objects but knows and evaluates them in terms of the concepts he has learned and the way they aid or obstruct his activities. This general epistemological approach has strong affinities with pragmatism as developed by Peirce and many others[42] and was the model for Existentialist theories of knowledge.[43] Understanding, the cognition of mental contents, involves the presuppositions required for any kind of knowledge as well as additional ones. The first of these is that the knowing subject shares with the object of his knowledge, i.e. other human beings, common, fundamental features, so that under-standing is, as Dilthey pithily put it, 'the re-discovery of the I in the Thou'.[44] In this sense, he assumed a common human nature but, as he sided with the historical school against the 'system of nature', in maintaining the variability of man, he had to specify clearly the characteristics which he presupposed to be universal. So he lists the following features with which we are familiar from experience.

(a) The mind has an innate structure which gives rise to typical connections between mental processes. For example, perceptions give rise to memories, memories awake desires and desires prompt us to action.

(b) Our mental life is purposive.

(c) We are aware of affecting the environment and being affected by it.

(d) We express, both intentionally and unintentionally, our mental states by physical manifestations.

(e) We not only perceive the world around us but evaluate it in terms of the feelings it arouses and the way it affects our purposes.

These and similar features (Dilthey did not claim to give an exhaustive list) are the source of the forms taken by our judgments about the human world. Dilthey called them the categories of life.

There is ample evidence – among it his use of the term critique for this portion of his work – that Dilthey modelled his theory of the categories on that of Kant. His *Critique of Historical Reason* was intended as a sequel to Kant's Critiques, supplementing the epis-temological exposition of the *Critique of Pure Reason*. By category

[41] See pp. 161–2.
[42] See J. Habermas, *Knowledge and Human Interests*, London, 1971.
[43] See M. Heidegger, *Being and Time*, London, 1962.
[44] See p. 208.

15

Introduction

Kant meant a general form of judgment which governs the way in which we acquire knowledge and, in his *Critique of Pure Reason,* he was mainly concerned with the way in which we apprehend physical facts and events in terms of such categories as substance and causality. The crux of his argument is that such relatively simple knowledge as being aware of a house in front of us or a ship sailing past presupposes – among other things – that the mind organizes the sequence of sense impressions in terms of a causal order.

Dilthey argued that additional categories which fulfil an analogous role were required in historical knowledge and, indeed, in all knowledge of the human world. To comprehend Caesar's crossing of the Rubicon as a historical fact, we need knowledge of certain physical events as well as awareness of his intentions, the fears he aroused in his opponents and the rule which he broke by his action. So we have to understand, on the one hand, the thoughts, feelings and aspirations of individuals, and on the other, the Roman constitution and the political situation. This involves the categories of life of which Dilthey provides the following list. (The name of each represents a concept, or pair of concepts, in terms of which we interpret manifestations of the human world.)

(**a**) The '*Category of Part and Whole*' is relevant to the knowledge of the physical world but has special significance for the understanding of the human one. To understand the crossing of the Rubicon one must appreciate what it consisted of (putting one legion after another across the river) and what it was part of (a march on Rome). If only a few soldiers had crossed and then returned it would not have had the significance we attribute to Caesar's action. We have already encountered other illustrations – words and sentences, Plato's individual dialogues and the body of his work, the individual and society. The primary experience from which we derive this category is that of our own mental structure.

(**b**) The '*Category of Means and Ends*' derives from our awareness of purposes. To demonstrate that the categories must be used in combination, I shall stick to the same illustration. To understand the crossing of the Rubicon we must know what Caesar was aiming at and the means he used to achieve it. In the same way every sentence has a purpose which the individual words serve.

(**c**) The '*Category of Power*' reflects our consciousness of affecting and being affected by the environment. We understand Caesar's crossing in terms of the physical and political obstacles in his path and the force he exerted to overcome them. One aspect of understanding words involves the impact they have.

(**d**) The '*Category of Inner and Outer*' corresponds to our capacity to express mental states through physical processes. The movement of legionaries across the river and down the roads of Italy (unlike logs floating in the water, or leaves drifting before the wind) can be understood in terms of the intentions and plans of which they are expressions. Words, too, are understood by relating sounds to ideas in the speaker's mind.

(**e**) The '*Category of Value*' represents the approval or disapproval with which we respond to situations. Caesar's act may thus be understood as the crime of an usurper or the liberation of Rome for future greatness.

While Kant's categories provide us with the means of knowing the physical world, Dilthey's enable us to grasp meaning in human life. Things become meaningful to us because we see them as parts of a whole, goals we desire or means for achieving them, physical manifestations of mental states, products of human effort, or sources of satisfaction or dissatisfaction. *What* they mean is, of course, a matter of empirical investigation.

This definition of the categories as categories of meaning contains an element of interpretation because Dilthey's late and unrevised MSS are a little ambiguous on this point. (At times he speaks of meaning as one of the categories.) However, I believe it to be justified by the general trend of his argument.

Kant in his so-called schematization related his categories to the temporal form of experience. Though Dilthey did not try to reproduce the pattern of Kant's argument explicitly it cannot be an accident that he discusses the temporality of experience in the context of his theory of the categories.

Unlike Kant, who was concerned with the concept of time as a uniform succession of moments which can be measured by clocks and is used in the sciences, Dilthey was interested in the subjective experience of time as a constant flow in which the future becomes the present and the present the past. For him the present is not an extended instant but a small, structured, part of the flow in which the immediate experience is always enriched by awareness of the past and anticipation of the future. So every moment of life has a distinctive meaning according to its place in the temporal sequence. (A second love affair can never be quite like the first.) This connection between the temporal structure and the categories of life makes man a historical being. He is aware of his life as history and this enables him to understand, record and contribute to general history.

Here, too, Dilthey's thought proved to be seminal. Heidegger, in particular, acknowledged – in *Being and Time* – his generation's indebtedness to Dilthey's analysis of temporality.

Though modelled on Kant's approach, Dilthey's theory of the categories also diverges from it in important respects for he took a different view of the origin of his own as well as Kant's categories. For Kant the categories were a finite number of *a priori* forms of judgment which could be established, once and for all, by a transcendental deduction. He thought that if such a deduction were impossible and we had to derive the categories from experience we would be involved in the vicious circle of accounting for the possibility of experience in terms of experience. Dilthey who, as we have seen, was not worried by this kind of circle which he considered inescapable, had no hesitation about deriving the categories from structures of the knowing mind which can be discovered through direct experience or systematic study. What is more, he considered the categories not only as reflections of unchanging human characteristics but also as historical products determined by the way languages, sciences and intellectual or cultural systems had developed. No complete list of categories can, therefore, be given *a priori*. New categories may emerge or old ones change their meaning as changing historical conditions shape our minds. Dilthey mentions 'development' as an example of a concept which in modern times has become more important for the categorization of our experience.[45]

As well as the common features of human nature understanding requires, as its second presupposition, a common sphere of mind to which I have already referred in my section on methodology. Dilthey, following Hegel, called it 'Geist' but, unlike his predecessor, used it in an unmetaphysical, down-to-earth sense.[46] There is nothing mysterious or philosophically sinister about the nature and origin of this sphere. Knowing that two plus two make four, that 'to dream' is a verb, that the law of England prohibits marriage between siblings, that 'Stadt' in German means town or that, in chess, the bishop moves on the diagonal, is neither knowledge of the physical world nor information about what goes on in particular people's minds. So it is convenient to describe what we know in these cases as belonging to a distinct sphere whether we call it 'Geist', culture or simply a third realm.[47] Languages, traditions, religions, philosophic systems, traffic regulations and parlour games are all part of it. This sphere obviously does not *exist* in isolation, but is embodied or objectified in material things like books,

[45] See pp. 208–17 and 231–45 for Dilthey's treatment of the Categories.
[46] See pp. 190–5 and 221.
[47] See K. R. Popper, *Objective Knowledge*, Oxford, 1972.

Introduction

buildings or formal gardens; it is the product of human minds and only becomes completely real when present in the consciousness of individuals. It must be treated as a distinct object of knowledge. Knowing how the bishop moves in chess is not like knowing how a snake moves, neither is discovering how the law applies to a particular case like knowing how the mind of a particular judge works. The method of coming to know the objects of this world of mind is called interpretation and we have already encountered the methodology governing its approach under the name of hermeneutics.

The reason why the re-discovery of the I in the thou is not enough for understanding but must be supplemented by reference to the common sphere of mind is obvious enough – human beings differ enormously. The individuality of each person is determined by his physical make-up and personal history and his thinking is shaped by cultural and historical factors such as his education and membership of a class or nation. If we were all exactly alike any effort to understand others would be superfluous: if we were entirely different it would be vain. Because we are partly alike and partly different understanding is possible but often difficult.

By referring to the common sphere of mind we can bridge the gulf between men of different ages or cultures who are divided by different beliefs and ideologies. If the problems of historiography or sociology prompt us to ask how an atheist can understand religious fervour, the simple answer is that he can discover what it is to be a Christian by reading the gospels, the lives of saints and other literature of this kind. The middle-class intellectual writing about the workers can learn about working-class life by looking at working-class homes, reading working-class literature and studying working-class hobbies. Modern Englishmen can gain insight into the minds of the ancient Greeks by reading their literature and contemplating their architecture. If a Western liberal finds it hard to understand the mentality of communists he will find reading Marxist literature more illuminating than interviewing party members. The source of our knowledge about the range and potentialities of human nature is the record of what man has done and thought. We cannot know what man is by introspection alone but only, as Dilthey never tired of stressing, through history.[48]

Knowledge of the objectifications of mind is thus an epistemological condition for understanding human beings in all their variety. Indeed Dilthey adds, such knowledge helps us to discover our own less obvious potentialities and understand ourselves better. But when we ask about the epistemological conditions needed for understanding this world of

[48] See pp. 84 and 93.

mind we encounter, once again, the circularity of argument which is so characteristic of Dilthey's thought. In principle we can understand the world of mind, because we – our minds – have created it. So, in embracing Vico's principle that the mind can understand what the mind has created,[49] Dilthey uses our immediate awareness of how our minds work as a key to unlock the impersonal world of mind.

A simple illustration will make these theoretical points clear. If I had no emotions I could not even begin to understand the love-poetry of the Elizabethans, but I can only understand it properly by reading about the period. Once I understand the poems I can gain insight into the thoughts and emotions of people very different from me and this extension of my imaginative insight into human nature will, in turn, help me to understand my own muddled feelings better. We are familiar with this to-and-fro movement in everyday life and in scholarship. The achievement of Dilthey's epistemology is that it formulated and justified theoretically this groping from incomplete to fuller understanding.

9. *Dilthey's philosophy of life*

Dilthey's epistemology and philosophy of science and the methodology of the human studies which followed from them were rooted in his general philosophy. He did not think of this as a system because he considered philosophic systems to be one-sided simplifications of reality. Sceptical of the mind's capacity to gain complete and final knowledge of reality and critically aware of the limitations of his own formulations, he continuously revised and modified his ideas and sought new ways of presenting the truth as he saw it. This lack of definitiveness and these continuous attempts to be faithful to conflicting aspects of reality can be exasperating for the interpreter and make his task harder, but the absence of complacent dogmatism may also be counted as one of Dilthey's chief virtues.

Though not believing in the possibility of an authoritative and adequate system Dilthey yet strove to be systematic and did not advocate a piecemeal approach. All his varied enterprises were part of a single, comprehensive, search. Like most great philosophers he sought the solution of individual intellectual problems within the context of a coherent framework so that all the themes he touched on in his long working life were interrelated.

[49] See *The New Science of Gambatisto Vico* (Garden City, New York, 1961), also *G. Vico, An International Symposium* (Baltimore, 1969), particularly the contributions by Hodges and Rickman.

Introduction

Dilthey described his approach as a 'philosophy of life' by which he does not mean a philosophy of all living things but one which deals with human life with all its social and cultural ramifications. Though he fully accepts that man represents an evolutionary stage of organic life he does not particularly emphasize man's biological features. The individual's life is the sum of his experiences from birth to death and is embedded in the life of mankind (social-historical reality). Because this life is conscious, reflective and organized by thought, Dilthey identified it (particularly in his later writings) with the world of mind, which he did not think of as a pure sphere of disembodied intellect, just as he did not treat life as only a biological concept.[50]

Dilthey described himself as a philosopher of life because his thinking rested on three related theses. The first was his version of the empiricist principle that all knowledge is based on experience.[51] The second was the theory that all philosophy arises from and refers to the problems of everyday, human life.[52] The third embodied the idea that philosophy must be closely linked to the knowledge of life acquired by the empirical human studies.[53]

According to the first thesis, life, as the sum of all our experiences, is the source of all our knowledge. Dilthey never tired of proclaiming himself a committed empiricist, siding with Hume, J. S. Mill and the positivists against metaphysicians like Plato or Hegel; but he considered that most empiricists had misconceived their starting-point in that they substituted an emasculated, metaphysical, construction of experience in terms of sense-data for the experience of life. Dilthey insisted that we must start from the richly varied experience of normal, mature observers who see trees in bloom, talk to other people, read newspapers, enjoy poetry and music, play chess, worry about the future, remember past holidays and resent noisy neighbours, who are citizens of a state and members of a family, who tend their gardens and earn their living. This complex experience which makes up life is the basis of all science and all study of the human world and provides the starting-point of all philosophizing.

Dilthey's empiricism was profoundly influenced by the impact of Kant's Critiques on his thinking. To him experience was not, as it was for the main tradition of empiricism, the imprint of the external world on a passive mind. He rejected the conception of experience as the sense-data received by the mind, and also the assumption of naive realists that the complex world of things and events which we

---

[50] Note the identification of mind and life in the title of vols v and vi.
[51] See below, pp. 170 and 211–12.   [52] See below, pp. 178–80.
[53] See below, p. 128.

encounter in experience is a mirror-image of objective reality. To him, as to Kant, experience itself was the product of the mind's activity which shapes and structures the data it receives. Experience remains the starting-point but it can and – if we seek criteria of knowledge – must be epistemologically analysed in terms of the structures of the knowing mind which permeate it. The physical world that the sciences study, the world of mind which is the subject-matter of the human studies, and the distinction between them are constructions by which the cognitive subject organizes his impressions.[54]

The organizing principles are, of course, the categories and, when I discussed these earlier, I indicated how Dilthey – in his radical empiricism – differed from Kant by assuming them to be accessible to experience.

So we can see how Dilthey's epistemology is based on his philosophy in which he defines life as both the sum and the source of all our experiences. We are part of life and the complexity of the knowing subject makes the complexity of our experience possible.[55] We interact with the physical world because we are physical creatures, evaluate things because we have feelings and purposes, understand history because we we are ourselves historical beings and are able to understand the expressions of others because we produce them ourselves.

It is natural for man to reflect on himself, his doings and his experiences and when such reflection becomes systematic and comprehensive it becomes philosophy. As life includes all our activities and experiences – this is the second thesis – it is the only subject philosophy can have and provides the impulse to philosophize. The different problems of philosophy and its different branches which deal with them arise – as Dilthey tried to show with a wealth of historical illustrations – from the varied requirements of life. Changing circumstances in politics, art, law, morality and the pursuit of knowledge make it necessary from time to time to improve methods, adjust attitudes or justify what is challenged. The fundamental examination of each subject gives each its own philosophy, for example the philosophy of law. This philosophy, then, affects the sphere on which it reflects.[56]

Dilthey believed that when philosophy examines the methods, concepts and epistemological foundations of a particular discipline it can be cogent and scientific and, at the same time, make the discipline or sphere of human activity it is dealing with more rational and scientific.[57] But most philosophies also aspire to a comprehensive vision

---

[54] See below, pp. 164–7 and 170–1.   [55] See p. 195.
[56] See pp. 125, 128, 143.   [57] See p. 125.

linking a general picture of reality, basic principles of valuation and final purposes. Dilthey called a system of this sort *Weltanschauung*, a view of the world, or world-view. But he considered such all-embracing systems incapable of being scientifically cogent because he could see no compelling, logical reason for treating one of the areas of experience – cognition, valuation or aesthetic vision – as the basis of the others, which would be necessary for successful systematization. Such systems cannot reflect objective truth but only a point of view determined by the author's temperament, character or historical circumstances. They are, inevitably, subjective and one-sided; though they contain genuine insight they can only present facets of the truth. Instead of a system of his own Dilthey therefore attempted a typology of philosophic systems based on the historian's awareness of the relativity of all systems.[58] He also believed that the human mind, as it contemplated the limitations and positive contributions of different philosophies, would be liberated from dogmatic narrowness.

10. *Philosophic anthropology*

Put slightly differently, an adequate philosophic system seemed impossible to Dilthey because we are embedded in, and part of, the life we are trying to understand and so cannot see it objectively from an outside point of view. Yet, through everyday experience and scientific knowledge, made more rigorous by philosophic criticism and reflection, we are constantly increasing our understanding of life and of ourselves. So the progress of philosophy reflects man's growing awareness of himself.

We see here the circles in which Dilthey's philosophy moved – in which he believed all philosophy must move because 'Life grasps life'.[59] We must start from the complex experience of life, observing, for example, housing estates, church services and business organizations which are meaningful to us because they are the products of mental activity. To understand them fully we must go back to the capacities and structure of the human mind which created them and can therefore recognize them. If empiricism is one side of the coin the epistemological point of view, derived chiefly from Kant's critical philosophy, is the other. We know nothing, not even our own minds, except through broadly-based experience; yet the central clue to all this experience lies in the working of that mind.

This critical empiricism meant that philosophy and the sciences, in

[58] See pp. 112 and 133–54.
[59] See p. 181.

particular the human studies, were for Dilthey involved in a circle of mutual dependence. This is what I have called the third thesis. History provides us with the accumulated experience of what man and his world is like while the systematic human studies – psychology, sociology and economics – examine the structural regularities within that human world. Philosophy, in turn, must reflect on the nature of the knowledge thus gained, justify its claim to validity and consider how the contributions of the different disciplines are limited and slanted by their starting-points and methods, and so co-ordinate their contributions into knowledge of the whole man. But, while reflecting on the knowledge derived from experience and the contributions of the human disciplines, philosophy must also make use of this knowledge. It cannot give man insight into himself, a critical epistemology, or the principles of moral action by introspection or pure, rational speculation alone but must derive its knowledge from a conception, based on a critical examination of our experience of what man is like.[60] So, the fact that Dilthey was both a philosopher and – as a historian of ideas, literary critic and student of psychology – an enquirer into human nature is not an accident but arises from and is justified by his whole outlook.

Dilthey's final aim was to co-ordinate and integrate all the disciplines concerned with the various aspects of human life, ranging from man's physiology to his intellectual and cultural products, from the working of individual minds to the functioning of social systems. He called this proposed systematization of knowledge 'anthropology'.[61] He believed that its foundations must be laid and its principles justified by a 'philosophic anthropology' which draws on the findings of empirical research but also spells out the fundamental features of man already *presupposed* by it. For example, when we look for – and possibly discover – the meaning of a particular action we have already assumed that human behaviour can be meaningful.

Philosophic preoccupation with human nature is not new. Plato discussed the parts of the soul and man's social propensities; Descartes and Spinoza, Hobbes, Locke, Hume and Kant all discussed various human tendencies and man's cognitive capacities; man's power to devise and use languages and his capacity for making rules and obeying them have been discussed, or merely presupposed, in modern philosophy. Dilthey drew attention to the central role of this preoccupation in most philosophizing by treating it as a distinct branch of philosophy. This, too, proved seminal and thinkers like Heidegger and

[60] See pp. 127, 134, 240.
[61] See pp. 240–1.

Introduction

Scheler,[62] and, more recently, Helmut Plessner[63] have developed the idea of a philosophical anthropology.

The general idea of an anthropology, too, has not lost its fruitfulness. At a time of increasing specialization it is important to look beyond economic man, or *homo sociologicus*,[64] to a conception of man which incorporates and integrates all the findings of the separate disciplines concerned with him. A common framework and guide-lines for inter-disciplinary co-ordination and co-operation are still needed and we could do worse than look for them in Dilthey's philosophy.

We have conflicting and inconclusive theories on education, politics and social reform. In spite of the vast expansion of the social sciences we are generally baffled about the unrest of the affluent young, the bitterness of worker–management confrontations, the growth of violence and the spread of nervous disorders. There are, of course, no simple remedies to all these problems and I am not suggesting that Dilthey's work contains specific solutions for our social ills. (Though he did, for example, apply his philosophy to the development of educational theories which have been taken up in Germany today.) But one of the conditions for tackling these problems is the building up of a comprehensive, co-ordinated body of knowledge about man – what Dilthey thought of as anthropology. I have stressed these dismal – and familiar – aspects of modern life because it is important to remember that Dilthey's work is ultimately about the problems of living as a human being in the human world and not about the abstruse technicalities of philosophy. To the social scientist, let alone the social worker, philosophy may seem remote, but, in Dilthey's case, it is a massive attempt to lay the foundations for understanding man, which is of practical as well as theoretical interest. One might even say that it is practical because it has so substantial a theoretical basis. The infantryman may have to take the brunt of the battle but he could not fight effectively without a general staff and a logistic system. In the same way effective social action and the practice of specialists in the social sciences depends on a broadly based philosophic framework.

[62] See M. Scheler, *Die Stellung des Menschen im Kosmos* (Darmstadt, 1928) *Philosophische Weltanschauung* (Bern, 1953).
[63] See H. Plessner, *Zwischen Philosophie und Gesellschaft*, Bern, 1953.
[64] See R. Dahrendorf, *Homo Sociologicus*, London, 1973.

Introduction

11. *The selection of texts*

The texts reproduced in this volume represent less than five per cent of Dilthey's published writings. Excluding so large a proportion of his work involved very careful sifting. I thought it desirable to preserve something of Dilthey's astonishing range of interests, to emphasize what seems most important and original and to include what is of greatest interest to English readers.

No doubt, a good deal of the material contained in the collected works can be excluded without much misgiving. His contributions to Prussian history, his writings on Music or his extensive notes on Schleiermacher's theology can only be of interest to specialists. His occasional articles and book reviews are ephemeral compared with his major writings. This still left major decisions to be made.

The philosophic consideration of the human studies takes pride of place among Dilthey's works. It occupied his mind for many decades, contains, in the view of most commentators, his most original ideas, and is particularly relevant to present-day debates on the methodology of the social sciences. I have therefore given, proportionally, the largest space to this and presented it in long, continuous, passages so that the reader can get the impression of how Dilthey developed his arguments.

Even in this one area difficult choices had to be made. The collected works contain alternative, overlapping, texts which develop the same theme but date from different periods. In some cases there are early sketches, the work as originally published and notes for altering and continuing the published text. Dilthey did a good deal of re-writing, re-formulating, amending and expanding of his ideas in the very last years of his life when he was well into his seventies. These writings which he did not live to publish himself are less polished and coherent than his earlier ones. One must ask if they can be discarded as the products of declining power or if they are the maturest achievements of his thinking. My selection is based on the conclusion that the latter is the case and, wherever possible, I have chosen later rather than earlier texts.

Dilthey's general conception of philosophy and his own philosophic outlook also deserve space for, after all, he was a professional philosopher. I have been more sparing in selecting from his works on this subject because his great influence on modern philosophy has been felt more directly in Germany, and the Continent generally, than in this country. So I have concentrated mainly on the general framework of his ideas which is also relevant to his philosophy of the social sciences.

Introduction

The main question is how far Dilthey belonged to any school of philosophy. He professed to be an empiricist but was also something of a Kantian. He adapted Hegelian themes to his purpose, was sympathetic towards Spinoza, and, undoubtedly, influenced by Schleiermacher. These ingredients are, I believe, finely balanced in his philosophy and it is important that any selection should not disturb this balance.

To avoid giving a one-sided picture of Dilthey I have also included passages illustrating his work as a biographer, historian of ideas and theoretician of psychology. Here the choice was particularly difficult because there is a wealth of interesting material to choose from. Also, it is not easy in short excerpts to give an impression of Dilthey's patient and persistent scholarship. The passages chosen are intended to illustrate the problems which prompted his theoretical enquiries and show how he practised what he preached.

Deciding on what areas of Dilthey's work to include and what space to give to each, chosing particular passages and arranging them in a meaningful order, involved an interpretation of his work as a whole. I could, of course, easily have drawn attention to certain obscurities and contradictions in this great corpus of material, but I believe that Dilthey's writings, though varied in subject-matter and spanning over half a century, show continuity of aim and a generally coherent and consistent approach. I have tried to represent this in my selection and underline it in my introduction.

Such an interpretation is, inevitably, coloured by the interpreter's interests and the intellectual climate in which he lives. In the case of minor authors with a limited and well-defined output this may make little difference. But it is well-known that different interpreters and different generations have, because of their different experience and outlook, seen a different Plato or Kant. From the rich variety of their work they picked what spoke most eloquently to their own condition. This gives such authors continued relevance. To speak of having to interpret Dilthey in this way is merely another way of saying that he belongs to the company of major philosophers.

12. The translation

Little needs to be said about the vexing but familiar problem of translating from one language to another and of putting what was written in another age into a modern idiom. Something of the flavour of the original should be preserved and – in the case of a philosophic text in particular – the meaning reproduced as accurately as possible. Yet it is essential to make the modern English reader's task as easy as

possible and that sometimes means sacrificing sentence constructions, metaphors, allusions and similar characteristic features.

These problems are worth mentioning because the style of a man like Dilthey reflects his philosophic attitudes and his method of working. Dilthey's scholarship and wide reading encumbers his sentences with cross-references and casual allusions. Because his approach was tentative and undogmatic he constantly qualified his assertions. The fact that he wrote, or dictated, rapidly under the constant pressure of thoughts crowding in on him is mirrored in occasional bursts of telegrammatic style. He had a strong sense of the interconnectedness of things and passed from idea to idea in a single paragraph. Continuous absorption in his ideas led him into unceremonious returns to the main argument after long asides. He believed in the practical relevance of philosophy and coupled technical jargon with colloquialisms. I mention these idiosyncrasies because a translation, to be easily readable, must gloss over or eliminate at least some of them.

A particular problem arises from some of the key terms Dilthey used to spell out his philosophy. Apart from the usual technical terms of philosophy – such as epistemology, *a priori*, or induction – Dilthey took ordinary German words and used them philosophically. Some of these have no proper English equivalents, or equivalents which carry misleading associations. What is even harder to present in English is the relationship between ideas effortlessly conveyed to the German reader because the words derive from the same root. A translation either eliminates the connections which are clear in the German or superimposes technical jargon. So I must explain some of these key terms and the policy I have followed in translating them.

Geist, geistig, die geistige Welt, der objektive Geist, die Objektivationen des Geistes, and *die Geisteswissenschaften* form a group of terms which, as we have already seen, are crucial to Dilthey's philosophy. Most of these terms cannot be translated consistently by the same term in different contexts. Still less can the linguistic connection between the terms be preserved.

Geist, of course, means spirit, mind, or intellect. It depends on the context which of these words renders the German meaning most accurately and idiomatically. We usually speak of 'the spirit of an age' but of a man's 'mind' or 'intellect'. In contrast to matter we refer to 'mind'. In most cases I have used 'mind' but one must remember that Dilthey is usually talking of something more general and impersonal than an individual's mind.

Geistig can sometimes be translated as 'mental' but often it is essential to avoid phrases in which this might be understood as

Introduction

meaning 'psychological' or even 'psychologically unbalanced'. 'Intellectual' or even 'cultural' frequently conveys the meaning most accurately. So according to context *die geistige Welt* has been translated as 'the intellectual world (or sphere)', 'the world of mind', or 'the cultural world', because 'mental world' would be misleading as it suggests the thoughts and feelings of an individual. The world of mind consists of the *Objektivationen des Geistes*, i.e. the 'objectifications of mind' by which Dilthey meant any permanent manifestations like books or buildings which the mind has constructed. This is why the world of mind can also be translated as the 'cultural world' or the 'mind-constructed world'.

Geisteswissenschaften, used in contrast to *Naturwissenschaften*, presents a double problem. *Wissenschaft* has a wider meaning than science because it describes any disciplined search for truth. I have used the word 'science' for *Naturwissenschaft* and called other *Wissenschaften* 'studies' or 'disciplines'. I also thought that it would be misleading to preserve the connection between *Geist* and *Geisteswissenschaften* by speaking of 'mental disciplines' or 'studies of the mind', as those are not usually thought of as covering such disciplines as sociology or economics. I believe 'the human studies' conveys the meaning most accurately.

Another difficult group of terms is *Leben, Erlebnis, Lebenserfahrung* and *Lebensbezug*. There is no difficulty about translating *Leben* as 'life' as long as one remembers the sense in which Dilthey uses it (human life) but it is not so easy to preserve the reference to life in the other two terms.

In German *Erlebnis* is contrasted to *Erfahrung* while English uses 'experience' for both. The latter has the sense which the O.E.D. gives as 'the actual observation of facts or events, considered as a source of knowledge'. An example of this use is learning from experience that nettles sting. *Erlebnis* corresponds to the meaning defined by the O.E.D. as 'the fact of being consciously the subject of a state or condition, or of being consciously affected by an event. Also an instance of this: a state or condition viewed subjectively: an event by which one is affected.' In this sense we speak of 'going through an experience' or 'something having been quite an experience'. Dilthey frequently and emphatically used *Erlebnis* because he wanted to distinguish his own empiricism from that concerned with sense-data, by stressing personal, emotionally coloured, experience. I have avoided the use of 'vital' or 'personal' to distinguish *Erlebnis* from *Erfahrung* because it is awkward, and relied on the context to make clear which of the terms is being translated by experience.

Introduction

In 'Lebenserfahrung', Erfahrung means experience in a third sense which the O.E.D. gives as 'knowledge resulting from actual observation or from what one has undergone'. I have translated this phrase as knowledge of life.

Lebensbezug refers to any relationship by which human life is consciously affected, for example my house being a source of pride to me, or the weather interfering with my holiday plans. Here I saw no alternative to using such phrases as 'relationship of life' or 'vital relationship'.

Finally there are three more terms frequently used by Dilthey. The first is Weltanschauung which in the past has often been left in German. I have translated it as 'world-view'.

Grundlegung is another term which plays a prominent part in Dilthey's writing because it describes what he is trying to do for the human studies, namely laying foundations or providing grounds for their methods. In this sense it figures in the sub-title of one of his main works, the Introduction to the Human Studies. As the word also occurs in the title of one of Kant's works there is a traditional translation – 'fundamental principles'. This will do in some contexts but does not convey the sense of doing something. This is why I have sometimes preferred 'justification' (the actual giving of a foundation).

The third term is Zusammenhang, which is fairly common in German and which Dilthey used in different combinations such as Bedeutungszusammenhang, Wirkungszusammenhang and Natur-zusammenhang as well as by itself. It is a noun meaning the state of hanging together or being inter-connected and its constant use by Dilthey reflects his sense of the inter-connectedness of things. I have translated this term in different passages as context, system, order or pattern, according to what makes best sense. Sometimes it could simply be omitted. (To say that something occurs in the context of nature means little more than saying that it occurs in nature.) I have usually translated Wirkungszusammenhang as 'system of interactions', Natur-zusammenhang as 'pattern or order of nature', or simply 'nature', Bedeutungszusammenhang as 'context of meaning', Structurzusam-menhang as 'structure' and Seelenzusammenhang as 'mental struc-ture'.

These are the essential points about the translations and I have discussed them here rather than inserting cross-references to the original German into the translation because I think Dilthey's texts are served best if the reader can follow the arguments without having to consult footnotes about shades of meaning.

Introduction

In this introduction I have tried to sketch the broad outlines of Dilthey's thought and indicate the point of view which guided my selection. I wanted to show, above all, that these extracts from different works can be read as parts of a meaningful whole. But what I have said is neither a full summary nor a detailed commentary on the selection which follows. I hope that it will speak for itself.

I
Dilthey as a Historian
of Ideas

The Schleiermacher Biography
EDITOR'S INTRODUCTION

I have started my selection with three sections from the Schleiermacher biography because this was Dilthey's first major work and established him as a scholar of distinction. The first volume of this work, from which these passages are taken, covers the first half of Schleiermacher's life and was widely hailed as a masterpiece. The biography was never completed. There is a second, more fragmentary, volume and a mass of material on Schleiermacher's philosophy and theology which has recently been published as volumes XIV/1 and XIV/2 of Dilthey's collected works.

Schleiermacher, a contemporary of Schelling, Hegel and the Romantic poets, was an outstanding philosopher, theologian and translator of Plato. He also played an active part in the regeneration of Prussia after the Napoleonic wars. In writing the life of such a man Dilthey developed and exemplified his conception of biography and its relation to history. For him the biographies of historically influential men are the natural building blocks of history because the pattern of a man's life provides a principle of organization for diverse themes. At the same time the life of such a person can only be understood in terms of the historical developments which influence him and with which he interacts.[1] As a result the original feature of Dilthey's biography is that the incidents of Schleiermacher's personal life are embedded in very substantial accounts of his philosophic, cultural, social and political environment. There are detailed accounts of Spinoza's, Kant's, Fichte's and Schelling's philosophies because Schleiermacher was influenced by them and took issue with them. Literary developments which shaped Schleiermacher's mind are described in detail. The beliefs of the religious order in which Schleiermacher grew up, the social conditions of the cities in which he lived and the founding of the University of Halle, at which he became professor of theology, are all patiently explained. Thus, many of the subjects which continued to occupy Dilthey's mind for the rest of his life, were first explored in this context. The Classic and Romantic poets, the development of Prussia and Hermeneutics are outstanding examples.

Biographical sketches designed as contributions to the history of ideas abound in Dilthey's works. He wrote about Hegel, Leibniz, Frederick II, Goethe, Schiller and Dickens. But none of these accounts is on as massive a scale as his Schleiermacher biography.

The preface indicates Dilthey's approach, the plan of the work and some of the methodological problems he faced. The chapter on Berlin speaks for itself. It is, I think, an entertaining picture of the development of this city, its morals, literary cults and intellectual life. We get lively pen-portraits of its journalists, satirists and the rich Jewish ladies who aspired to a prominent place in society.

[1] See page 184 on biography and history.

Dilthey as a Historian of Ideas

The chapter on German literature is an illuminating exercise in the history of ideas. Besides illustrating his approach it makes interesting and important points. He argues that, as a result of particular historical development, the literature of Schleiermacher's time provided not only entertainment and aesthetic pleasure but also a philosophy of life which shaped the outlook and thinking of educated Germans. He also shows that this is related to the fact that the outstanding poets were also serious thinkers and scholars who felt that their poetry and their scholarship were equally important and interdependent.

This chapter also has a direct bearing on Dilthey's philosophy of the social sciences because it shows how Spinoza and Goethe developed an intellectual approach which proved vital in the study of man.

The Schleiermacher Biography[1]

INTRODUCTION

Vol. XIII/1, pp. xxxv–xlv

This is the life of man who, more than anyone since the Enlightenment
and its most powerful exponent, Kant,[2] has influenced the development of European religious attitudes. Schleiermacher saw religion as a
profound experience springing from our relationship to the universe.
For him it was the soul's emotional response to the world through
which untrammelled by religious dogma, philosophy or moral concepts, it perceived the invisible pattern of things. During his many
years of ecclesiastical and theological activity he struggled to secure a
place within the protestant church for what he had experienced in his
youth; only in that church (as it was gradually reformed) could religion
become the free activity of the individual. Unlike all earlier manifestations of the religious spirit, Schleiermacher's experience took place in
the plain daylight of scientific enlightenment and worldly *joie de vivre*;
indeed, what was now required from a religious genius was to
overcome the autocratic tendency inherent in religion, by his understanding the great, new and independent historical forces at work in
society. A basic striving for experience and understanding soon
became part of Christian piety and informed the work of the clergy; it
spread to different fields of scholarship and permeated social life,
aesthetic enjoyment and artistic expression, the family, the educational
system and politics.

Schleiermacher, a profoundly thoughtful man surrounded by the
highest achievements of scholarship, turned his philosophic attention
to this universal experience and form of understanding. He tried to
grasp what was central to every sphere of life and so achieved a
universal view of the cultural world. In this context his youthful
understanding of the Christian religion and ecclesiastical organization
inevitably developed into a unified theological system; this affected all
spheres of research into religion and, finally, penetrated to the
ultimate depths of being and knowledge. He seemed to radiate a mild,
clear, light which illuminated all forms of life. A higher consciousness
was always present within him, making him, in the midst of life's
struggles, superior to fate. In this bravest of fighters there was the
divine peace which fills saints who renounce this life.

[1] E. Schleiermacher, 1768–1834.   [2] I. Kant, 1724–1804.

37

Dilthey as a Historian of Ideas

The background of this account of Schleiermacher is the great German intellectual movement which starts with Lessing[3] and Kant and ends with the death of Goethe,[4] Hegel[5] and Schleiermacher. The latter's historical position must be understood in terms of the conditions, context and character of that movement.

These conditions differ significantly from those in which comparable intellectual movements developed in other countries of modern Europe. Germany was splintered. Only Prussia, under Frederick II,[6] achieved military greatness. He promoted a mighty upsurge of national confidence, but suppressed its social and political application. The size and culture of the middle classes made them intellectually preponderant, but they found themselves excluded from political influence. People in the middle classes reached a fixed position early. They had no great goals but neither did they have a hard struggle for existence. So, at the height of their powers all their vitality and energy was turned inwards. Personal culture and intellectual significance became their ideals. The atmosphere was one of moderate desires, modest possessions and serious conscientious striving. The international background was completely becalmed: from the peace of Westphalia to the time of Frederick no political or social event affected the nation deeply. Nothing hindered the widespread development of introspective life; every circle of cultured society was affected by the achievements of this inner world: it was a development of historical significance.

When the scholarly and literary movement which had spread from Italy since the sixteenth century affected this land in the middle of Europe[7] it encountered a pronounced religious trend; this had been fostered for centuries by a rich, deep, popular sentiment and was sustained by the great past of Protestantism in the German-speaking countries and a learned, profoundly active, preaching profession; allied to it was an idealistic turn of mind. In Leibniz[8] these features were combined with European scholarship into a world-view made popular by the Enlightenment. The formation of this world-view was dominated by some of the great, fundamental features of the Christian world-view which was interpreted as being in harmony with the ancient philosophers and with the results of modern science. Central to this view was the dignity of man, his bond with the divine and the infinite

---

[3] G. E. Lessing, 1729–1832.   [4] 1749–1832.
[5] G. W. F. Hegel, 1770–1831.   [6] 1712–86.
[7] 'Land der Mitte' in the original. This is more than a stylistic flourish; Dilthey wants to stress the cultural and historical significance of Germany being surrounded by, and lying between, other nations.
[8] G. W. Leibniz, 1646–1716.

perfectability of every individual and of mankind as a whole. However the Enlightenment may have sinned, one must never forget that it impressed these ideas on the mind of our nation.

The union of the clergy, the universities and the people, created by the Reformation, bore fruit in the unified culture of German Protestantism; in Prussia, in particular, to which Schleiermacher belonged, this unity of intellectual culture culminated in the enlightened autocracy of a great king.

The Enlightenment forms the background for the history of Schleiermacher's development. In protestant Prussia it gave the office of preacher the freedom without which Schleiermacher could not have developed his uncompromising integrity. It passed on to him the results of Biblical criticism which liberated his mind from the old dogmatism. His youth, up to his move to Berlin in 1796, coincides with the great period in which Kant's main works appeared one after the other and in which our classical poetry reached its zenith. At that time all Germans interested in Philosophy were observing the emergence of Kant's system with bated breath as his main works followed each other. This system completed the critical position of the Enlightenment and justified its faith in God, immortality and infinite development: it also initiated a new age. Schleiermacher developed by taking issue with Kant; even the work of his later years, including his second main publication, *The Christian Faith*, and the *Lectures on Dialectic*, was influenced by him. This is why the history of the scholarly career of the great theologian will have to start with a description of this system and Schleiermacher's relationship to it. The influence of our great literature and poetry on the spirit of the young preacher who lived in north-east Prussia far from the centres of the poetic movement was much more quiet, calm and slow. It filled the atmosphere of the small, quiet towns in which he worked, and particularly that of the castle of Schlobitten. From the writers who followed Shaftesbury, Lessing and Wieland he derived a freer feeling about life and above all – like all the young men of that period – he owed them the transformation of his ideal of man and his world view.

The historical conditions described above make it understandable that it was a poetic movement which set out to revolutionize our view of life and the world. The liberation of thought in the Enlightenment was followed by the release of all the powers of feeling, passion and imagination; this was intensified by the influence of society, foreign literature, Frederick's warlike deeds, and finally by Rousseau and science: it found our nation with narrow customs, and old-established ideas, inward-looking, pre-occupied with emotions: this inner world was acted on by these most powerful forces, and so the national character was shaped.

In the inexhaustible imagination of men like Shakespeare, Calderon, Corneille and Racine was mirrored the passion for glory and domination, love and honour felt by brilliant and powerful nations. These men depicted the struggle for power, the bloody road of ambition, the reward of loyalty and the tragic fate of love in a world of ruthless egoism; in short, the inner and outer destinies of active passions. The greatness and the prejudices of a conscious national spirit colours, and speaks in, these works.[9]

The world of our poets was the inner world of the sensitive, contemplative man. It was not meant to represent a view of life and the world which already commanded the nation's enthusiasm; on the contrary such a view had to be created to overcome the narrow circle of outdated and now intolerable ideas; the vital urge of a strong, spiritual nation sought an escape in it which the outer, political, apparently immutable external conditions obstructed. The narrow traditions of custom, society and the view of life and the world had to be broken by poetry in order that something new could be created. So the nation which listened to our poets was not one eager to hear gay or bloody adventures while resting from daring enterprises with which its energy was fully occupied, not one which desired the poetical expression of all the ideals which animated its life. Instead the nation expected an enrichment of its actual life, a powerful elevation and liberation of the inner world in whose magic circle its vital urge was enclosed.

This was the central motive which, in the midst of a chaos of unleashed forces, determined the steady course of our poetry. A new picture of life, the need for a new freedom and an attempt to see the world without the blinkers of tradition are alive in this poetry and frequently come to the surface. The highlights of the movement were the vivid descriptions of an ideal of life in such literary works as *Götz*, *Werther*, *The Robbers*, *Nathan*, *Faust*, *Iphigenia*, *Wilhelm Meister*. These descriptions characterized its different stages and their content had the effect of a new philosophy. But in the midst of this creative activity our poets seemed to be dissatisfied; they turned to scholarly reflection in order to express this ideal of life conceptually and defend it against the dominant moral-religious views. Mirabeau[10] had already noted that our poetry arose at a time when scholarly reflection was highly developed and, so, he says, German poetry bears the character of a period in which reason was victorious over imagination: this is why it had to produce fruit rather than flowers. So our poets do not only

---

[9] See pp. 79ff.   [10] 1749–91.

combine scholarship with their poetic activity; their poetic development is directly conditioned by the progress of their research. They
themselves produced a magnificent scholarly movement, new directions in research and indeed a new world view. This explains why the
following generation was not very good at poetry but creative in
scholarly research, in the production of moral ideas and in the shaping
of a world view. These creations were only the completion of what their
predecessors had begun.

Let us now turn to this new generation. After Schleiermacher's move
to Berlin his contemporaries began to influence him. The completion
of Kantian Idealism by Fichte[11] had prepared the ground for this
generation: within the quiet walls of the Tübingen Seminary, Hegel,
Hölderlin and Schlegel developed and, after 1790, came in contact with
each other. In the same decade the members of the Romantic
movement began to associate with each other in Leipzig, Göttingen,
Dresden, Jena and Berlin. As relationships developed between the two
circles of the younger generation, after 1797 Schleiermacher made
many contacts with these young men of genius through his friendship
with Friedrich Schlegel, and only then, in the romantic circle which
emphasized the impact of Goethe's personality on poetry, ideal of life
and world view, did our classical literature really change him. From
now on Fichte determines his philosophic thought. Schelling affected
him from a distance. From the ferment of these years his main religious
work emerged. Infinite tasks spread before him.

Moral life and ethics had to be transformed by the new ideal of life.
Fichte had once described his task as transforming the world through
Kant's Philosophy. Schleiermacher's vocation for ethical reform was
based on the results of this great movement in the midst of a powerful
moral ferment which emerged most strongly in metropolitan society.
The poets were followed – in his person – by the moral philosopher,
the self-sufficient description of an ideal world was followed by a deep
conviction which sought to spread the new achievements to everybody.

When he turned to the spiritual forces affecting reality, he had to
embrace with deeper understanding the most important of them all in
modern European culture, the Christian religion. He had to show its
eternal significance in a revolutionized world view and thus stimulate
its declining influence into greater effectiveness. It was a stimulation, as
Claus Harms put it, 'to an eternal movement': he gave religious life a
greater depth. Schleiermacher's influence in Europe rests on the
particular form he gave to the Christian religion.

The revolution in world view which the poets had started also had to

[11] J. G. Fichte, 1762–1814.

41

be completed. Starting from Fichte's presuppositions, Schelling used a conception of Goethe's, the inter-related ideas of Leibniz, Kant and Lessing, the scientific and historical research of Goethe, Herder,[12] and other contemporaries, as a basis for that magnificent world view which – in different forms – determined the philosophy of our nation for nearly half a century. The power of this great conception, which had already emerged in Goethe rather than Hegel's logical explanation, was to prove influential for many years. Only late in his last period did Schleiermacher – with admirable thoughtfulness – sketch the simple outlines of his world view: in doing so he retained Kant's critical achievements and combined them with the recognition – set out in his 'addresses' – of the significance of the religious contemplation of world harmony to every view of the world. These outlines do not contain the charm of a poetic grasp of the world-pattern, but a deep, true, insight into the motives and development of all world views: this was the fruit gleaned by his critical spirit from its experience. These outlines retain a permanent attraction, even though put together from notes and lectures, and are relevant in many ways to the most significant aspirations of today. His second main religious work, the doctrine of faith, originated from his critical reflection and was sustained by profound study of the sources and history of Christianity.

So Schleiermacher stands in the centre of all the aspirations of his generation. He embraced all the greatest impulses of his time and the preparatory work of the previous generation. He re-directed the mood of the preceding era towards practical life, towards the dominance of ideas in the world.

The events of world history forced idealism to prove itself during the crisis in our fatherland. We can now abandon the misconception that idealism as represented by Schleiermacher, Fichte or even men like Friedrich Schlegel, was at any time, before or after the foreign domination unpatriotic or indifferent to what happened. In this respect one can even recognize a profound difference between this generation and the preceding one. The reforming interest of the former turned it towards practical life; only there did some of its leaders show their full capacity. Schleiermacher was predominantly preoccupied with country, state, and Church. He had to embody the ideas of his life in the land he loved. What a life! He had started as a Herrenhuter:[13] his mind had extended over the wide field of disparate disciplines: he had been affected by the poetic movement of his period and his youthful works have the aura of a poetic environment, of poetic

---

[12] J. G. Herder, 1744–1803.
[13] A rather austere Protestant sect.

attempts and plans; he was one of the first to make social life an art, controlling a wealth of relationships which swamped the lives of other, by no means insignificant, people around him; he was one of the first, in a great age, to live for the state and to become a power in it. Surrounded by indifference, he began, before anyone else, to assert the great historical task of the Church which many years of preaching, serving the Church and theology had impressed upon him: he became the spiritual head of the Church of his time. He experienced and lived through all this not as the plaything of fate but driven by an inner power which led him through all the circles of human existence until the whole cosmos of the moral world arose before his contemplative spirit. Here was a universality not of research but of life. One can see that he, himself, was more than all the notes or research he left behind.

We can see the significance of this great existence in the historical context of the spiritual movement in which it occurred. The influences of three generations interacted in him. In lively competition with highly gifted companions, Schleiermacher combined the far-reaching results of the Enlightenment, of Kant and of our classical poetry, yet he stands alone in his deep reflectiveness in the inspired vision which was his; at the same time he turned these ideas towards a reform of the moral world and the development of the Christian religion; thus he turned men's minds towards the great tasks of the present.

If this is taken into consideration the great movement with which Schleiermacher was significantly connected appears to be more than the sum of individual aspirations; what had inspired the whole nation for decades was made fully explicit by the men of this movement: the popular spirit itself, at this almost unique moment of great upheaval and deep concentration, inspired their work. As a whole this is imperishable, the property of our nation, open to criticism but not to scorn.

In the light of these considerations the charge against this period of inner culture does not seem justified. For too long, it is said, this urge for a rich inner life has consumed the vitality of our nation; for too long we have been reforming ourselves instead of the world; now we must transform the natural, social and political conditions of life on which happiness and unhappiness rest; we must investigate the laws which govern such changes and use them for our purposes. So we pass from one kind of one-sidedness into another. We may want happiness and well-being for our generation as the highest, indeed the only goal of our existence, for religious and philosophic reflection is not everybody's concern; but this happiness and well-being only arises from the effect of the external conditions of civilization on man's mind. This involves a second constituent as changeable as the environment; for what is more changeable than the human heart? In the midst of oppressive conditions an aspiring attitude to life or a harmonious contemplation of the world find sources of happiness everywhere and no abundance of material things can make an impoverished mind happy. It is not being realistic but parodying good sense to imagine that chasing after the outer trappings of happiness automatically brings happiness itself. So a purely inner culture can be justified even in the face of unalloyed hedonism.

But these accusations are least justified in the case of a man like Schleiermacher. They are completely based on a historical misunderstanding. They are automatically refuted by Schleiermacher's historically significant position in a changing world, in moral reform and in the active life of society, state and Church. He is, indeed, an idealist, but only in the important sense of insisting that active life must be guided by ideas. The questions which moved him and his period are as eternal as the human mind and as the claim of ideas to govern the world.

Finally we must discuss the sources of the first volume of this story. The history of intellectual movements has the advantage of reliable records. One can be deceived about the intentions of these movements but not about the mental content they express. But though the records are reliable they do not by any means reveal everything the historian needs. They do not express the causal nexus, the origin of ideas from an older context of thought or from experience and observation of reality. Here one must rely on letters and diaries. Though the most important part of what seems intelligible in a collection of letters is published I could not have tackled the task as I conceived it if the Schleiermacher family had not generously given me access to all the papers including the most intimate letters. The material is more comprehensive and well arranged than almost anything available for other biographies. In the course of time it expanded in other directions; access to the relevant part of the A. W. Schlegel papers was most valuable. It has already been noted that it is dangerous to use impressions, even confessions and personal plans, which emerge in letters because they are spontaneous, determined by the moment and the thought of the addressee. There is only one critical antidote: comparing the same person's letters to others at the same period, where it is a matter of impressions, comparing the impressions of others. For the thoughts of most important figures of this volume – beside Schleiermacher the two Schlegels in particular – I have been able to establish a firm basis through their most intimate letters to very different people. So I hope to have gained a truly

The Schleiermacher Biography

objective insight. I am offering a story based on a wealth of manuscripts which supplement each other.[14] But to oral communications I thought I could concede a deeper significance at only one point: the criticism of Varnhagen's notes on his attitude to Schleiermacher; it comes from a most trustworthy source.

For, when I compared the direct sources with the notes of others, particularly those of Varnhagen and Steffens, Varnhagen's emerged as those of a man ignorant of the issues and not an intimate of those historical figures, a man who, from a distance, put together daring speculations based on appearances and hearsay. He extolled – though, to my mind, in an exaggerated way – the world in which he lived and which he knew well (I am not speaking of the political one) but what he says of the representatives of the intellectual movement not only lacks intimate knowledge, it is also coloured by hidden likes and dislikes based on personal circumstances. Steffens, in contrast, wrote as a participant from the centre of the intellectual movement with an open, impersonal enthusiasm for its aims and a true insight into what moved individuals; his memory, too, was admirable.

Hardly less important than the letters are diaries and unpublished manuscripts. It is regrettable that in the case of Schlegel and Novalis the material of this kind which has survived is still published without accurate investigations of its origins. I trust that, by working repeatedly and infinitely laboriously through Schleiermacher's papers, I have succeeded in establishing their true chronological order. In the *Denkmalen* I have given their essential content in chronological order. They are made available for general use so that any fellow scholar can check my investigations.

[The final paragraph referring to the arrangement of the material has been omitted.]

[14] Dilthey edited Schleiermacher's letters in *Aus Schleiermachers Leben und Briefen* (3 volumes of letters to and from his friends up to his move to Halle) (Berlin, 1866) and *Leben Schleiermachers in Briefen* (letters to and from his friends from his move to Halle to his death) (Berlin, 1863).

THE DEVELOPMENT OF
A NEW WORLD-VIEW
IN GERMAN LITERATURE

Vol. xiii/i, pp. 183–207

In September 1796 Schleiermacher went back to Berlin which now became his spiritual home. Until then in the environment of Southern Germany he had been very little affected by the power of our literature. His inner development seems to have been dominated by the theological Enlightenment, by Kant and by other philosophical thinkers, his existence filled by the simple customs of Christian Enlightenment. He confronted the world as tutor, country preacher and simple adviser of his friends but was outstanding in that he asked nothing of fate beyond the harmonious development of his emotional life. Now an entirely new world opened up to him. Wherever he had lived he would, inevitably, have been affected by the great events in the world of thought. But sometimes external circumstances providentially help a man's inner strivings to come suddenly to fruition. Such circumstances transferred the man of twenty-eight to Berlin where he suddenly found himself face to face with the great poetical and scientific movement of that period and saw all its features collected and concentrated in this city.

Here we come to a turning point in our narrative where a significant view quite suddenly opens up.

Two spiritual powers moulded every one of Schleiermacher's generation, though other influences affected individuals: the philosophy of Kant, and our great poets. Philosophers as well as scientists owed the critical foundations of their world view to the immortal works of Kant but their ideal of life, indeed the crucial content of their outlook, to our poets. What these great and fortunate men had seen, the philosophers tried to think out in conceptual systems. In the introduction I have indicated this true relationship in our intellectual history. I explained the peculiar interweaving of poetry and research in terms of German cultural conditions. Our poets themselves repeatedly interrupted their poetic creation with scientific work which, in turn, provided a basis for their poetic creations; this had the effect of a kind of philosophy so that from their influence scientific work and philosophic world views originated. Now we must turn to the content of this development in the literary and scientific works themselves. The first of the two great spiritual powers which moulded Schleiermacher and his generation, the philosophy of Kant, dominated all his ideas and writings in the first period of his life and its influence lasted the whole of it; for this reason its impact has been described in the first part of this work. Fichte derived a new conception from Kant's analyses and this for a while eclipsed Kant's direct influence on Schleiermacher. Only half a dozen years older than Schleiermacher and a few more than Hegel and Schelling, he is the first of the generation of younger philosophers and, at the same time, dominates them. Now I shall turn to the second power: the ideal of life and outlook of our great poets. For here Schleiermacher, like his most significant contemporaries, found a complement to the critical philosophy which went beyond the Leibnizian Enlightenment.

Lessing must be discussed first because the characteristics of the period which, as I have already indicated, show why he must be considered the true founder of our literature. My account explains how, in the midst of so many significant forces, the development of our literature rested on his shoulders. His most outstanding contemporaries, foremost among them Goethe, testified to this. He was the first to impart great moral and intellectual content to our literature and so he is the first to have a contemporary significance. Before him there were only the chaotic elements needed for this development – the growth of our language, the fashioning of its rhythms and the power of imagination to understand nature and the play of sensuous feelings. None of the work of his contemporaries has remained truly modern for us.

Even Wieland had not got beyond the point reached by the ideal of life in England and France: He had an immense impact because, for many years, his rich poetical talent poured forth untiringly and generously the inventions and ideas of world literature: but in all this wealth there is nowhere an original answer to the needs of his age. Klopstock, on the other hand, who expressed with such inspired energy the urge for emotional experience as it had developed in the middle classes nevertheless surrendered to the narrow, stifling, religious sensitivity which he found there. Thus, like Wieland, only in another form, he failed to move forward. He remained eternally youthful and enthusiastic, his tongue was never capable of simple speech, his head never liberated by scientific thought; he grew old in a narrow circle of admirers and ended up like a parody of his youthful ideals. Lessing arrived and, in his great masculine soul, all the budding individual aspirations around him matured into a conscious ideal of life and a liberal world-view.

His conscious and decisive will dominated even his first literary expressions; clearly and serenely he surveyed the world and felt an irresistible temptation to intervene in its activities. Later he transmuted everything into action, struggle and energetic movement. This expressed itself in a style which conveyed step by step a dynamic struggle towards knowledge. He felt as compellingly his affinity to the stage, the ideal mirror of the life of action. It was this personality which Lessing, the only north-German genius except Kleist among our poets, contributed as a fortunate and indeed unique dowry to our literature. The conditions he encountered endowed him with brittle independence. If it is the characteristic of the writer – in contrast to the scholar – that he is concerned with his effect on the nation and not exclusively with the progress of scholarship, then Lessing was a born writer as he was a born dramatist. He dared to base his existence on this profession. Several of his generation like Weisse, Engel, Moritz and Dusch tried it, too, but soon escaped into secure positions. From the traditional centres of German culture, the universities and the courts which represented the old spirit, Lessing the journalist turned to the emerging public opinion of Berlin and the rising German theatre, which, as they were only just beginning, proved too weak to provide for him. The undeveloped state of the social factors in Germany on which a writer of those days could rely explains the unrest and touching lack of happiness in that great existence. But it also explains how a great character, whose position was comparable with that of Frederick in his Age, could develop as a writer at his desk. His ideal of life arose from his character.

Poetry, like science, expresses the universal, though not in an abstraction from many cases, but in the representation of one. In it man can express vividly and, therefore, with great emotional power his insight into his nature, destiny and highest moral ideals. What is thus expressed is the ideal of life of an epoch. Poetry's moral greatness depends on the truthfulness, as well as on the reconciling and purifying energy, with which it accomplishes this, its highest task. This aspect of poetry never appeared greater than when we had to shape an ideal of life using a creative moral spirit and not just distil it from an existing reality. This is why Schiller later sought creative power in practical reason, i.e. in the moral capacity. In Lessing's moral power, i.e. in his great character, we find the basis for the harmonious ideal of life which he created.

This was already the background of his critical activity. His personality and character gave rise to his reforming ideas about the nature of poetry as the expression of a great soul. This he contrasted with descriptive, musical or even philosophic poetry, with a cold, dramatic, ideal based on the virtues of respectability, with an anxiously supine theological morality which reduced the life of the emotions to mediocrity and weighed poetry down. In contrast to the pictorial arts the essence of poetry is action; this action represents inner perfection, the truly poetic because completely human and truthful character, which appears in the free movement of great passions; it is recognized in shared sorrow or joy, in inner empathy with the strong, natural movements of the passions.

So his mighty soul conceived that poetry had a more powerful effect than that envisaged by any contemporary poet or critic and he became the reformer of our poetry. Indeed his vast conception left what he could produce far behind and because, and only because, none of his works measured up to his own conception, he rejected the label of poetic genius.

Yet anyone seeing *Minna von Barnhelm* felt with great pleasure the breath of a new age. Where were the equals of these proudly self-contained, inwardly alive characters, whose likes and dislikes are emotionally controlled and whose speech is laconic? This could be felt even if it could not be expressed. Only after extensive scholarly disputes and reflection could Lessing himself express it fully. *Nathan* was produced. The reader not only felt the breath of the new age unseen around him, he learned to understand it, indeed to be its citizen. In *Nathan* the idea of the Enlightenment was transmuted into perfect beauty. Around him Lessing created a poetic world in which the forces that he knew were locked in bitter, unreasonable struggle, were reconciled by understanding and brotherly joy based on the highest moral ideal. This world is, as it were, the Enlightenment's dream of the future, bringing consolation to the great fighter who had already begun to despair and collapse. No serious investigator of human nature can read this poem (or *Iphigenia*), in which Lessing's ideal of life is expressed simply and fully, without being moved deeply: for in them a pure greatness of soul appears so truly embodied that we reach – beyond experience – to higher conceptions of human nature.

This ideal of life achieves its most intensive power in the poet's intuition: but he only gains clear insight into himself through moral reflection, through the development of a world view and insight into its presuppositions and implications. Here the position which the founder of the new spirit of the German nation inevitably took up towards science becomes plain. Our poetry arose in an age when theoretical views of life, systems of morality, text-books of theology and philosophic enlightenment had penetrated every pore of our nation.

The poet – confronted by the dominant, scientifically justified, world-view – had to become fully conscious of the content and presuppositions of his ideal of life if he was not to perish, like Klopstock, in dismal narrowness. Lessing dared to do this. It is a risk but the poet is, in all ages, allowed to express in attractive images what, expressed conceptually, exposes thinkers to hatred and even persecution.

I have shown in the first part that our national culture as Lessing found it, and still in Schleiermacher's youth, was wholly under the influence of theology. To reform the convictions of the bourgeois and the concepts of the scholars thoroughly, and so change this national culture, Lessing had to take issue with theology. He did not shrink from the endlessness of this study or the risk of such confrontation. The historical limitation of Lessing's position is defined by the fact that this confrontation with theology dominated him even when he conceptualized his ideal of life and sketched a corresponding world view. Nevertheless both contained the seed of the future.

His analysis of moral concepts appears to us today extremely incomplete. This alone explains why Kant's ideal of life, though based on a less rich and mature human personality and therefore more one-sided, had an incomparably stronger impact. Kant was a master of conceptual analysis. Lessing's moral reflection stammers, as it were, when it undertakes an analysis of the fully mature man as he envisaged him. The essence of man is action and will; motive determines the value of action; the motive of the perfect action or the perfect will is the good for the sake of the good, irrespective of any consequence, any reward or punishment. 'No, it will come, it will surely come, the time of perfection when man, the more convinced his reason is that this future will be increasingly better, will have no need to borrow motives for action from the future, when he will do good because it is good not because it is linked to an arbitrary reward – it will surely come the time of a new, eternal gospel.' In the same way the true motive of our striving for truth does not lie in an infinitely remote goal but in the openness of a human soul turned energetically and freely towards the truth. It was this thought which made a complete break with the theological Enlightenment; the core of the new sense of life which emerged in Germany with Lessing, became visible. Instead of using up life like worthless material day by day in plans and expectations, subordinating the present moment and your emotion to an uncertain future, fill yourself with the intrinsic value of every unique day, the unconditional value of every act of will irrespective of its success. 'Why can we not anticipate a future life as calmly as a future day?'

Here Lessing moved towards his two great contemporaries Frederick the Great and Kant. In royal isolation these three, all belonging to northern Germany, more specifically to Prussia, move on parallel lines without really knowing each other, one the founder of the Prussian monarchy, the second of modern philosophy, the third of our literature. So, quite independent of each other, they meet in this great thought that the sense of duty, irrespective of consequences, is the true interpretation of conscience. 'We', said Frederick, 'who forego every reward, who do not believe in eternal torment, are not corrupted by our interests. The welfare of mankind, virtue alone – a sense of duty – prompts us.' One should die, he said, in a royal image – leaving the good consequences of one's actions behind as the setting sun leaves its last rays. But only Lessing of the three developed a full, harmonious ideal of life from this outlook. Man, as Frederick's astringent spirit saw him in the mysterious order determined by the Highest Being, appears as if standing at a post at which his strict sense of duty bids him to remain in a kind of subordination to the Highest Being. Man, as Kant's abstract thought conceived him, is determined by respect for the form of the moral law, irrespective of the consequences of his actions. But when Lessing spoke of good for its own sake and was filled by the intrinsic value of every day he felt this valuable content of our existence quite differently. His feeling for it sounds forth in the beautiful words of Philotas: 'I am a man and like to weep and laugh': other related expressions about true heroism show his emphasis on a will towards good sustained by the fulness of emotional powers and purified by progressive insight into our task; but here he fails to provide an analysis.

Only in the context of a world view which explains and justifies the ideal of life is the vital urge of this period satisfied. Lessing grew up with Leibniz' world view which he shared with Kant. But once Kant conceived the passage of time as a subjective form of intuition the great idea of the infinite development of the individual soul which he takes from Leibniz had to become an enigma. Once Kant introduces freedom into the realm of nature and grace as conceived by Leibniz, Leibniz' world-order acquires a different outline. Lessing, on the other hand, developed Leibniz' own ideas through a free, inspired study of human nature and the moral world. Here the thinker and poet within him met and here his problems lay. He was troubled by the historically determined distinctions among man which were not part of their essential nature, a problem as yet insoluble in that unhistorical age; there was also the fact that most men had remained, through no fault of their own, on a low level of development. (This was a problem of real significance to him because of his determinism, i.e. his conviction that there was a strict causal connection between all events even in the moral world.) Finally, there was the fact that the old religion revealed to the Jews was morally and intellectually imperfect, and this raised the question of the relation between mankind and natural religion and the revealed religions which only then acquired its full significance. To solve it he developed the basic ideas of Leibniz.

The magnificent picture of an all-embracing divine consciousness (comparable to a creative genius) arose in his mind; the all-embracing divine foundation gives rise to all the phenomena of the universe; the all-embracing reason produces the plan which is realized in all these phenomena and, by a particular combination of the senses, constructs types and stages of sentient beings; all is steady, upward-striving development; our own life, apparently circumscribed by birth and death, is only a point on the infinite path of the individual soul which has unfolded into this particular life. It will continue to unfold into higher forms of life under ever new and less limited and stimulating conditions. Thus the dreadful discord of an inner unhappiness caused by God is dissolved in the thought that this is only a necessary stage in a steady intellectual and moral development; all the puzzles which the facts of the history of religion seem to pose are solved by the idea of this same steady moral and intellectual development applied to the whole of history; they are solved by the conviction that everything within this development of society, state, religion and history serves the moral and intellectual growth of individuals.

Thus Leibniz' principles yielded the first comprehensive philosophic understanding of history in Germany; its core was a steady intellectual and moral development which advances through an ascending and regular series of epochs. This understanding was the culmination of Lessing's whole system of thought. But this system was to be trans-formed in terms of more comprehensive premises.

A new wave carried to the top those men who, independent of Kant's investigations, were destined to accomplish this trans-formation – Herder and Goethe. In the sixties and seventies of the eighteenth century a strong change in the attitude to life becomes noticeable. The reform of the historical sciences which had taken place in England and France, English studies of Homer, Hebraic poetry, folksongs and Shakespeare, French science, particularly Buffon's comprehensive view of the unity of nature encompassing physical and mental phenomena and, finally, Rousseau's new ideal of life – all interacted with events in Germany; some of this memorable develop-ment, particularly Hamann's cultural history, is still insufficiently explained. But a significant step forward was made in the conception of the goal, the inner conditions and true course of human development.

The Schleiermacher Biography

Lessing had conceived, in the spirit of his age, the clarification of our concepts as the most outstanding condition of our general development. Now the formation of concepts was traced back to the most elementary operations of the human mind. Man, using his eyes, in control of his body and the power of his senses and emotionally free now seemed to be the true material for the development of a higher ideal of life. The reform of education, inspired by this spirit, became a common national concern. Lavater's Physiognomic, a typical product of this age, tried to see the shaping structure of the soul behind the appearance. Nations and individuals were considered in the context of their natural conditions; the independence and many-sidedness of historical phenomena came to be appreciated; the historical character of every human ideal emerged.

So the true foundation of the highest mental achievements was sought for in the form and strength of the most elementary operations, quite apart from the power to form concepts and determine the will by them. This foundation is described as genius. But the essence of genius is – according to Lavater–Goethe's description – a certain way of sensing and seeing, 'the inspirational', the 'apparition' and 'given-ness'. This genius precedes all abstract conceptualization and is most fully understood in its original manifestations such as folk poetry unaffected by intellectual culture, folksong, Ossian and Shakespeare. Even today, when it appears among us, it only achieves its purest development where it remains free from rational, aesthetic rules and abstract moral laws, for these are merely generalizations derived from its original power and its manifestations. Here the significant problem of the relation of the moral genius to abstract moral concepts emerges. It was Friedrich Heinrich Jacobi's main interest in the first half of his career (in *Allwill* and *Woldemar*).

This new generation sees in the ideal of genius it developed not merely the special, inner basis of poetic power (as Kant had defined the limits of genius) but the general basis of all creative power. This inspired capacity for sensing and seeing must prove its worth by its revelations. All the powers of the soul must work together to reproduce the innermost being of the object; everything human must be revived by being understood at a depth only attainable by imagination and living empathy; nature itself should reveal its secret to the sympathetic soul. On this Herder's infinitely fruitful activity is based and so is that of Winckelmann. Winckelmann was the first to achieve great scholarly results by means of inspired intuition and so established its method. It is not necessary to discuss him in detail as da Justi, in his significant biography of Winckelmann, has, on the basis of his scholarly diaries, demonstrated how he studied the new historical method of the French and English, that of Montesquieu above all, for a long time, with the intention of producing a great work of political history and how he then transferred certain main points of this method – the doctrine of the connection between climate and mental phenomena and the doctrine of the constant causes which explain the origin, flowering and decline of historical phenomena – to the history of art. This explains the peculiar phenomenon of a man who approaches a difficult subject late in life and, without any apprenticeship, moves with sure steps towards the solution of a great task. Winckelmann's great work was later joined by Herder's *Ideas towards a Philosophy of History*, the second, comprehensive achievement of inspired intuition in historical science to which we shall have to refer later. There is a link between these two works and the later, scholarly achievements of the Romantic Movement; its method was also inspired intuition. To it we owe epoch-making works in the sphere of the human studies, outstanding ones in that of the descriptive physical sciences, but errors, starting with Goethe's colour theory, throughout the philosophy of nature, wherever it approached other parts of the physical sciences, the general philosophy of science or metaphysics. Our achievements in chemistry, physics and physiology at this period were, with the possible exception of Ritter's work on electricity, due to the opponents of this great movement among us. On the other hand we owe to it the fact that to this day our human studies hold the first place in European scholarship.

In this context the poetic vision of man changes too. *Werther, Götz, The Robbers, Faust* and the poetry of *Sturm und Drang* were produced. I consider highly questionable the attempt to abstract general truths from poetry or even their quintessence as the world view of the poet. Poetic creation is most closely related to the organization of sensation into perceptions and to the origin of our insight into people (*Menschenkenntnis*). It is a matter of forming a picture of something unique. The mental procedures involved here have two features which, if we look more closely, we see are related to each other. They consist mainly of inferences from the particular to the particular and they occur in the depths of the unconscious. The universal which seems to permeate the events and characters of true poetry need not be present in the form of a previous, rational insight. So what the reader abstracts from the interweaving of characters and destinies is his own, subjectively formulated, idea which he derived from the enjoyment of the poetry, though it is not inherent in the poem itself. This explains the infinite variety of a poetic work which allows its content to be expressed in quite different conceptual interpretations but exhausted by none. We confront the poet's creations like the world itself, which also defies any final interpretation through concepts. For this reason the conceptual interpretation of a poetic work can only be accepted as strictly true in so far as the poet has become his own interpreter, either through rational expositions in his works or through scholarly investigations. So Lessing's scholarly works throw light on the ideal of life and world-view in his *Nathan* and, retrospectively, on some of his earlier plays. The conscious idea of brittle, moral independence is stamped on them; these heroes are moved neither by powerful natural passions as are those of Shakespeare, not by historical ideas like those of Schiller: their core is an irritable, moral confidence, a concentrated will subjected to principles, a sensitive feeling of justice and capacity for infinite devotion. Even Orsina, Lessing's most pathological character, is filled more by ethical emotion, a moral disgust, than by a natural desire for revenge. This is why Lessing's poetical world does not coincide with the concept and task of tragedy. In the youthful works of Goethe, Schiller, Lenz, Klinger and Fr. H. Jacobi we can perceive quite a different view of life. We notice also that this change is related to the new scientific movement which I have described. In these youthful works genius sometimes appears at odds in combat with existing scholarship, sometimes with the dominant laws of society and moral requirements. When we take into account letters and notes like that strange 1769 travel journal of Herder's which shows what went on in the most exciting head of the time yet more points for consideration arise. If we put the individual features in our history of literature together we get a most vivid picture of the wealth of these phenomena. But it is impossible to express this new, exciting view of life by means of a conceptual abstraction from the poetic works of these years. Only since Schiller and Goethe began to explain these views scientifically – Schiller through the study of history and morality, Goethe through that of nature – can we recognize intelligible, general insights even in their poems. By contrast the new content of *Götz, Werther, Faust* or *The Robbers* seems inexpressible as a sum of general thought; now, as then, it has to be recaptured by sympathetic feeling; contemporary accounts show how today's most powerful emotion is only a faint echo of the impact which these poems achieved then. This is why I shall not describe either the content or the effect of this poetry on Schleiermacher's generation but only discuss a few leading ideas of Goethe and Herder; these together with the works of scientists, philosophers and historical thinkers determined the world view of the next generation.

In the eighties Goethe and Schiller had started to analyse scientifically what made the best minds of their time tick. Schiller's great mind included among its interests two outstanding phenomena: the contrasts and conflicts which religious reform produced, and Kant's philosophical reform. From these materials he constructed his own system of views and ideas. His noble simplicity, the expression of his powerful and straightforward nature, was bound to coincide with the general need of the nation. But the circles of the younger generation which we are describing here were only affected by his philosophic works. They were captivated by Goethe's whole existence, his poetry and his investigations, for all this seemed to point out a new way of life and give it a new ideal. So he was looked-up-to as the quintessence of everything life could grant to man. There are innumerable valid testimonies that for a time in his own person he entirely fulfilled his generation's ideal of life. 'Goethe is one with life itself' Rahel said. *Iphigenie*, *Tasso* and *Wilhelm Meister* are vivid renderings of the meaning his life had during this period of fulfilment.

Some of his great insights into the position and destiny of man in the universe, which break through in his purely poetic works in the 1790s must be emphasized. Man is the final link in nature; his destiny is to understand its purposes and to complete them. Goethe's active, manly existence in these years is mirrored in Lothario and the uncle. 'Man is born into a limited situation; he can understand simple, near and definite goals and he gets used to employing the means at hand.' 'Decisiveness and consistency are, in my opinion, to be admired most in man.' 'The whole essence of the world lies in front of us like a great quarry in front of an architect who only deserves his title if he constructs an original creation with the greatest economy, purpose and firmness from these accidental natural materials. Everything outside us, indeed, I may even say everything within us too, is merely material: but deep in us lies this creative power which is capable of producing what ought to be and does not allow us to rest or pause until we have achieved it one way or the other either within us or without' (*Wilhelm Meister's Lehrjahre*).

This man, active by nature, finds himself confronted by men and fate. Towards men, Goethe teaches, we need a sublime tolerance for the individuality which reflects the value and unity of human nature. Towards fate, resignation. 'Everything calls us to resignation.' 'We replace one passion by another.' 'There are only a few people who, anticipating this intolerable emotion and in order to avoid all partial resignations, resign themselves entirely once and for all. They are convinced of the eternal, necessary and law-governed reality and seek to form concepts which cannot be destroyed and, far from being denied by contemplation of the transitory, are confirmed by it.' By this resignation the human mind is purified of self-seeking passions; satisfied by contemplation and knowledge of the world and no longer striving for possessions, it rises to intellectual majesty. One cannot think about this without seeing Iphigenie before one's eyes, without hearing the great pronouncements of Spinoza's final book, without listening to the wonderful words of Goethe at this time; lonely and free from the egoistical desires of his prime he absorbed – by the gentle light of a sympathetic view – the whole of nature into his soul.

But Goethe's poetry can only be fully understood in this period of scientific thought by referring to the works in which he struggled for clarity of thought about his new views of the world, man and destiny.

I shall start with an authoritative testimony about the main direction of his work. Schiller was by far the greatest man to observe Goethe, who opened his whole nature to him as to no one else. After they had lived together for several weeks Schiller summarized his view of Goethe's spirit in the following way (Letter of 23rd August 1794): 'You look for necessity in nature but look for it on the most difficult path. You survey all nature to gain light about something particular; in the universality of its manifestations you look for the means of explaining the particular. From the simplest systems you ascend, step by step, to a more complex one in order to construct genetically from the materials of the whole of nature the most complex of all, man. Thus by, as it were, imitating nature's creation you try to penetrate its hidden technique. A great and truly heroic idea.'

The starting-point of his researches lay in nature. He wanted to solve the puzzle embedded in the confused longing his generation had for it. It is the way science captivated him that distinguishes his outlook entirely from that of Lessing. It is also entirely different from that of the German Enlightenment in that the development of his world view is guided by science. Through the first period at Weimar runs, full of naive power, the urge to live with the eternal order of nature, with sun and air, with plants and waters as if they were friendly powers. He saw and felt the steady progress of the year and the circle of stars above his head at night. The expression of this relationship constantly recurs in new forms; it was given to him to look into nature as into the heart of a friend. This tendency was furthered by the very favourable conditions of his official duties at Weimar: his feeling for nature which clung to the wealth and splendour of appearances, led him to serious science. In this he found the basis for a consistent activity to help the national economy. His thorough, steady and progressive mind was willing to begin at the beginning. So he started his mineralogical studies up and down the valleys of the Ilm and the Saal, in the mountains and mines of the neighbourhood, particularly in the mines at Ilmenau. Buffon's geological surveys had attracted the interest of the European public from the middle of the century. A paper on granite from this first period in Weimar shows how even then Goethe began to envisage the vast, overall, pattern of nature of which man is a part. This was the conception which, as we have already seen, Schiller ascribed to him. 'I do not fear the accusation that it must be a spirit of contradiction which led me from the contemplation and description of the human heart, the youngest, most variable, mobile, changeable and sensitive part of creation to the observation of the oldest, firmest, deepest, most unmovable part of nature. For it will be granted that all natural things are precisely related to each other.' From this 'foundation which reaches to the deepest places of the earth' the 'first, firmest beginnings of our existence' he turned to the history of plants, to the anatomy of the animal bodies which animate the surface of the earth. Methodically, by thorough research, he sought the answer to the Faustian question of his youth.

This first sketch of his life's work – grasping the phenomena of nature as an articulated whole – becomes completely clear in his exchange of letters with Jacobi, the companion of his first, burgeoning plans who adopted the opposite starting-point for looking at the world – the mind and its manifestations. Here it becomes plain that he was able to make use not only of Buffon's approach (unfortunately he did not know Aristotle) but also of Spinoza's related efforts. 'When you say one can only believe in God I must tell you I put a high value on intuition and when Spinoza speaks of the "scientia intuitiva" and says this kind of knowing advances from an adequate idea of the formal essence of certain attributes of God to the adequate knowledge of the essence of things[1] these few words give me courage to dedicate my whole life to the contemplation of things which I can reach and of whose *essentia formali* I hope to form an adequate idea. . .' 'Here I am on and among mountains and seek the divine in plants and stones.' 'Forgive me for staying silent when the divine being whom I can only know in and through individual objects is referred to. . .'

This was Goethe's state of mind when his creative conception of the newer pantheism arose: for many years all his mental powers had been concentrated on the articulated whole of nature of which man is an integrating link. He (unless the idea can be traced even further back) and not Schelling or Hegel produced the inspired view which distinguishes this pantheism from that of Spinoza, of antiquity and of the Renaissance (i.e. both from the pantheism whose creative point of view consists of the relation of the world of thought and body to each other and to the divine unity and from that which rests on the analogy

[1] Ethics Part II, Prop. 40, Note 2, translation by W. H. White, p. 186.

of a world soul). The first sketch of Goethe's pantheism is the essay
'Nature'. 'Nature. . .we live in its midst and are yet strangers to it. It
talks to us incessantly and yet does not reveal its secret. . .it seems to
have staked everything on individuality and yet does not care for
individuals. . .it lives in children and the mother, where is she?. . .it
thinks and reflects incessantly; but not as man but as nature. . .it loves
itself and has for ever innumerable eyes and ears turned upon itself. It
has unfolded to enjoy itself. It allows new creatures to grow up to enjoy
it in order to communicate itself insatiably. . .life is its finest invention
and death is its trick to increase life.'

The conception that nature has unfolded in an ascending order of
living creatures in order to enjoy itself in sensation, vision and
comprehending reason is the true core of Schelling's and Hegel's world
view. The turning point for the philosophic spirit of investigation
comes in Kant; that of the world-view, which is entirely independent of
the armour of philosophic arguments, lies in Goethe, in that great,
persistently pursued plan of his life, to grasp the unity of nature in the
steady evolution of its phenomena up to the highest spiritual ones, and
in the form of pantheism which emerged from it. This form is
distinguished from every preceding one because it conceives the total
world system as a process, as a history in which nature becomes
conscious of itself. With this began the sequence of ideas which was
anticipated (but on the basis of different presuppositions) in Leibniz'
world view and Lessing's education of mankind and finally led to
Hegel's philosophy of History.

When Salomon Maimon, basing himself on the critical approach,
renewed the hypothesis of a world soul in 1790, there was nothing new
in his approach, which reaches beyond the old hypothesis and
approximates to a development from unconsciousness to consciousness. The world soul is, according to him, an active force inhabiting
matter; it has different effects according to the modification of matter.
It is the basis of the special composition in everything, is itself the
organization in every organized body, the life in every animal, reason
in man. Maimon finds in this idea a guide to widen our insight into the
unity of nature. Goethe, who esteemed Maimon, may have seen here a
welcome confirmation of his own direction.

So the creative idea of modern pantheism in Goethe had sprung
from his great urge to grasp the phenomena of nature as an internally
articulated whole. This point of view led him to a number of significant
discoveries.

But before we consider these results we must trace the direction of
Goethe's research further. A deeper insight into the progress of the
intellectual movement which we are describing depends on it. Goethe,

himself, felt this need, though at a later date. There we must look for an explanation. It was 1828, half a century after the composition of that essay about nature, when it came again into his hands. Now its view of nature seemed to him to be a prophecy which had been abundantly fulfilled. He described this fulfilment as the growing interlocking of phenomena into a technology of nature. It seemed to him that this was how the being which 'thinks but not as a man' had to be revealed. But he explained the power which designed such a technology of nature with the aid of Kant's *Critique of Judgment*. It was the same inspired intuition which is active in the poet and which his generation had begun to introduce into science. How delighted he must have been to see the poet's active power and the capacity to design the technology of nature grasped by Kant as a unity. 'Here I saw my disparate preoccupations placed side by side.' One of Kant's ideas seemed to illuminate profoundly the direction his research took. 'We can envisage an understanding which, because it is not like ours discursive but intuitive, proceeds from the synthetically general, the contemplation of a whole as such, to the particular, from the whole to the parts' (Kant, *Critique of Judgment*). While Kant assigns this procedure to divine understanding alone Goethe replies: 'Just as in the sphere of morality we are meant to approach the highest good so, in the intellectual sphere, contemplation of an ever creative nature is intended to make us worthy of participating in its productions.'

This expression is like a signpost. In the famous passage to which Goethe refers Kant touches the limits of the intellectual world. There is no knowledge except through the synthesis of given intuitions by means of understanding. For we are not capable of forming a world within us by a creative process without something being given to us through the senses. So the particulars of nature given to the senses remain strangers to its unity which is derived from our minds; their harmony appears to be an accident; only when we envisage a truly intuitive divine spirit does this accidental harmony become a necessary unity. Goethe takes up Kant's line of thought. To him it is linked to the mysterious passages in Spinoza about intuitive knowledge which rest on individual things without being mediated by abstract concepts. By starting from the divine understanding in nature and our absorption in it he, like Spinoza and Schelling, justifies an intuitive understanding[2] – or, according to Schelling's reversal of the expression – an intellectual intuition.

[2] The whole passage is highly relevant to Dilthey's methodology. See Dilthey's own theory of understanding and its role in the human studies, pp. 220–31, and the Editor's Introduction, pp. 9 and 19–20.

The Schleiermacher Biography

So Goethe was already preoccupied with the nature and justification of this intuitive understanding which, in another sphere, Winckelmann and Herder had first undertaken to develop into a method of research; after them it remained, throughout the period we are discussing, the dominant intellectual procedure in Germany. It competed with the inductive methods, frequently separated from them by the errors of thinkers and, again and again, linked to them by the true positive investigators. No philosophy of science has, as yet, properly investigated this great research movement. There is a scientific interest which is satisfied simply by understanding the unique and incomparable; the stellar constellations, the formation of the earth, the geographical distribution of life on it, social differentiation and the historical inter-connections within (mankind down to the individuality of the single person) are the subjects of such interest. From these valuable individual insights there follow the general conceptions (schemata) formed by abstracting differences which, to us, are irrelevant. Thus we form ideas which, within the flux of appearances, sketch something permanent that nevertheless does not exist anywhere. Such schemata were the basic forms which Goethe undertook to establish. This whole world of ideas belongs to scientific research. It is an error to consider only abstract insights, the recognition of laws as valuable; it is understandable in Mill or Buckle but was refuted here from the outset because of the direction such important German research took.

The direction which Goethe's research took converged with the state of the descriptive sciences. Enough logically ordered material was available in botany and comparative anatomy to make a comprehensive survey possible, yet it had not even been begun. In botany in particular the great systems of Linnaeus and Jussieu were available.

If the intuitive understanding which is permeated with the idea of the totality of nature becomes a method of research which tries to penetrate the uniform structure of the whole, it finds its most powerful tool in analogy. Its justification lies in this idea of a uniform structure of nature. By means of analogy, the comparative procedure, Goethe made progress within the descriptive sciences.

His first guiding idea for the study of organisms was that of the analogy between the different parts of one and the same organism. The individual organisms display a disguised, as it were, repetition of the same parts. This, in plants, in which it could be studied most simply, he called metamorphosis. It is the same leaf which appears first as the shoot, then the stamen, the calyx, the bloom, the pollen, the pistil and finally the seed-pod. Under unusual circumstances it seems to change from one form to another, apparently at random. This Goethe discovered in the gardens of Palmero in 1787. Then in 1790, a fortunate glance at a half broken sheep's skull which he saw by chance in the sand of the Lido of Venice taught him to apply this law to the structure of the vertebrates and to conceive of the skull as a series of strongly adapted vertebrae. We are still arguing about the number and formation of the individual vertebrae in the skull but the principle has been retained. The metamorphosis of plants has also become an established part of botany.

A second guiding idea led even further. Goethe taught us to think of the differences in anatomical construction of individual classes of animals as variations of a common design or type, conditioned by different modes of life, habitats and foods. Camper had already based his research on the idea that throughout the animal kingdom from fish to man, similar parts emerge where similar purposes exist. Meanwhile in 1786, Goethe had already made the peculiar discovery of the intermaxillary bone in man: this established a case in which a uniformity of structure given in the original design may exist in contradiction to the requirements of the completed structure; so the structural part in question had to be adapted to these requirements through a later coalescing of parts which originated separately. In 1795, at the request of Alexander Humboldt, Goethe elaborated his draft into a general introduction to comparative anatomy. 'In it he teaches', Helmholtz judged, 'with the greatest decisiveness and clarity, that all differences in the construction of the species of animals have to be considered as variations of one basic type; they were produced by merger, transformation, enlargement or reduction in size or even by the elimination of individual parts. In modern comparative anatomy this has become the leading idea. It has never been expressed better or more clearly than by Goethe and few significant changes have been made subsequently; the most important of these are, that one does not assume an underlying common type for the whole animal kingdom, but one for each of the main divisions established by Cuvier.' Johannes Müller said of the ideal of comparative physical science which he envisaged, 'Whoever wants to gain a clear conception of it should read Goethe's masterly description of the rodent and its social relations to other animals in *Zur Morphologie*. There is nothing similar to compare with this explanation in terms of the central organization. If I am not mistaken this hint contains an anticipation of a distant ideal of natural history.'

'The proper study of mankind is man'; this saying, in Schiller's view, Goethe made his own; according to the former Goethe explored the series of the organized wholes from the simplest up. Finally from the materials of the whole of nature he constructed man, in order to understand him genetically and to recreate him as it were in an imitation of nature. Here was the goal of his wandering through nature. But our account of Goethe's research must stop at the point before he reached his genetic conception of man. Here we are looking at Goethe as he presented himself in the last years of the 1790s when he influenced Schleiermacher's generation. The development of his thoughts about human society, based on his insight into the whole of nature, belongs to his last period.

At that time he tried, under the influence of this new movement, to solve the very problems raised in Schleiermacher's circles. These were the origin of the *Elective Affinities* and *Die Wanderjahre*. He was preoccupied with marriage, property and education. Research in this field led him to the thought of Schleiermacher and his friends. 'Everyone is an individual and can only be properly interested in individual things. The general emerges on its own, intrudes, persists and multiplies. We use it but we do not love it.' To this last period also belongs an opening up of his world-view corresponding to the extension of his research into the moral world. It extended beyond the pantheistic thoughts of his youth to a significant agreement with Leibniz and Lessing, i.e. with the Christian world view conceived in harmony with Plato and Aristotle. 'Neither thought nor will can be separated from its object.' In this God-nature man is an imperishable monad which can pass through a thousand transformations but destined to rest at every point of this infinite existence in the full possession of the moment. 'If yesterday is clear and open to you and if you are acting strongly and freely today you can hope for an equally happy tomorrow' (Goethe). Here we are only anticipating the completion of Goethe's world view.

But in the earlier period, from 1784 Herder, whose intellect had a deep affinity with Goethe's, achieved what he had aimed at; the understanding of man and history in the context of the world whole. Goethe's ideal as a natural scientist was not the product of fantasies which transcend the conditions of human existence but of his highest insight into the order of nature itself. This approach could only find fulfilment in genetic understanding or in a comparative science or man. Even in the later years Goethe's works only contain individual insights of genius which are of great scientific value, for example, his notes to the *West-Östliche Divan* and his history of the theory of colours. But, by his methods and their scientific results, he created a strict scientific foundation for the long-prepared work of Herder. That extraordinary man made it his mission to show what is human in all its forms and to assert, in opposition to Lessing, that humanity realizes itself in relation to mother earth and to the national environment and that there is no unvarying ideal of what is human in historical change. From the autumn of 1783 Goethe had shared all his ideas. I shall not try to separate what they derived from each other or both owed to others; but it was under Goethe's influence that Herder's only mature, undistorted work, designed in a great style, originated – his *Ideas towards the Philosophy of History of Mankind*, the first volume of which appeared in April 1784.

Nothing harmed the understanding of this magnificent work more than Herder's book *Philosophy of History for the Education of Mankind* which had appeared ten years earlier. There he worked out the analogy between the ages of the individual and those of mankind. When referring to whole epochs and the consolidation of many beliefs and customs in individual nations this analogy is not unfruitful and was taken up by Roscher. However, there are not that many parallels between the abstract idea of mankind and individuals. But there is something stimulating about analogies. In vain did Herder protest against variations on this immature attempt, and, indeed, as good as withdrew it. Even Gervinus, the great expert on philosophic treatments of history, regretted that Herder had dropped the physiological law of the life of nations which he had suggested in the early work.

Through all the books of *The Ideas*, as throughout Spinoza's Ethic, runs a stream of opposition to fictitious ideas and, in complete agreement with the latter, which was acknowledged by Goethe and Herder as the basis of their world view, the introduction of the concept of purpose in history is treated as the enemy of true research, as something that had to be traced in all its disguises. 'The historian', Herder says, 'will never try to explain an existing fact or event by another which does not exist.' With this strict principle all ideals, all the phantoms of the magic circle, vanish. 'So we shall try not to invent hidden, individual purposes of unknown design for the facts of history. To the question: Why did Alexander march to India? there is no answer except: because he was Philip's son, Alexander. Once we abandon the search for a plan of history we are rewarded by insight into the sublime and beautiful laws of nature which man obeys even in the wildest excesses and passions.'

Whatever happens anywhere on the earth is 'what can happen, partly according to the position and need of the locality, partly according to the circumstances and opportunities of the age, partly according to the inborn or acquired national character'.

From this there arises the idea of a genetic approach which starts from the universe then proceeds to the position of the earth and the conditions of all life on it. It goes on to a picture of the distribution of water and land, mountain and plain and the distribution of organic life which results: the basic construction of plants and animals can be developed until, according to Ritter,[3] the individuality of the earth is completely revealed, with all the conditions which it places on human history. One cannot illuminate this great plan of Herder's better than did Alexander von Humboldt's and Ritter's immortal works which are the fruit of this method pioneered by Herder and his contemporaries.

But in *The Ideas* this great design of Herder's was merely the basis for a comparative study of man. Man is the highest link in the development of the genetic power active on the earth. Here Herder follows Goethe's research completely and sharply diverges from Kant. Here, where we are dealing with the explanation of man in the context of nature, we recognize the decisive contradiction between the Herder–Goethe point of view and that of Kant, for whom man, taken out of the order of nature, was a link in an invisible, higher order. The progress of nature's design is directed towards the production of an ever more subtle, and relatively larger brain to give the creature a freer centre of sensations and thoughts. The more the head and the body of an animal lie in a continuous horizontal line the less room there is in him for a higher brain: the more the body tends to be raised and the head separated, the more subtly is the creature formed. This is the general explanatory basis for the facial angle discovered by Camper. This scientific point of view makes it clear what a well-justified meaning the significance of upright carriage has in Herder's chain of thought. 'The inner spatial relationship of the parts and the place of the head in the organization of the whole makes for the difference of instinct or activity in an organism, whether animal or man.'

This organization, an elevated, unrestricted human chest, gave man the conditions for speech. Education and culture were based on it. Reason must be understood as deriving from it and not, we may add, as Kant proposed, as an original endowment common to angels and men. So the highest goal of mankind can only be humanity. A morality which transcends it produces phantoms. 'Even when we imagine angels or gods we imagine them as ideal, higher men.' Divinity 'has tied the hands of men by their conditions in time and space and by their innate powers'.

The mother of the manifold organizations of mankind is the genetic power of nature affected for good or ill by the climate. The unifying link is to be found in the fact that mankind is one species. A magnificent

[3] Karl Ritter, German geographer, 1779–1859.

law of nature asserts itself in the struggle of the manifold human powers. All the destructive powers must – in the course of time – succumb to the preserving ones. A particular case of this general law is that fewer destroyers than preservers are born in mankind. The conditions of the animal kingdom allow fewer carnivorous than herbivorous animals and a similar relation is preserved in the historical world, because here irregular passions and unnatural tendencies must combine with corresponding outer conditions to produce a destructive historical force. On the other hand the progress of the arts and sciences weakens 'the animal strength of the body as well as the propensity to wild passions' and provides stronger means for controlling them.

We cannot follow in detail how far Herder got in the study of the persisting causes of great historical phenomena or how penetratingly he described them. Spinoza was his model in his basic conception, Kant in his research, which proceeded from the evolution of the universe to the position of the earth in it and on to man, Goethe in his conception of the genetic power of nature and the sequence of its formations, but Winckelmann for his view of Greek history and Montesquieu for that of Rome. Could anyone do it all by himself? But a great beginning was made by him and Goethe.

The reader should now be able to survey quickly the world-view I have presented which was not developed by professional philosophers. It would be quite impossible to appreciate, let alone understand, the great achievements of Schleiermacher's generation, still less those of this extraordinary man unless we start from what this generation found in existence.

An ideal of life had been developed in poetry and moral reflection and was to reform the moral sciences. It converged with the philosophic movement which, motivated by the same striving for a new ideal of life, had been developed by Kant and Schleiermacher. One of the profound characteristics of Schleiermacher's nature could only find its fulfilment in combining these two factors.

A world-view, magnificently developed from free contemplation of the world, confronted that of theological enlightenment. Indeed a conception was formulated according to which the universe could be conceived as a genetic development from unconscious nature to the highest forms of consciousness. Here is the first, original form from which, through the addition of the philosophic movement, the new German Pantheism developed in Schelling and Hegel. On the basis of this conception these two men tackled the problem of human knowledge; the true meaning and content of nature dwells in the human mind and is developed when its concepts are developed because mind is merely nature which has become conscious of itself. In essence and content it is identical with nature. Can we imagine a more magnificent conception of the universal system? Only by referring to it can we appreciate what Schleiermacher was undertaking when he sought to establish the metaphysical connection between mind and nature from the way in which nature is given to us as permeated by reason and at the same time to prove that the religious mind can gain an intuitive grasp of this metaphysical basis to world harmony.

Inspired intuition had penetrated from the realm of poetry to that of the sciences; here it developed into a truly fruitful synthesizing and comparative approach which became a powerful method for the study of the whole earth. This prepared the way for the greatest achievement. Two great men followed in Winckelmann's, Goethe's and Herder's path. Humboldt described his goal as making 'contemplation of physical things in terms of a totality of nature moved and animated by inner forces, into a separate science'. Ritter formulated his ideal as follows: 'The earth is a cosmic individual with a particular organisation, an *ens sui generis* with a progressive development: the exploration of this individuality of the earth is the task of geography.' In the sphere of the human studies it is superfluous to mention names: here the intuitive method achieved most: the Schlegels, W. v. Humboldt, Bopp, the Grimms, Boeckh and Welcker form a series. At the same time this great tendency of the German intellect to start with the whole and then to distinguish the parts, distribution and structure provided the grounds for the gross errors of that period. It is as difficult as it is necessary to seek in the scientific spirit prevailing at that time an explanation for the philosophic and scientific methods which prevailed from Kant to our time and to separate its great inspirations from its errors.

The swelling stream of our great poetical epoch brought many things: new ideals of life, a new world view, even new methods of scientific research. First of all this particular ferment presented itself in moral and social conditions and views which sprang from the new ideals of life.

BERLIN

Vol. xiii/i, pp. 208–28

In Berlin Schleiermacher joined the stormy controversy between the new ideal of life and the traditions, convictions and forces which had accumulated in the preceding centuries. In the capital of Frederick the Great's monarchy this tradition had more vitality than anywhere else. He and his friends spent their effervescent, youthful energy on this controversy. Much-praised and much-slandered personalities come to the fore. They can only be properly appreciated in terms of the spirit of this emerging metropolis. From an early period it, more than any other city in Europe, showed a historically determined individuality which it impressed on all the movements which arose in it. It was involved in everything that Schleiermacher did and was the historical basis of all his activities until he died. Let us try to grasp the development of the city's unique character and understand the position of the parties and the conditions that Schleiermacher found.

When Frederick the Great left Berlin, in the throes of a carnival on the morning of 13 December 1740, he went to join his army at Krossen, and, in a youthful spirit, started what was to commit him to a lifetime of victories, dangers and restless work. The capital he left was entirely different from contemporary Berlin; it was a town of about the size of today's Cologne (from the registers of deaths Süssmilch estimates its population at about 100,000); it was little more than a residential and garrison town; the population, always lively and sharp-tongued, was used to strict obedience; literary interests were not much in evidence. Patriotism, submissive to hard, oppressive duty, was allied with firm convictions inclining towards Pietism.

From the peace of Dresden (1746) onwards the size, customs and mentality of the city changed with striking speed; modern Berlin emerged. Court festivals still formed the central interest of the town and, according to a reputable city historian, the Berlin public was kept in a good mood by them. An amazing age in which the citizen enjoyed furtively watching festivals paid for from his pocket! But other things happened which began to transform these cosy conditions. The city grew rapidly in the years of peace that followed. In 1747 there were, including a garrison of over 21,000, about 107,000 inhabitants: from then on, until 1755, it grew by about 3,000 a year. Prices rose, marriages decreased, a more luxurious life rapidly emerged; the rich Silesian aristocracy sparkled at court. Frederick allowed freedom to speak and write on religious topics and surrounded himself with companions who were so full of wit and frivolity that it seemed permissible to say and do anything which was not against the state. Frederick broke the old tie between state and church interests. 'This, so called, refinement gradually eroded the principles of the inhabitants which, till then had been their motives in civil life.' These simple words express what is essential for judging the civic enlightenment which had its centre in Berlin in that century. The motives of the great king contained something alien to the general spirit, something mysterious. His great soul felt itself bound by the idea of duty without any motive of fear or hope, of faith or philosophic conviction; but the time had not yet arrived when duty towards the state would become a powerful motive among other sections of the community. Yet his special kind of will-power, without the garb of French philosophy – and it was only a garb when one compares the shaping of the will in Frederick and Voltaire – began to influence individuals of outstanding intelligence or great political position. He was acceptable to the middle classes because of his admixture of homely philosophy. Journalists found it quite natural that he should prefer the welfare of the state to moral and religious issues. Active, searching criticism, a negative trait, which has remained characteristic of Berlin, came freely to the fore.

This spirit found its first social expression among the middle classes in the Monday Club, founded, on the suggestion of the Swiss theologian Schulthess, by the poets Friedrichs, Ramler and Sulzer, and joined by Nicolai and Lessing. Here the new spirit achieved its highest poetic and literary power. It first appeared in the 'learned' articles of the *Vossische Zeitung*. Their light epistolary tone, their daring form and the strong sense of real and healthy life evoked Nicolai's letters about literature. A shy, lonely Jewish merchant, excluded from the scholarship of the time, joined the club – Moses Mendelssohn. It can be said that, in 1755, when Lessing, Nicolai and Mendelssohn came together, the older literary school of Berlin was founded. Its character has long been overshadowed by Nicolai's later misdeeds. These writers did not wear the pigtail common in the universities of the time; they received no ducal pensions; they felt that they represented the thinking of a powerfully growing bourgeoisie which was sustained by the interests, moods and intellectual needs of a rapidly expanding metropolis. Thus began the splendid period in which Berlin led the intellectual movement in Germany.

It is most peculiar that this emerging spirit was powerfully furthered by the Seven Years War. While the size of the population fell on the whole, though not steadily and only insignificantly, the mood of the city was far from depressed. There were traces everywhere that a public opinion was forming about political matters. A flood of political pamphlets from both camps, above all, Hertzberg's inspired *mémoire raisonné*, aroused the public to lively debates. The war – as it does today – brought forth newspapers which spread the latest news among the masses. Cheap pamphlets about events made booksellers rich. Nothing shows the connection between life and literature more strikingly than the decisive energy which the war imparted even to the belletristic enterprises of Berlin. Nicolai expressly testified that it put Lessing in the mood to dispose boldly and summarily of Seraphim, Catones and Daphnes in the world of German poetry. So his letters on literature originated. In the midst of Prussia's crisis Berlin stayed in the van of the intellectual movement.

A dynamic age had produced communal feeling, political sense and realism. How did Berlin develop socially and intellectually after the victorious conclusion of the great war? It is a less brilliant, but very informative, picture which confronts us.

Hardly any cultural phenomenon has been praised more uncondi-tionally and then ridiculed more completely than the older intellectual movement which had developed and become dominant in Berlin from Lessing's departure in 1766 until the 1790s. Schleiermacher and his friends, either individually or together, found themselves constantly forced to fight it either mockingly or seriously. Here its character as well as its strength and weaknesses becomes plain. This old Berlin school originated because Frederick the Great's absolutism hindered, distracted and even demoralized the aspiring intellectual movement I have described.

From 30 March [1763] when the king, awaited by festive crowds of citizens since the morning, rode to his castle through the suburbs in the evening – alone in the midst of his enthusiastic people – a series of fatal disappointments were in store for the public spirit of the city created by the war. Various factors had combined to change the king's character enormously: the ingrained habits of camp life, the tendency of a commander placed in terrible circumstances to treat everything as a means to an end and to consider that obediently facing death is man's sole virtue. All these and other experiences, which no autocrat is spared, had made his propensity to despise men all-powerful. The slim shoot had become gnarled. His harshness fell heavily on commerce and finance. If one looks at the growth figures of Berlin after the peace one is surprised to find that the increase of the population is smaller than at various periods before and afterwards. His regulations cut mercilessly into the citizens' simplest pleasures. Smokers and snuffers grumbled about interference with the natural rights of man; a witty conversation among a few old invalids about coffee, and a farewell song of an old maid to her coffee-pot, circulated in the city. The king left to his Berliners only the right to ridicule and even this was considerably limited by the fear of the old lion at Sans-souci whose paws were incalculable. The rising spirit of serious discussion about the common good was limited to literary or religious questions or degraded into miserable trivia and sycophancy. The spirit still existed, even in Nicolai's description of Berlin and his journey through Germany, in Biester's essays about particular administrative questions and institutions in the respectful *Monatsschrift*, in the debates of the Monday Club – but debased and confined. Scholars like Büsching and Süssmilch had lively response from the public but only certain conclusions were drawn from their statistical compilations. Dohm, the most important political writer living in Berlin, became silent once he had to deal with major issues in the foreign office. A variety of private lecture courses revealed the strong intellectual interests of the city; there were no less than twenty-one of these in 1786; Herz lectured on experimental Physics and Moritz on belles-lettres. The prevalence of a practical, realistic tendency was also evident in them. Even poetry, what little there was of it in this respectable society, seemed realistic and allied itself to practical but, of course, non-controversial interests. One must grant that Nicolai attempted something significant when he tackled the social novel; he gave a realistic picture of society by focusing on certain tendencies and produced a noteworthy example in his *Sebaldus Nothanker*. Even in the mediocrity of the characters, their doings and sufferings, Nicolai's novel is a faithful mirror of the citizens, officials and scholars of Berlin at that period. Engel and Moritz made similar attempts. But the Berlin spirit was most at home in the periodicals and their topical, practical and informative journalism. Their number is terrifying. They were all outdone by Nicolai's *Allgemeine Deutsche Bibliothek*; after Lessing's departure he never doubted that he represented Berlin's intelligentsia and that care for the education and enlightenment of Germany was his life's task. So, first of all, he took charge of what was then called religious enlightenment and has been described in the first volume of this work. But in his and his friends' hands it lost its own peculiar spontaneity and simple, healthy self-limitation. They acted as if they were the governors of enlightenment. They brought to this sphere something of Frederick's absolutism and thought that enlightenment could only be protected in the same way as his government protected it. The *Monatsschrift* and *Bibliothek* instituted an enquiry into the aesthetic and religious feelings which creep in the dark and cannot be dissolved by common sense. This kind of enlightenment prevailed among judges, academics and church authorities; Teller and Zöllner represented it among the clergy, Gerike in the educational system, Biester, Engel and Ramler, as well as Nicolai, in literature. As late as 1796 Nicolai was elected to the Academy. The creators of the Prussian common law were of the same generation and their code was based on the same attitude of mind.

This was the older Berlin spirit. But the very sharp judgment about a man like Nicolai, justified by his narrow-minded and passionate criticism of cultural phenomena he could not understand, recedes when different considerations are taken into account. All his other mental inclinations were insignificant compared with his enthusiasm for the common welfare of the citizens, for the glory of his king and the position of Prussia in Europe. He hastened to make all possible sacrifices in 1806 and was so prostrated that he never recuperated from the illness which overtook him then. Patriotism and a realistic and practical way of thinking represented the strength of men like him but, in the circumstances of the Age it was also the basis of their ill-humour, growing sterility, indeed their incapacity to appreciate the greatness which another tendency of the age was to bring forth.

Towards the end of the king's life a little-discussed but important effect of absolutism on the intellectual life of the budding metropolis became noticeable in different circles of Berlin. A series of pamphlets, spiteful attacks and satires emerged; it was the natural expression of a lively, alert, metropolitan society which felt itself cut off from practical and active political interests. In the more self-contained and refined Parisian society the same ugly product developed under absolutism but it was more elegant and biting. . .In both places it sprang from the same growing-pains. The manifestations under Frederick were predominantly confined to small bourgeois gossip. The miserable scribblings of the war-office official, Krantz, who began to play the role of a Rabener and disguised his muck-raking as patriotism (for example *The Berlin Correspondence* and *Pictures from Contemporary Berlin*) were eagerly devoured. He depicted the luxury and frivolity of the Berlin of 1783 in exaggerated colours. He talks as if all upper-class women were venal then. This had appeal and was continued by others with even greater pleasure. This kind of thing was considered to be rather strongly expressed but talented and useful. Moral lessons once received from the pulpit were now the respectable job of the satirist. This tendency to take intellectual interest in the details of private life increased in the subsequent reign. The literature of scandal spread widely. Krantz, who had had to leave the country when Frederick was alive because he had stolen from an account and had sold a horse three

The Schleiermacher Biography

times, was now allowed to return. Indeed the minister had to fight off appeals to re-employ him. In this class of nameless journalism Garlieb Markel stood out: together with Falk he analysed the private life of the young generation, that of F. Schlegel, Schleiermacher and Tieck.

Because they are conditioned by the requirements of satire these descriptions of morals have to be taken with a pinch of salt but there is little doubt that the morals of Berlin society did decline rapidly from the 1780s onwards. The causes were at first a court without women and Frederick's French sympathies; later the sensual and passive character of his successor. In 1779 Foster found Berlin's former hospitality and tasteful enjoyment of life debased into vulgar display and debauchery, free enlightened thought replaced by impertinent gaiety and un-bridled free thinking, and women generally corrupt. Under the great king's successor political interest declined and the pleasures of private life had increasingly to compensate for this. One must read Mirabeau's secret letters from Berlin, the first of which starts 'The king of Prussia is going to die' to get a feel of the depressed mood in which the Prussian capital watched the king's struggle with death which lasted for several months, to see with what little hope the first steps of the new government were accompanied and to what depression its further steps led. 'In a word', Mirabeau says, 'just as everything had expanded into greatness everything now shrinks into pettiness.' One can see from the descriptions how this affected morals. It is true that some things singled out for blame represented healthy progress, for example, that the upper-classes began to live more spaciously, surrounded by lighter, more comfortable furniture; mahogany furniture was introduced to the city. Other things were inevitable parts of the development of a metropolis, for instance, the liking of the lower classes for luxury in dress, for the novel and for comedy. But some immoral features were undoubtedly connected with a decline in the social sense of honour which pervaded court and city. Uncertainty about marital faithfulness resulted in impertinent words about the honour of women being heard frequently and with pleasure; affaires played a prominent part in the interests and lives of people and revelations of these became a favourite topic of the – in this respect only – incredibly unbridled press. These features are in strange contrast to others: the religious compulsion introduced when Wöllner took over the ministry of education in 1788, the narrow, middle class form of society which, without free social contact between men and women, sought its enjoyment in recreational societies, playing cards and Iffland's middle class plays, the morality of which was soon diluted into the weepy, forgiving and forgetting of the Kotzebue heroes.

73

Dilthey as a Historian of Ideas

These were the intellectual and moral conditions of old Berlin, which Schleiermacher still found dominant in the nineties. Though the new generation decisively opposed the trend of old Berlin it was still subject to the same conditions. Indeed the new tendencies were shaped and coloured by the way public spirit had been formed. The claim to lead German culture remained and it was promoted by lively journalism; but this was coloured by the tendency to point sharply and generalize unconditionally in order to affect a busy society; the social and moral problems which at times of political lethargy come to the fore were separated from the poetry and scholarship of German culture; something of the spirit of frivolous enjoyment combined with moral scepticism, something of metropolitan restlessness, of the thirst for life which does not allow a balanced existence to arise, imparts itself to the moralists and poets.

In these conditions the new spirit, the new ideal of life, the world view described in the previous chapter entered the young generation of Berlin.

It is true that Nicolai and Mendelssohn, too, claimed Lessing, who had fought his first aesthetic campaigns in their company, for their own; but Friedrich Schlegel was right when he considered it necessary to explain to them that the most powerful factor in his existence was his great and free style of life which ultimately found conscious expression in his philosophy. His article of 1797 about Lessing robbed the great man's old companions of their highest authority, the basis of their continued dominance. The influence of Goethe, in whom the new ideal of life emerged fully and freely, then became decisive. It was only *Wilhelm Meister* which made Goethe truly comprehensible to these circles.

Now the young generation learned to appreciate the true value of personality, to dedicate itself joyfully to a wealth of human relationships, to trust the moment, to enjoy the manifestations of one's own personality while remaining sensitive to the individuality of others. Life, containing a wealth of poetry, seemed to open its shining eyes. Once again poetry had accomplished its great task of disclosing the infinite content of existence which emerges in the restless urge of feelings, passions and will as well as in serene contemplation.

This initiates a splendid – indeed, to this day, the most splendid – period of Berlin society. Periods when social life flourishes have been scarcely more frequent than those of the highest artistic development. If they are to occur outer conditions of prosperity and tranquillity are as necessary as those of free delight in individuality and its expressions which unite different classes in the value placed on

74

personal culture. A flourishing social life is only achieved when people feel a strong impulse to assert their personalities but no special desire to achieve anything practical. Such a period of not only brilliant but truly significant social intercourse, of the kind which at different times developed in Athens, Florence or Paris, then began in Berlin. An expression of the conception of life on which it rests is preserved in Varnhagen's writings: here a man of brilliant descriptive gifts felt himself impelled to preserve for posterity the picture of men who played a large part in society without being active in practical matters. This urge itself, the spirit in which this picture was composed, characterizes the period as much as the people whose portraits it has preserved. Everything rests on a strong interest in the individual and his intrinsic value in society. Only this uncommonly intensified interest can produce so brilliant, significant and lively a society as then existed.

Which section of Berlin society precipitated the flourishing social life that inevitably developed in that period of the highest poetic conception of life has often been a matter of debate. There was in Berlin a group which strove upwards, was eager for culture and was motivated by wealth, distance from court and office and untiring ambition to create for itself a sphere where it mattered. The rich merchants were predominantly Jews. Mirabeau notes that there were few merchants in Berlin who owned 150,000 to 200,000 *livres*, and infinitesimally few who owned 400,000 *livres*; but these were almost exclusively Jews. In 1798 there were about four and a half thousand in Berlin in a population, without the garrison, of 142,000: they stood out by their wealth, their display and their desire to set the tone. Mendelssohn made immense efforts on behalf of the German culture of his nation. In Dohm they found a weighty champion of their claim to full citizenship. His pamphlet *Improving the Civil Status of the Jews* of 1781 was followed by a lively literary debate which Mirabeau joined in 1787. Efficient Jewish scholars, like Friedlander, Herz, Bendavid and Maimon came to the fore with Mendelssohn. In spite of his straitened circumstances, the latter was, with the conductor Reichardt, one of the first in Berlin to keep an open house, and entertained distinguished strangers. The wives and daughters of the Jewish merchants now came to the fore; they were clever, restlessly enthusiastic, had plenty of time and were alive to culture; they were married early without their hearts having been consulted. At first the living spirit of Mendelssohn's home shaped their development. In 1778 Mendelssohn's daughter Dorothea, barely 17 years old, had married the banker Veit on her father's instructions but could not come to love him. She introduced the hospitality and cultured social life of her father's home to the more ample circumstances into which she entered. A year later her beautiful friend, Henriette de Lemos, who had also sat at the feet of the Jewish philosopher, married the great physician Markus Herz while she was still half a child. She, too, soon gathered a large circle around her and her beauty was so unique that all men of importance visited her home and even Nicolai, a refined and reserved man in society, paid her homage.

This was still under Frederick the Great and the literary interests of the older school of Berlin predominated in the salons of these ladies. At Dorothea Veit's weekly reading circle David Friedlander, Herz and Moritz were to be found: Dorothea, like her friend Henriette, looked towards the chair of the aged Mendelssohn to catch a sign of his approval. In the great reading circle which gathered, under Engel's experienced stage directions, in 1785 at Frau Hofrat Bauer's in the royal castle, Moritz, Teller, Zöllner and Dohm were joined by the brothers Humboldt, then only very young men mainly interested in the beautiful ladies. This idyllic scene was soon to change.

Goethe himself had been in Berlin in 1778 but he was liked by the Berliners nearly as little as he liked them. Moritz who grasped the inner spirit of Goethe's poetry deeply and enthusiastically, the conductor Reichardt and Zelter (the two first composers of his songs) and many other individuals worked on his behalf. But it was a different matter to grasp the meaning of Goethe's poetry fully and to understand life from the point of view of this great poet. Of this only the young generation was capable and so it freed itself from the influence of the old Berlin school. Goethe became the symbol of the complete separation between the old and the young generations. Only now, under Goethe's influence, was the new society formed. Even in August 1795 Rahel wrote 'Goethe is the focus for everything which can, and wants to be, called human'.

Nothing conjures up the brilliance and the deep shadows of this new society more clearly than the life of this burningly passionate woman; this one must get from her unabridged letters to Veit, as they have now been published, and not from their arrangement by Varnhagen. Her father was a well-to-do, not very educated, jewel-merchant whose witty despotism lay heavily on his family and who entertained many people, mostly actors. Rahel, herself, was ten years younger than the wives of Veit and Herz and had no close contact with them; she knew mainly actresses. Various sections of society met at her house and she formed her own judgment of them. Gentz and Miss Eigensatz, his mistress, visited her; so did Prince Louis Ferdinand and Pauline Wiesel. One is shocked by the passion with which – in her intimate correspondence – she feels the fate of being a Jewess: she feels like an outcast. At the same time one notices how, in spite of her sense of the moment, she systematically pursues the plan to rise from the circle of her youthful background and associate with the upper classes on an equal footing. We know to what extent she succeeded; the salon of Frau von Varnhagen and that of Frau von Arnim represented, decades later, that flourishing social life of Berlin which, finally, had to give way to other forms of social intercourse.

Other friends, too, penetrated into high society. Two sisters, one Frau von Grotius, the other morganatically married to Prince Reuss, an elderly, ugly man, played a prominent part; the latter was eventually given the title of Frau von Eybenberg. The justified urge to count in society appeared in less significant people in not very agreeable forms. One noticed that the ladies hurried to climb the highest steps of culture without having touched the middle ones.

This new society which spread over the whole city influenced the talents of the younger generation considerably. There is an important, but as yet scientifically unexamined connection, between great social movements and those of intellectual activity. Periods of great poetry are invariably linked with the lively development of social life and a high degree of individual freedom in society. Goethe created conditions for himself in Weimar which met these requirements. With naive directness he lived as he wrote. But when his ideal of life had been accepted by this metropolitan society, with its scepticism about ideal emotions, widespread independence and alternating periods of desire and enjoyment, it gave rise to the doctrine of the unlimited right of passion. Society was deeply permeated by this. To some extent, Genz, Tieck, Bernhardi and Friedrich Schlegel must be considered as products of this society. Sharp, realistic knowledge of men and social skill give scope to unlimited desire; intellectual creation itself is pressed into the service of this life of passion; tendencies threatening the family spring from this soil. A phenomenon like Genz only has its equivalent in the Italian or French society of the Renaissance. But even if we believe that freedom of the passions must be firmly limited in the interest of the whole society and that there is a deeper, inner law which links the true value of a person and his existence with purification, justice and steady faithfulness, we must contemplate with admiration the rich unfolding of *joie de vivre*, individuality and lively social intercourse.

Now Schleiermacher entered this society; he was the man who was to give imperishable expression to everything of lasting value in its desire for freedom.

The Great Poetry of
the Imagination

EDITOR'S INTRODUCTION

The passages selected come from an essay written by Dilthey in the 1890s. It first appeared in 1953 with other literary articles selected by Dilthey's disciple, H. Nohl and previously published in periodicals, and provided the title for the collection.

The title *Die Grosse Phantasie Dichtung* does not refer to a general type of poetry (narrative or lyrical poetry) but is the name Dilthey gives to the literature produced in England, France and Spain in the sixteenth and seventeenth centuries. Cervantes, Molière, Marlowe and Shakespeare are outstanding representatives of this movement.

Specialist students of literature must judge for themselves if this article – eighty years after its composition – contains any fresh insights. They may find the width of Dilthey's scholarship which refers with equal familiarity to the literature of several countries and makes comparisons between them stimulating.

To me the interesting thing is the extra dimension which literary criticism acquires when it comes from a philosopher interested in the history of ideas. The essay stands or falls by the thesis that this whole literary movement is influenced by, and can, therefore, be better understood in terms of, two factors. One is the politics, particularly the international politics, of France, Spain and England. The other is a common world-view, or philosophy, which gives this literature a distinctive character.

The Great Poetry of
the Imagination

pp. 22-5

A unifying intellectual force deriving from the scholarly literature of the Renaissance emerged in the midst of all these national limitations. Its influence freed the poets from ecclesiastical and national limitations by producing an awareness of the connectedness of things, of the value of life and of the nature of man. Even Calderon's[1] most philistine fanaticism for ecclesiastical and national conformity was deepened by the influence of this universal spirit. It gives the highest artistic creations and poetic works of the Age the power to overcome national and ecclesiastical limitations, to rise to universal validity and thus to become part of world literature. It contributed to all the most profound descriptions of man and reflections on the course of the world; it deepened, strengthened and shaped the imaginative comprehension of life by placing emphasis on the individual, his physical appearance and his relationship to world events and invisible powers.

The philosophic background to this age of imagination was a faith that the world was completely permeated by mental processes. But it did not, like the philosophy predominant in Antiquity and the Middle Ages, relate the divine power to substantial forms,[2] i.e. to the forces active in the species – but to individual things. This is the new contribution in the world view of that Age. The individual is now a quintessence, image, or mirror, of the godhead. The world-power, meaningfully creative, expresses itself in individuals. This Age sees mental power in whatever exists and its mental attitude is invariably artistic and poetic. Everything which is inanimate to us had, for the man of that time, power and soul; it was as if the primitive ways of looking at the world had returned. Being manifestations of divine power all individual things are linked in an embracing harmony which seems to produce an ineffable music. A spiritual quality floats over everything like a fine mist or moonlight and illuminates it in a particular way. The poet's empathy with inanimate nature here is not deliberate symbolism but the natural result of how he sees things. This comprehension of nature merges by subtle, imperceptible degrees into

---

[1] P. Calderon de la Barca, 1600–81.
[2] Refers to the emphasis in medieval philosophy on 'universals' (i.e. what makes thing belong to a class).

79

the fantastic superstition which with a force incredible to modern man enveloped the original geniuses of the Renaissance, Pico[3] and Cardano, Luther and Melanchthon and researchers like Paracelsus and Kepler. Only in Italy did the transmission of divine power through substantial forms exercise an effect on art and literature at that time: clearly the new Platonism influenced the artistic ideals of Raphael and Michelangelo via the Florentine Academy. On the other hand a sceptical spirit and rational thought developed among Italian Renaissance writers and, in France, Montaigne[4] became influential in art and poetry. The former movement did not diminish the power of the imagination, only changed the way it was expressed in art. Scepticism mainly influenced the Italians and French while imagination continued to rule among the Spanish and Teutonic nations.

The power which the imagination exercised over the men of that period expressed itself in their way of perceiving and thinking and in their style of speech. Especially among the Nordic peoples, poetical vision was inseparably related to thought. The writers of this epoch speak in images – not deliberately but spontaneously. The language of an inductive philosopher like Bacon[5] is of greater sensuous power than that of any modern poet. The medical disquisitions of a Paracelsus are permeated by such a breath of imagination, by such a feeling for the mental life in everything and for the transformation of all being into power, that compared with them, any modern poem appears laboriously artificial and philistine. In Luther's youthful writings and letters there is a responsiveness, a visible, almost tangible, presentation of inner states, a sense of life, power and soul in the objects of nature, a fantastic magical and terrifying power of imagination, an awareness – to the point of hallucination – of supernatural forces in conflict, and a power of expression that borders on the brutal. Compared with these all religious poetry from Klopstock to the present day is the lifeless product of a literature remote from life. Kepler in his search for a science of the cosmic approached even astronomical problems with such powerful images that few later poets can match the energy of his imagination.

This is the general intellectual atmosphere in which Spenser, Marlowe, Shakespeare, Ariosto,[6] Cervantes,[7] Lope,[8] Calderon and Corneille[9] lived: it alone makes the origin of their great works comprehensible. The power of their imagination confronts modern

[3] Pico della Mirandola, 1463–94.
[4] Michel de Montaigne, 1533–92.
[5] Francis Bacon, 1561–1626.
[6] Ludovico Ariosto, 1474–1533.
[7] Miguel de Cervantes, 1547–1616.
[8] Lope de Vega, 1562–1635.
[9] Pierre Corneille, 1606–84.

man as something totally incomprehensible – as if it were the product of an extinct race of giants. Their works become a little more comprehensible if one sees them as the highest expression of an imagination which naturally dominated the world-view, the prose style and even the picturesque everyday speech of the time.

The belief that everything is alive and colourful because it is a manifestation of the godhead gives new strength to superstition. Every body is power and everything spiritual seeks its body. Medieval faith combines with the surviving doctrine that the heavenly bodies have spirits, plants have souls and spirits can be conjured up by magic. Such notions, going back to ancient times, can never be eradicated from popular belief; at this period they were accepted and defended by the pan-animistic philosophers. So all this was real for those who heard or read the poetry of imagination. All the pulsing life in river and wood – the spirits which move so terrifyingly in the moonlight and animate the scenes of Spenser's *Faerie Queen* or Shakespeare's comedies, the mighty shades who, attracted by murderous thoughts or blood, enter the visible from an invisible world – were, to the poets of the time, manifestations of the divine order expressing itself in spirits and powers of every kind. They did not ask if Brutus or Richard III encountered such shades, if the prophecies of which historical tradition is full really came true, if spirits really can appear; perceiving the universal pattern through pan-animistic feelings, they considered all this a comprehensible revelation of divine power.

The manifestation of this divine power in the individual thing or person is the key to the secret of how the poets, the Nordic ones especially, saw and described man. Their characters are not types like those of the Greeks: still less are they merely products of nature or hard fact, nor are they fully accounted for by their social context. For men of that time the individual was the quintessence or mirror of the godhead. In the same way, the gipsy in Cervantes, Calderon's religious figures and Shakespeare's Imogen, Julia, Hamlet and Richard III confront us as living wholes radiating a kind of inner splendour by which they are removed from everyday life. This conception of man culminates in Shakespeare. He has a strong sense of the ambience (climate, landscape and social structure) which surrounds his Nordic kings and the heroes of his Roman tragedies or Italian comedies; we seem to breathe the exhilarating air of Venice or the fog and heath of the North. Each of his plays appears steeped in a colour of its own. But, though the real setting of the dramatic action and characters, the particular historical and political background, provides the atmosphere he never uses it to deduce the inner life of the characters and their inevitable fate. This is why he was content to accept as history what he read in stories, sagas, chronicles or Plutarch and was not interested in pursuing the matter further. He takes the structure of the individual as something given. His characters are not shaped by circumstances nor is the impetuous course their energies take affected by them. They do not develop before our eyes. They appear to burst forth from the heart of reality and to force their way through the world. All Shakespeare's characters reveal a highly personal, individually structured, life – even though they may appear for only a few minutes and show limited aspects of themselves. Daemonic power radiates from some, an aura of confidence in their divine beauty surrounds others; or they appear as the teasingly gay creations of the poet's boundless, divine capacity. But they all have an inner vitality and a stronge sense of their own identity.

pp. 29–31

The structure of this great imaginative poetry is determined by the laws of imagination themselves. This is what is predominantly meant by the Romantic character of the poetry of that period.

Any social background which forms the setting of a literary work contains a complex combination of circumstances and these condition the characters and their development, the composite interaction of the characters and, finally, their fate. Reason grasps these causal relationships by means of the conceptions we have formed about the uniformity of events. Such relationships form the backbone of every literary work and even the Romantic poets are tied to them. But what distinguishes their work from ancient, as well as modern poetry is that the causal connections are much less important than the overall literary arrangement based on the laws of imagination. By imagination we do not, of course, mean one particular mental power. The memory of impressions is not static; whenever they are recollected they are changed – more or less subtly – by the context of mental life. Every experience, and every historical event, is increasingly liable to change. So the acquired mental structure constantly exercises a shaping influence; our feelings and instincts permeate our nostalgic memories, passions and eager or anxious images of the future. Spontaneously or deliberately these processes are at work in saga, myth, religion and art. Artistic imagination is merely the quintessence of these processes intensified in a particular mind. Such a mind sees and experiences vividly, remembers with pictorial and emotional power and of itself creates a heightened artistic reality which, like another world, extends above that of actuality.

It is clear that the power of imagination increases when the men of an age are less governed by reason which adjusts its ideas of reality strictly according to the rules of induction, mathematical concepts and the laws of nature (in short, by producing an objective, law-governed order of reality). Whenever a conceptual framework has perished and another is about to emerge we see that a new openness to experience and imagination dominate mental life.

There was a period like this when the medieval world of ideas had lost its dominance and mathematical science, which was to become the basis of modern thought, had not yet developed. Here one sees the way opened simultaneously to art, literature and religious experience.

The predominance of the imagination at that time first showed in the desire to transform life itself into a work of art and enjoy it as such. The individual strove to regard himself as of intrinsic worth and to display, in every possible form, his standing and dignity. This trend manifests itself in splendid, colourful clothes and artistically shaped rooms and gardens. The period was characterized by public jollifications, festivities, gorgeous court ceremonies and indulgence in every kind of spectacle. This tendency of the imagination to enjoy life as a spectacle culminated in drama and recitation. Poetry was not locked away in the reader's room or in playhouses where the productions were completely divorced from everyday life. It was life itself which produced this upsurge in art and poetry and gave exceptional zest to living.

Life in the Iberian peninsula and England provided the most colourful and magnificent subject-matter for the imagination – consciousness of world power, discoveries and wars on land and sea in India and America, pomp, adventure, and the internal struggles of an aristocratic monarchy.

The most general feature of imaginative poetry is that it is based on extensive experience of a rich and varied life and is not something that literary men transfer from paper to paper. The poets of this movement were craftsmen. It is characteristic that the two greatest dramatists of the period, indeed of the whole modern age, were actors. This gives their plays their expressive power. By this I mean that the poet keeps the stage in front of his eyes, treats words as adjuncts to gestures and actions, and has the power to give dynamic movement to the action. The poetry of this period culminates in this power. Lope, Cervantes, Shakespeare and Molière are the models for all time. The inner structure of their works is determined by the principle that the causal nexus and the laws of imagination are equally relevant. The emotionally barren is eliminated like dead wood. The essential parts of the plot are also the emotionally powerful moments and the appearance of life is produced by arranging these moments just as pictures are created by using blobs of colour.

pp. 32–4

I am not afraid of being misunderstood. None of the great turning-points in human history can be seen as the inevitable result of preceding circumstances. If man were a rational being, as Hegel assumed, or if he were determined by the succession of his ideas and concepts, as a modern school of psychology which also has adherents among historians assumes, then we could infer every later stage of human intellectual life from a previous one. Everyone knows from his own experience how little we resemble thinking machines. It is the whole man with his imagination, emotions and follies who is involved in any intellectual change. His human nature is always on the point of breaking out and overthrowing every intellectual construction or system within which it had dwelt for a time. In the Middle Ages it proved impossible to discipline him: the revolutions of later centuries have demonstrated this even more strongly. Never at any time did he show his formative and creative power so forcibly as when he shed his medieval chains and moved forward to the enjoyment of unlimited freedom – hot-bloodedly, passionately and with his imagination released. What happened then was not determined by previous circumstances, nor could it be explained by the social conditions. These only precipitate great historical actualities as the rays of the sun make flowers grow. What there is in human nature is revealed by the great turning-points of history. For history alone shows what man is.[10]

[A few lines referring to particular persons and places omitted.]

...The works of that time reveal an understanding of man as an individual which, so far, leaves any scientific analysis behind and, in a sense, will always do so. These works reveal that life and the emergence of individuals is unfathomable. A constructive energy which transcends the empirical and aims for the uniquely individual or typical is the main feature of this approach. In the finest achievements of this literature men are seen as energy in motion. Their development is ignored. The soil from which they grew was not seen in relation to the plant. They stand divorced from the social and historical context in which they emerged. The dynamic plots into which they are placed, their relationships and their location are all purely mental constructions. Man is the goal, not nature, society, or history.

[10] This paragraph represents a central theme of Dilthey's thinking – see p. 93 and Editor's Introduction, p. 19.

II

Dilthey's Approach
to Psychology

Ideas about a Descriptive and Analytical Psychology

EDITOR'S INTRODUCTION

The *Ideas about a Descriptive and Analytical Psychology* first published in 1894 contains some striking suggestions and aroused a good deal of controversy. Because of this, as well as its relevance to other portions of Dilthey's work, I have included portions of this work which indicate the drift of its argument. But I have been more severely selective than in most of my other translations because many of the detailed proposals and criticisms of contemporary psychologists have been outdated by eighty years of development in psychology. Indeed, and this influenced me more than any of the other reasons, some of Dilthey's formulations have been overtaken by later one's of his own which he considered more precise and illuminating. (I am thinking particularly about some of the fragments collected in vol. VII.)

Yet some of Dilthey's points are very eminently worth making and may not have lost their relevance even today. Here are some of these:

(i) A psychology which establishes causal laws for mental life by postulating some simple entities and mechanisms is, in the state of our present knowledge, premature and speculative. It is also of insufficient value to the disciplines which require insight into human nature like history or sociology.

(ii) Instead we need patient, careful and searching descriptions and analyses of mental processes. This is not merely, or even mainly, a recommendation to look into oneself rather than study behaviour. It stresses rather the examination of the structure of languages, myths, legal codes, novels and autobiographies because these manifest the working of the human mind in all its complexity. We must understand complex mental processes as they occur in or affect mature human beings if we want to understand the human world.

(iii) Patient study of these processes allows the following tentative and modest generalizations: (a) there are common, typical ways in which the human mind functions, i.e. thinks, feels, remembers and strives and in which these processes are related to each other; (b) on the inborn structural features of the mind an acquired structure is superimposed. This is the product of cultural influences and adjustment to the environment. (c) This mental structure forms a unity and affects individual human responses.

(iv) In the human sphere, as in any other, description can serve as a preliminary stage of explanation, just as description of an experiment often precedes its explanation in terms of the laws of physics. But description in the human studies does more than this. In the alien world of matter the links between events must be hypothetically constructed, but because we are at home in the world of mind, we experience the connections themselves.

Ideas about a Descriptive and Analytical Psychology

1894

Vol. v, pp. 139–40

Chapter I. The Task of Laying a Psychological Foundation for the Human Studies

Explanatory psychology, which at present absorbs such a large measure of work and interest, establishes a causal nexus which claims to explain all mental phenomena. It tries to explain the constitution of the mental world according to its constituents, forces and laws, in the same way as physics and chemistry explain the physical world. Particularly clear representatives of this explanatory psychology are the association psychologists,[1] Herbart,[2] Spencer,[3] Taine,[4] and different types of materialists. The difference between explanatory and descriptive science assumed here, corresponds to ordinary usage. By an explanatory science we understand the subsumption of a range of phenomena under a causal nexus by means of a limited number of unambiguously defined elements (i.e. constituents of the nexus). This concept describes an ideal science which has been shaped particularly by the development of atomic physics. So explanatory psychology tries to subsume mental phenomena under a causal nexus by means of a limited number of unambiguously defined elements. This is an extraordinarily bold idea containing the possibility of an immeasurable development of the human studies into a strict system of causal knowledge corresponding to that of the physical sciences. Every psychology wants to make the causal relationships of mental life conscious but the distinguishing mark of explanatory psychology is that it is convinced that it can produce a complete and transparent knowledge of mental phenomena from a limited number of unambiguously defined elements. It would be even more precisely characterized by the name constructive psychology. This name would also emphasize its great historical context.

[1] W. D. Hartley, 1705–57, and A. Bain, 1818–1903, are outstanding representatives of this psychological approach advocated by such philosophers as Locke, Hume and Mill.

[2] J. F. Herbart, German psychologist who combined associationism with a rationalism derived from Leibniz, 1776–1841.

[3] H. Spencer, 1820–1903.

[4] H. A. Taine, French philosopher/psychologist/historian and critic, 1828–93.

Descriptive and Analytical Psychology

Explanatory psychology can only reach its goal by a combination of hypotheses.

The representatives of explanatory psychology tend to justify their extensive use of hypotheses by reference to the physical sciences. But here, at the outset of our investigations, we are staking out the claim of the human studies to determine the methods they consider appropriate for their subject-matter. Starting from the most universal concepts of a general methodology the human studies must work towards more definite procedures and principles within their own sphere by trying them out on their own subject-matter, just as the physical sciences have done. We do not show ourselves genuine disciples of the great scientific thinkers simply by transferring their methods to our sphere; we must adjust our knowledge to the nature of our subject-matter and thus treat it as the scientists treated theirs. We conquer nature by submitting to it. The human studies differ from the sciences because the latter deal with facts which present themselves to consciousness as external and separate phenomena, while the former deal with the living connections of reality experienced in the mind. It follows that the sciences arrive at connections within nature through inferences by means of a combination of hypotheses while the human sciences are based on directly given mental connections. We explain nature but we understand mental life. Inner experience grasps the processes by which we accomplish something as well as the combination of individual functions of mental life into a whole. The experience of the whole context comes first; only later do we distinguish its individual parts. This means that the methods of studying mental life, history and society differ greatly from those used to acquire knowledge of nature.

Any empiricism which foregoes an explanation of what happens in the mind in terms of the understood connections of mental life is necessarily sterile. This can be demonstrated in any one of the human studies. Each of them requires psychological insight. So every factual analysis of religion involves concepts like feeling, will, dependence, freedom, motive, which can only be explained in a psychological context. It must deal with the context of mental life because in it alone the consciousness of God originates and gains strength. But it is conditioned by general, regular, mental connections and can only be understood through them. Jurisprudence is confronted by mental constructions in such concepts as norm, law and accountability which require psychological analysis. It cannot possibly describe the context in which respect for the law originates, purposes express themselves in the law and the will of people is subjected to law unless it has a clear understanding of the regular connections in all mental life. The political sciences, which deal with the outer organization of society, find the psychological factors in community, domination and dependence in every association. These require psychological analysis. The history and theory of literature and art must refer to the composite, fundamental, aesthetic moods of seeing something as beautiful, sublime, funny or ridiculous. Without psychological analysis these moods would remain dark and dead *ideas* to the literary historian. He cannot understand any poet's life without knowing how the imagination works. This is true and no departmentalization can prevent it; the systems of culture, commerce, law, religion, art and scholarship and the outer organization of society in family, community, church and state originated from the living context of the human mind and, ultimately, can only be understood through it. Mental facts form their most important constituents so they cannot be grasped without psychological analysis. They contain connections because mental life forms a context. So our knowledge is always conditioned by our understanding of this inner context. These systems and organizations could only become powers which control the individual because the uniformity and regularity of mental life permits the same order to apply to many people.

The development of the individual human studies is tied to the progress of psychology, so the combining of these disciplines into a whole depends on understanding of the mental context in which they are linked to each other. Without reference to the mental context on which their relationships are based the human studies are an aggregate, a bundle and not a system. Any, however crude, conception of their mutual links rests on some crude conception of the nexus of mental phenomena. How commerce, law, religion, art and knowledge are related to each other and the outer organizations of human society can only be understood in terms of the comprehensive, uniform, mental context from which they sprang side by side and on the strength of which they co-exist in every person without confusing or disrupting each other.

p. 151

The relationship of psychology to epistemology differs from that of any other discipline even from mathematics, mathematical science and

Descriptive and Analytical Psychology

logic which were singled out by Kant. *The mental context forms the basis of the process of cognition* and this process can, therefore, only be studied and its capacity evaluated in this mental context. It is a methodological advantage for psychology that its subject-matter, mental connections, are a directly experienced reality. It is necessary to experience these connections in order to understand all mental, historical and social facts whatever the degree of elucidation, analysis and investigation. The history of the human studies is based on these connections which it clarifies step by step. Here the problem of the relationship of epistemology to psychology can be solved. The human consciousness and a valid description of its mental context is the basis of epistemology. It does not require a fully developed psychology but all fully developed psychology is only the scientific completion of what also forms the basis of epistemology. Epistemology is psychology in motion towards a particular goal. It is based on the reflection which embraces the *whole* content of mental life: it is this which determines the meaning of validity, truth and reality.

pp. 157–8

To contemplate life we must describe the *whole*, powerful reality of the soul's potentialities from the lowest to the highest. This must be one of the aims of psychology if it is to achieve as much as ordinary knowledge of life and poetic intuition. It is also necessary to the human studies. Their psychological foundations must describe and accommodate all mental powers and configurations, including the religious genius, the prophet, the hero or artist who move history and society onward.[5] Given this definition a way opens up for psychology which promises a much higher degree of certainty than the methods of explanatory psychology can achieve. We must start from the culturally shaped human being, describing the connections within his mental life and highlighting its most important manifestations as clearly as possible by every artistic means; we must analyse the individual connections within this comprehensive context as accurately as possible and take the analysis as far as we can; we must explain the origin of things we can analyse and describe accurately those we cannot. In each case we must state clearly how certain the explanation is, constantly resorting to comparative psychology, evolutionary history, experiment and the analysis of what history has produced. Psychology will become a tool for the historian, the economist, the politician and theologian: so it will guide both the observer of human nature and the man of affairs.

[5] See Editor's Introduction, pp. 6–7.

pp. 176–7

Descriptive and analytical psychology

The general part of such a descriptive psychology describes and names [mental processes] and so contributes to a future agreement on psychological terminology. For this analysis is necessary. The structure of fully developed mental life must also be clarified. Here analysis must deal with the architectonic structuring of the complete edifice; it does not enquire about the stones, the mortar and the labour first but about the inner connection of the parts. It must discover the structural law which links intelligence, instinctive and emotional life and acts of will into the whole of mental life. The connections described in this law of structure are vivid experiences of the individual connections between mental components. Their meaning impresses itself insistently upon us in inner experience. According to this law of structure the character of the mental components is simultaneously teleological and causal. A subsequent chapter will describe these structural connections.

The second fundamental law of mental life results from the teleological character of these connections; it operates in time and is the law of *development*. If mental structure and the forces producing it were not teleological and did not involve valuations which push it in a certain direction, then there would be no development in life. The development of a human being cannot be inferred from Schopenhauer's concept of blind will or from the play of isolated, individual, mental powers described in the systems of Herbart or the materialists. Development in man is directed towards producing a pattern of mental life adjusted to his environment. All mental processes co-operate within us to produce such a pattern, giving shape, as it were, to the mind; for even when we distinguish and separate we create relationships and, thus, connections. The formulae of transcendental philosophy about the nature of our synthesizing faculty are only abstract and inappropriate expressions for this quality of our mental life which creates development and pattern. H. Spencer has correctly described other features of this development in his doctrine of differentiation and integration. Another chapter will deal with the possibility of combining these ideas with those of the German speculative school, thus initiating a scientific theory of human development.

pp. 180–1

The way these connections are given to us determines the point of view from which we analyse them. I have tried elsewhere to prove that the acquired structure of mental life contains the rules on which the *course of individual mental processes* depends. It therefore forms the main subject of psychological description and analysis in terms of the three parts of mental life which are linked together in the structure of the mind; these are intelligence, instinctive and emotional life and acts of will. This acquired structure is given to us most directly in a developed human being, particularly in ourselves. But as it does not enter consciousness as a whole it can only be reproduced bit by bit or seen in its effect on mental processes. So we must compare its *creations* in order to apprehend it more completely and profoundly. We can study the vigorous working of particular forms of mental activity in the works of men of genius.[6] Language, myth, religious tradition, custom, law and outer organizations are products of the collective mind in which human consciousness, to use Hegel's phrase, has become objectified and so open to analysis. Man does not discover what he is through speculation about himself or through psychological experiments but through history.[7] Dissecting the products of the human mind which is designed to give us insight into the origin, forms and function of the mental structure, must combine the analysis of historical products with the observation and collection of every available part of the *historical processes* by which they were produced. The whole historical study of the origin, forms and working of man's mental structure depends on the combination of these two methods. Such vital processes are already revealed in the historical changes which occur in the products of the collective mind; in linguistic sound-shifts, in the way words change their meaning, and in the change of ideas associated with the name of a god. We can also learn about the inner processes which illuminate the origin of particular forms of mental life, from messages, diaries and letters. In order to study the nature of imagination we must compare the remarks of genuine poets about their inner processes with poetical works. What we know about Francis of Assisi, St Bernard and, particularly, Luther, is a rich source for the understanding of the mysterious processes by which religion develops.

p. 199

Psychology depends on the different approaches compensating for each other's defects. It combines awareness and observation of ourselves, understanding of other people, comparative procedure, experiment and the study of anomalous phenomena. It seeks entry into mental life through many gates.

[6] See Editor's Introduction, p. 6, also the section starting p. 99 where this theory is applied.　　　[7] See above, p. 84.

Dilthey's Approach to Psychology

All the methods which deal with processes are supplemented by the use of the objective products of mental life. In language, myth, literature and art, i.e. in all historical achievements we have before us mental life which has been, as it were, objectified; they are products of the active mental forces, stable configurations composed of mental constituents and subject to mental laws. When we contemplate processes in ourselves or others they appear as changeable as figures in space the contours of which are constantly altering: this is why it is invaluable to be confronted with permanent clearly defined creations to which observation and analysis can return again and again.

If we try to gain knowledge of the comprehensive and uniform pattern of mental life we shall see if a descriptive psychology can be developed. Psychological analysis has certainly established many individual connections in our mental life. We can follow the processes which lead from an outer impression to the development of a perceptual image; we can pursue its transformation into a memory; we can describe the formation of fantasies and concepts. We can also describe motive, choice and purposive action. But all these particular patterns must be co-ordinated into a general pattern of mental life. The question is can we pave the way for this?

p. 206

The decisive fact for the study of mental structure is that *the transitions from one state to another, the effect of one on another are part of inner experience. We experience this structure.* We understand human life, history and all the hidden depths of the human mind because we experience these transitions and effects and so become aware of this structure which embraces all passions, sufferings and human destinies. Who has not experienced how images thrusting themselves on the imagination suddenly arouse strong desire which, confronted with great difficulties, urges us towards an act of will?[8] In these and other concrete connections we become aware of particular transitions and effects; these inner experiences recur and one connection or another is repeated until the whole structure becomes secure, empirical, knowledge in our inner consciousness. It is not only the major parts of this structure which have an inner connection in our experience, we can become aware of such relationships within the parts themselves. The process of mental life in all its forms, from the lowest to the highest, is from the beginning a unified whole. Mental life does not arise from parts growing together; it is not compounded of elementary units; it does not result from interacting particles of sensation or feeling; it is

[8] See pp. 185ff.

94

always an encompassing unity. Mental functions have been differentiated in it but they remain tied to their context. This has reached its highest form of development in the unity of consciousness and the unity of the person and completely distinguishes mental life from the whole physical world. Knowledge of this context of life makes the new theory that mental processes are single, unconnected representations of a pattern of physical events, completely unacceptable. Any doctrine which pursues this course contradicts experience for the sake of a combination of hypotheses.

This inner mental structure is conditioned by the person's situation within an environment. The person interacts with the external world; the form this takes can be represented as an adjustment between the person and the conditions of his life; this is merely a general description of a fact about man as we know him and will be investigated later. In this adjustment chains of sensations and motor-activities are linked to each other. Even the highest forms of human activity are subject to this great law of organic nature. The reality surrounding us calls forth sensations. These show us the nature of the various external things which cause them. So we continually find ourselves physically and mentally conditioned by outer causes. According to this hypothesis our feelings express the value these external forces have for our bodies and instincts. Conditioned by these feelings, interest and attention select impressions on which they focus. This increased consciousness in attention is, intrinsically, a process. It consists of distinguishing, identifying, combining, separating and perceiving. This is the origin of perceptions, images and, ultimately, thoughts which enable the person to control reality up to a point. A firm system of reproducible ideas, valuations and acts of will is gradually formed. Now the person is no longer at the beck and call of stimuli. He inhibits and controls his reactions; he chooses when he will adjust reality to his requirements. What is more when he cannot control reality he can adjust his own vital processes and controls the unruly passions and the play of ideas by an inner act of will. This is life.

The third fundamental characteristic of this context of life is that its parts are not linked to each other according to the same causal law as external nature; i.e. cause and effect are not quantitatively and qualitatively equal. There is no compelling reason why ideas should give rise to feelings: one can imagine a creature which only has ideas and which, in the tumult of a battle, remains the indifferent, passive spectator of its own destruction. Nor do feelings necessarily give rise to acts of will. One can imagine the same creature observing the battle around it with fear and horror and no defensive reactions resulting from these feelings. The connection between these different factors, none of which can be deduced from the others, is *sui generis*. Its nature is not explained by the word 'purposiveness', for this expresses what is contained in the experience of the mental structure only in a conceptual abbreviation.

pp. 221–2

In this context we can clarify how descriptive psychology approaches the theory of development. An explanatory psychology would have to choose between conflicting hypotheses about the nature of development; descriptive psychology avoids these hypotheses which take one back to the most fundamental contrasts in human views of the world. It recounts what it finds and emphasizes the regular sequence of the processes which take place in human beings. In the same way as the botanist must first describe the sequence of events from the moment an acorn begins to germinate in the ground to that when one drops from the tree, the psychologist must describe the processes of mental structure in terms of the laws of development and the uniformity of succession. He gleans these laws and uniformities from the relationships between environment, structure, values of life, mental differentiation, acquired mental structure, creative processes and development; these are a vivid part of inner experience and are supplemented by outer experience without the need for additional hypotheses about causal relationships.

If, instead of this descriptive procedure, we attempt an explanatory theory which seeks to penetrate behind inner experience, the concept of unambiguously defined mental factors cannot deal with the problem; this is why explanatory psychologies which only use such mental elements in their construction of a theory usually avoid the subject of the development of mental life. Explanatory psychology must either place human development in a universal metaphysical context or try to grasp it in the general context of nature.

pp. 225–6

The acquired structure of mental life which exists in developed human beings embraces constant images, concepts, valuations, ideals and fixed directions of the will. It contains constant connections which are the same in all human beings as well as those which are peculiar to each sex, race, nation, class or individual. All human beings share the same external world so they produce the same number system, the same spatial relationships, the same grammatical and logical relationships.

Descriptive and Analytical Psychology

Because this external world is experienced by a common mental structure the same forms of preference and choice arise, the same relationship of ends and means, similar relationships between values and similar ideals of life are developed everywhere.

Schleiermacher's and Hegel's formulae about the identity of reason in all individuals and Schopenhauer's about the identity of their wills express the fact of human kinship in metaphysical abstractions. The uniformity of the individual products of man, the great and pervasive connections which link these products into systems of culture and the persistence of powerful organizations which relate men to each other provide psychology with solid material for real analysis of mental life, even its fundamental content.

Goethe's Poetical Imagination

EDITOR'S INTRODUCTION

The analysis of Goethe's imagination is part of a very long essay on Goethe which first appeared in 1877. In 1905 it was republished, together with essays on Lessing, Novalis and Hölderlin, in a volume called *Das Erlebnis und die Dichtung* (Experience and Poetry).

The section reproduced illustrates Dilthey's abiding interest in poetry and shows how his analysis illuminates the work under consideration as well as drawing lessons from it for the student of the human world. Here we also have a fine example of the kind of descriptive psychology he thought we needed (see p. 90).

Dilthey was interested in imagination in general because he believed it was involved in almost everything man does – his recollections and plans for the future, his scientific work and solution of practical problems, his artistic creation and political actions. He returns to this theme again and again. Here, as always, his approach has three distinctive features. Instead of considering samples of ordinary people or examining elementary forms of imagination in children or even animals he turns to the extreme case of a poetic genius in whom we can study imagination 'writ large'. Secondly he aims at the painstaking description of the working of the imagination rather than at explanations of it in terms of elementary processes. He did not deny the possibility or the value of explaining imagination in terms of physiological or environmental factors. But he believed they could not take the place of full descriptions, which are both theoretically illuminating and practically useful.

The third feature of Dilthey's approach is his choice of evidence on which to base his descriptions. He uses the poet's work, his spontaneous comments, recorded by friends, and his autobiographical remarks, rather than the results of tests and experiments. Even if Goethe had been alive Dilthey would have considered it futile and misleading to drag him to the psychologist's laboratory to get evidence of his imaginative processes. In his view the working of the imagination could only be distorted and emasculated by artificially controlled conditions.

But the Goethe essay is not only an exercise in descriptive psychology, it is also – and in this it is typical of all Dilthey's biographical essays – a contribution to the history of ideas. For the qualities of imagination which Goethe applied to his work influenced subsequent literature and scholarship – it was a formative factor in Germany's intellectual life.

Goethe's Poetical Imagination

Experience and Poetry pp. 188–96

Goethe's imagination is the classical example of the process in which powerful poetic creations emerge from elementary processes. The strongest zest for life permeates the young man's conversation and poetry; every mood is expressed with partisan energy and pictorially symbolized in images. Everything that Goethe said or wrote then contained the germs of future poetic works striving towards the light.

From this expressive power his incomparable *verbal imagination* emerged. Language is the poet's material. But it is more than this, for the sensuous beauty of poetry in rhythm, rhyme and verbal melody forms an independent sphere of intensive effects which can be divorced from what the words mean. Who would be fully conscious of the meaning of the words when, for example, he recites to himself Goethe's poem 'To the Moon'. Their meaning only chimes in quietly and mysteriously. The poet's verbal imagination concentrates on the shaping and forming of these effects just as the painter does with his lines and colours. Goethe is a sovereign in the sphere of language because, in him, experiences were constantly and directly linked to an urge for expression. In his youth his conversation often jumped from prose to the quotation of his verses. At that time when out walking he sang to himself 'strange hymns and dithyrambs' in which he expressed the rhythm of his emotions in sounds. So the art of creating great, free rhythmic poems in all their naturalness and vivacity arose within him; such a will to master life has never been expressed in such rhythms! In his youth he broke away from traditional language. Basing himself on Klopstock he created a new poetic style. He also turned to his local dialect and exploited the vital energy of verbs. He made his effects by new word formations. Thus he gave verbs new prefixes, combined the noun with a particle and the verb with its object or strengthened the sensuous energy of a verb by omitting the particle. He put nouns together into new, extended word-formations, he emphasized expression by repeating significant words, he ran through question, answer and explanation to reproduce agitation. Every mood found expression in a verbal melody of its own. Gradually, in his first years in Weimar, he used his local dialect less. He moderated violent expressions and gave a full description of emotions. He calmly conjured up objects by new means such as the increased use of significant adjectives; using the foundations laid by Luther's translation of the Bible he and Schiller developed our classical literary language. On this basis he formed his great style. In such achievements Goethe's unique verbal imagination stands revealed; so extensive is its power that it has dominated all our subsequent poetry and, to this day, his poetic language can evoke any mood in the reader.

This verbal imagination of Goethe's which developed from the urge and capacity to express experiences, is combined with an astonishing imagination in the whole visual sphere. So the pictorial beauty of the world of things overlies the agitated states of mind.

The following passage from his contributions to morphology throws light on the natural basis of such a capacity for pictorial creation: 'I possessed the following capacity: when I closed my eyes and, with head inclined, envisaged a flower in the centre of my vision, it did not remain in its original shape for a moment; it opened up and from inside it unfolded new flowers with coloured and also green petals: they were not natural flowers but fantastic ones, symmetrical like the sculptor's rosettes. It was impossible to stay this proliferating creation in its flow; it lasted as long as I liked, neither abating nor intensifying. I could produce the same effect by envisaging the decorations of a many-coloured pane which also changed continuously from the centre towards the periphery like the kaleidoscopes invented in our time.' Under favourable conditions, before going to sleep the observer may, as I have myself, manage to see the coloured fog emerging in his dark field of vision forming into shapes and changing; we observe with what ease and beauty Goethe's spontaneous shaping imagination gives rise to these creations. In *Elective Affinities* which, after all, is entirely permeated with the description of the way in which even the highest revelations of mental life are physiologically conditioned, he transfers this capacity in a modified form, to his beloved Ottilie; the description reminds one of what Cardanus tells us about himself; between sleep and waking she looks into a softly illuminated room in which she sees Edward, who is away at war. The power which the creations of the imagination exercise on the poet himself is repeatedly expressed with deep insight in *Tasso*: 'In vain do I try to halt the urge which fluctuates in my mind day and night' etc.: then, when he describes the future journey of the exile to Naples: 'I walk in disguise, I don the poor coat of a pilgrim or shepherd' etc., one shares Leonora's shudder which interrupts him as if to break the uncanny enchantment with which this fantasy envelops him. In *Pandora* Goethe gave the most comprehensive and vigorous poetic description of all this. He generalized the insight into the poet's nature which had resulted from such experiences as follows: 'One can see more clearly what it means that poets and all real artists are born. An inner, productive, power must – freely, spontaneously and vividly – project the images retained by the senses, by memory and by imagination; these images must unfold, grow, expand and contract, so as to transform fleeting shadows into true pictures before our eyes.' 'I am', he told chancellor Müller, 'so strangely constituted with regard to my sense-perceptions that I remember all outlines and shapes most sharply and am, at the same time, most vividly affected by disfigurements and defects.' 'Without this sharp perception and impressionability I could not produce my characters so vividly and sharply individualized. This clarity and precision of perception has for many years in the past lured me into the illusion that I had a vocation and a gift for drawing and painting.' In the same vein Goethe defines the goal of poetry in his aphorisms. 'The poet depends on representation. At its best it competes with reality, i.e. when the mind describes it so vividly that anyone would think it was present.' The intense co-operation of these two kinds of poetic imagination in Goethe produced a universality of poetic power unmatched in modern times. He depicted its power and unique quality in the description of his last years in Frankfurt. 'For some years my creative talent has not deserted me for a moment; what I had observed when awake in the daytime turned into clearly defined dreams at night, and when I opened my eyes I saw either a surprising new whole or part of one already in existence.' This natural gift was his whether he was alone or in company. At that time his proud consciousness of creative power found expression in Prometheus. He had to consider this gift as wholly natural. It occurred 'spontaneously, even against his will'. Occasionally it lay fallow for a long time and he could not produce anything even with an effort of will; at other times his pen could hardly follow his 'somnambulist writing'. Even his major works originated, after a long period of gestation, as one inspiration; he wrote *Werther* in four weeks 'fairly unconsciously', as if guided by a dream, without having previously committed to paper an outline of the whole or the treatment of any of its parts; he scarcely found anything to alter; this is how his most accomplished and homogeneous work before *Hermann and Dorothea* originated. In all the examples I have given the characteristics of poetic imagination confront us with exceptional strength. We see a spontaneous, law-governed creativity drawing on the fullness of mental powers and divorced from ordinary life and its purposes. This peculiarity of his youthful poetry continues into his later years, modified by tranquillity, reflectiveness and the declining power of imagination. Periods of intense creation follow long preparations; 'the pile of wood, gradually collected and arranged' – so he reports in 1795 during his work on *Wilhelm Meister* – 'at last begins to burn'. He isolates himself, preferably in the castle at Jena, to maintain the poetic mood and the inner continuity of creation. No amount of willing promotes success and the best work comes of itself. So his creations develop over long periods of time. 'Certain great themes, legends and ancient, historical traditions impressed themselves on my mind so much that I retained them, living and active, in my mind for forty to fifty years; I treasured the frequent imaginative renewal of these precious images which constantly changed and ripened – without losing their identity – towards a more formal and clear-cut presentation.' In other poets, like Schiller, every artistic work originated from strenuous, conscious labour. Perhaps this strong, forward surge of the will communicated itself to the action and lends it the dynamic quality which we admire in Schiller's plays; Goethe's finest creations do not exhibit these qualities. While at work Goethe was not wholly independent of the judgment of his friends about what he had started. In particular he was decisively influenced by Schiller as regards the continuation of *Wilhelm Meister* and *Faust*. In other cases criticisms made him give up the idea of a particular poetic work. Like other great storytellers he could be deeply moved merely by conjuring up the product of his imagination. When he envisaged the details of a situation in *Wilhelm Meister* 'he finally burst into bitter tears'. The same happened when he read aloud a just completed portion of *Hermann and Dorothea*: 'so one melts on one's own coals' he said, drying his eyes.

We get the most complete insight into the power and peculiarity of this imagination when we see how it affected every part of the organism which was Goethe. Its influence pervaded his life, his world-view, his ideals. In the young man imagination was predominant among his abundant yet uncurbed powers. In the years of effervescent, youthful power, it immeasurably heightened his joys and sorrows; it enveloped all reality in veils of beauty and endowed him with the gift to enchant and inspire both men and women; at times it idealized the present, at others magnified constrictions to the point of making them unbearable and, by conjuring up new images, made distant lands seem attractive; so it heightened the restlessness of youth and of his inspired consciousness; it drove him to the point of toying with suicide, made him unreliable in his friendships, love, work and aspirations; he acquired the almost daemonic qualities of the superman which he described in

Goethe's Poetical Imagination

the *Urfaust.* To Jacobi he then appeared like a man possessed who was rarely able to act freely. Again and again poetic imagination – by transforming this life into the world of make-believe – offered him temporary freedom from the restlessness of his life. He relieved his soul by expressing what moved him. He freed himself from the circumstances of his life by externalizing them as something alien, part of the realm of poetic imagination where their consequences unfolded far from what conditioned him. Poetry also helped him to discipline himself and achieve the mature ideal of his manhood. This ideal was based on raising the whole of life to its highest significance; so grasping and realizing this ideal – unlike following abstract moral rules – depended on images of the past, the future and what was possible because the life reflected in these images is the basis of any ideal conception of the self. Finally, Goethe's poetic imagination revealed the secrets of nature and art. Because his detached contemplation of nature was akin to artistic creation, nature revealed itself to him when he experienced the creative power of his own imagination. He saw it as a power governed by law and purposively active: it expressed itself in metamorphosis, in development, in the systematic arrangement of typical forms and the harmony of the whole.[1] Therefore, inevitably, art for him was the highest manifestation of the workings of nature.

[1] See pp. 57–62.

III

Dilthey's Philosophy
of Life

Dilthey's Conception of
Philosophy

EDITOR'S INTRODUCTION

Dilthey's general view of philosophy is represented by three separate texts. The first, 'Present-day Culture and Philosophy' is the MS. of a lecture Dilthey often used from 1898 in one of his University courses. It is characteristic of his style of approach and of the themes which intertwine in all his thinking. For him philosophy meant taking issue with the intellectual and cultural problems of his age. Among these are the challenge of our increasing knowledge and control of nature, the movement towards political reform and popular government and the growth of scepticism about ultimate beliefs and values illustrated by the rejection of metaphysical systems, traditional morality and established religions.

Characteristically all this is presented in historical perspectives. He refers to recurring periods of scepticism in human history; he describes the collapse of the rationalist system of the seventeenth and eighteenth centuries and its replacement by the views of the Romantic movement and the historical school of the nineteenth century; he sketches the development of science and individualism. Surveying the contemporary scene he sharply rejects the aridity of academic philosophy but criticizes, equally sharply, the kind of philosophy of life produced by philosophers like Nietzsche and literary men like Maeterlinck. Such a philosophy, he argues, tries to be undogmatic and close to the immediacy of experience, but ends up being unsystematic and idiosyncratic. Dilthey's own conception of philosophy emerges clearly from these discussions.

The Nature of Philosophy, from which I have selected representative passages, was first published in 1907. It is a comprehensive and systematic account of Dilthey's conception of the nature and functions of philosophy. He considered that philosophy was man's most comprehensive form of thought by which means he confronts the mysteries of life and reflects on himself and his doings. Particularly interesting in this context is Dilthey's account of the relationship of philosophy to the sciences and human disciplines.

The third work on philosophy from which I have selected passages is *The Types of World-Views*. First published in 1911 it was based on various earlier drafts. Here Dilthey looks at philosophic systems as a historian of ideas. But this is not merely a factual enquiry. In the light of a historical perspective we see that philosophic systems assume typical forms which conflict and cannot be reconciled with each other. This insight, Dilthey believed, frees the mind from bondage to any dogmatic system. It cures us of the illusion that philosophy can give an ultimate and comprehensive knowledge of reality which is many-sided. The different types of world-views – by which he means philosophies which combine a picture of reality, an assessment of its meaning and value, and moral principles – contain true insights but are inevitably one-sided. They err because they take their own points of view for ultimate truth.

Dilthey classifies world-views into three types, though he does not exclude the possibility of different classifications. Naturalism, which includes the atomists of antiquity, the materialists of the eighteenth century and the positivists and empiricists, is the philosophy which has empirical knowledge of the physical world for its basis. The idealism of Freedom of which Kant's and Fichte's philosophies are examples are focused on the experience of the active will. Objective idealism, exemplified by the work of Spinoza and Hegel, springs from the contemplative vision of the whole of reality. Preference for one or the other of these points of view is influenced by the philosopher's temperament and the intellectual climate and historical conditions of his age.

Present-day Culture and Philosophy

Vol. VIII, pp. 190–205

I

What I want to offer you is no mere academic philosophy. The right philosophic note can only come from an understanding of the present, so let us try to grasp the basic features of the present which shape today's generation and colour its philosophy.

The most general and basic feature of our age is its realism and the worldliness of its interests. We cling to the words of Goethe's Faust:

> Well do I know the sphere of earth and men.
> The view beyond is barred to mortal ken;
> A fool! who thither turns his blinking eyes
> And dreams he'll find his like above the skies.
> Let him stand fast and look around on earth;
> Not mute is this world to a man of worth.[1]

Since Goethe's assertion the progress of the sciences has constantly heightened our realism. The planet on which we live shrinks, as it were, under our feet. Every one of its constituents has been measured and weighed by scientists and the laws of its behaviour determined. Astonishing inventions have shortened and narrowed distances on earth. The plants and animals of all the continents have been collected in museums and botanical or zoological gardens and listed in reference books. The skulls of all races have been measured, their brains weighed, their faiths and customs determined. Travellers study the minds of primitive people and excavations reveal the remnants of perished cultures. Gone is the romanticism with which even the previous generation viewed the culture of Greece or the religious development of Israel and we realize that everything happened very naturally and on a human scale. In politics the nations now consider every part of the earth in terms of their own interest and pursue this ruthlessly, to the limits allowed by sober insight into the balance of power.

A single characteristic consequence of this realism appears in the poets and novelists. Idealistic pathos has lost its effectiveness. We can see the limitations of historical greatness, and are more clearly aware of the mixture in the draught of life. We want to get to the bottom of everything and not be taken in. Our mood is, in this respect, nearer to that of Voltaire, Diderot or Frederick the Great than to that of Goethe

[1] *Faust*, Part II, act 5, Midnight; translation by George Madison Priest (New York, 1950).

or Schiller. We feel that life is a problem and all contemporary literature and art – the paintings of the great French realists and the realism of our novels and plays – respond to this. The mixed style of Schopenhauer, Mommsen and Nietzsche impresses us more than the pathos of Fichte and Schiller.

A second fundamental feature of our age determines its philosophy. The methods of the physical sciences have established an area of valid knowledge and given man domination over the earth. Bacon's programme – knowledge is power, mankind should progress towards dominance over nature through discovery of its causal laws – is more and more realized by the physical sciences. They are the power which has furthered progress on our planet in the least controversial way. All the arts of Louis XIV have produced fewer permanent changes on this earth than the mathematical calculus which Leibniz and Newton quietly thought out. Thus a new stage began for mankind in the seventeenth century with the founding of the mathematically based physical sciences. No century accomplished a greater and more difficult task than the seventeenth.

(1) The development of mechanics provided science with a firm foundation. It was based on a combination of mathematics and experiment. Mathematics developed the relation between magnitudes, experiment showed which of these relations was realized in motion. The simplest and first example of this procedure was the discovery of Galileo; he ascertained experimentally the rate of continuous acceleration of a falling body under simple conditions.

(2) Once changes in nature could be represented by movement the new science proved itself capable of discovering the laws of nature. Light, heat, electricity and sound were submitted to the methods of science.

(3) Movements in outer space proved to be subject to the same regularities.

(4) Chemical processes became increasingly accessible to quantitative analysis. To conclude: In all these spheres a certain and valid science of nature developed and became a model for all science, reaching far beyond the sphere of mechanical science. In biology, too, the mastery of man over nature, by means of causal laws, became possible. Once the causes of change in nature become accessible to our will we can produce the effects we want. In other cases we can at least foretell these effects. A limitless prospect of extending our power over nature has opened up.

A third fundamental feature of contemporary culture is connected with this. Gone is the faith in an immutable order of society. We are in the midst of transforming this order according to rational principles. During the last centuries several factors have been at work in this direction: (**1**) The influence of industry and commerce grew gradually from country to country. The resulting shift in economic power also led to changes in the social position of classes. First the bourgeois came to the fore, then the working class demanded better economic conditions and more political influence; today these demands determine the internal politics of states. (**2**) Another factor is the growth in the consciousness of the right of the individual. It first asserted itself in religious movements, in the religious sects active in the peasant wars, in the religio-political movements of the Netherlands, and in English puritanism. A firmer foundation for this same right of the individual was then sought in the philosophical movements of the modern age. Hugo de Groot, Voltaire, Rousseau, Kant and Fichte mark the stages in which consciousness of this right was established. This consciousness demanded a corresponding order of society. But where is there a firm foundation for this? Here another factor enters. (**3**) This is the extension of the scientific method, which had proved so fruitful when applied to the study of nature, to the problems of society. Independent human studies developed. Following the physical sciences economics has developed since Quesnay as the doctrine of the laws of economic life; the natural laws, according to which individual systems of interaction combined within social historical reality were investigated, and so the new ideal of transforming society on the basis of these natural laws arose. (**4**) Finally, the subject who made these changes changed himself. The limited attempts at reform of enlightened rulers have, since the French revolution, been increasingly replaced by the sovereign will of the people to give themselves their economic, political and social order. Freedom of association, the increasing power of popular representation and the spread of direct, universal suffrage contained the possibility of putting knowledge of the laws of social life into practice.

2

Fill yourself completely with this realism, this worldliness of interest, this dominance of science over life! They represent the spirit of the last century and, however hidden the future may be, it will retain these basic features. This earth must become the stage for free action ruled by thought and no repression will hinder it.

But when, today, we ask what is the final goal of action for the individual or for mankind, the deep contradiction which pervades our time emerges. We face the enigma of the origin of things, the value of our existence, the ultimate value of our actions, no wiser than a Greek in the Ionian or Italian colonies or an Arab at the time of Averroës. Today, surrounded by the rapid progress of the sciences, we are even more at a loss for an answer to this question than any earlier period. For (1) the sciences have progressively dissolved the presuppositions which lay at the foundations of the religious faith and philosophic convictions of former centuries. The reality experienced by our senses has proved to be merely the appearance of something unknown. (2) The greatest achievement of philosophy in the last century, the analysis of consciousness and knowledge, has itself contributed most effectively to this destruction. Space, time, causality and even the reality of the external world were subject to doubt. (3) Historical comparison reveals the relativity of all historical convictions. They are all conditioned by climate, race and circumstances. Often in the course of history Ages have appeared in which all firm presuppositions about the value of life and the goals of action were questioned. Such Ages were the Greek Enlightenment, the Age of the older emperors in Rome, and the Renaissance. But if we compare these Ages and ours, we find that each was more fundamentally sceptical than the preceding one; the anarchy of thought extends in our time to more and more presuppositions of thought and action. Now that we can survey the whole earth we can see the relativity of the answers to the world's enigma more clearly than any previous period. Historical consciousness increasingly proves the relativity of every metaphysical or religious doctrine which has emerged in the course of the Ages. Something tragic seems to lie in man's striving for knowledge, a contradiction between will and capacity.

From this dissonance between the sovereignty of scientific thought and the inability of the spirit to understand itself and its significance in the universe springs the final and most characteristic feature in the spirit of the present age and its philosophy. The grim pride and pessimism of a Byron, Leopardi or Nietzsche presupposes the domination of the scientific spirit over the earth. But, at the same time, the emptiness of consciousness asserts itself in them because all yardsticks have gone, everything firm has become shaky; an unrestricted freedom to make assumptions, and playing with unlimited possibilities allow the spirit to enjoy its sovereignty and at the same time inflict the pain of a lack of content. This pain of emptiness, this consciousness of the anarchy in all deeper convictions, this uncertainty about the values and goals of life, have called forth the different attempts in poetry and fiction, to answer the questions about the value and goal of our existence.

Present-day Culture and Philosophy

3

What, then, is the position of philosophy in our present-day culture?
(**a**) Its first, and most obvious, task arises from the significance of the
sciences. They require justification for each of them contains presuppositions the validity of which has to be investigated. If the forces of
nature are conceived as a system of movements this presupposes space,
time and the reality of an outer world and the validity of these
presuppositions must be examined. When at the outset thought
assumes that by its own laws it can know outer reality this presupposition, too, must be examined. For these, and many other, reasons the
sciences require justification. Because of this need there was, after the
decline of the metaphysical systems,[2] a return to Kant. The movement
which at present dominates philosophy in all the universities[3] originated from the discovery that Kant's justification was insufficient. The
problem of knowledge must be posed as universally as possible and its
solution prepared for by new, reliable methods. A general philosophy
of science is the task of contemporary philosophy wherever it seeks
certainty of knowledge. Today we take a universal view. (**b**) The
individual sciences also set philosophy the further task of establishing
the connections between them. Originally the link was formed by
metaphysics, but once metaphysics is rejected and only the empirical
sciences acknowledged, this task has to be solved by a combination and
hierarchical arrangement of the sciences. Positivism undertook to
accomplish this task. Comte and the two Mills were the first representatives of this point of view. In Germany this task was accomplished by
Mach and Avenarius.

The common doctrine of the positivists is this: all human knowledge
rests on experience. Concepts are only the means of representing and
linking experiences. Science is a representation of experience which
enables us to condense and evaluate it. Philosophy is merely a
compendium of the empirical sciences. Where these end the unknowable begins. Positivism is the philosophy of the scientists; all cool,
scientifically trained minds accept it. They have found in the extension
of knowledge a firmly delimited purpose for their existence. Thus they
have personally solved the question about the value and purpose of
life. With cool resignation they accept the unknowable.

How can we overcome what is unsatisfactory in this position? Not
through metaphysics, though – with Aristotle, Thomas and Hegel
– she was once queen of the sciences.

[2] Dilthey is referring to the various forms of post-Kantian idealism.
[3] Neo-Kantianism and positivism.

Dilthey's Philosophy of Life

(c) Academic metaphysics:
The Philosophy of Possibilities and desiderata etc.

The same principle of an unjustifiable, spiritually blind, authority is asserted within Protestant orthodoxy and even extends into the theology of Ritschl. Here the sceptical spirit of our age is used to justify the plunge into the particular positive faith of Lutheran religion. Once the whole historical foundation of such a faith has collapsed belief in the truths of the Church, which have no link with reflection about human ideals, floats entirely in a vacuum.

In the present intellectual situation in which scepticism pervades everything and lies at the basis of all vital movements academic metaphysics has become a shadow. We need to achieve a clear, well-justified consciousness of the sum of human aspirations. Compared to this the empty possibilities of metaphysical conceptions reveal themselves if only by the anarchy in which they are at war with each other – as ineffective school saws. These shining fairy-tales may enrapture the young but I predict that they will collapse in the face of the serious work of subsequent life. Then the philosophic intoxication of the university years will only leave a philosophic hangover.

What empty noise and what metaphysical disputation! It is like the end of the Middle Ages when Scholasticism was taught in all the schools while the humanists conquered the world. This is how Carlyle, Schopenhauer, Nietzsche, Richard Wagner, Tolstoi and Maeterlinck[4] are effective today. When the possibilities of metaphysical speculation from particular premises are exhausted the solution of the enigma of life seems to vanish in the mist.

We are at the end of metaphysical thought in the traditional mould and think that we are at the end of scientific philosophy itself. It was then the philosophy of life arose. In each new manifestation it got rid of some metaphysical elements and unfolded more freely and independently. In the last generation it became a dominant power again. Schopenhauer, Richard Wagner, Nietzsche, Tolstoi, Ruskin and Maeterlinck took turns in influencing the young. Their impact was strengthened by their natural link with literature, for the problems of poetry are the problems of life. Their procedure was to experience life methodically while rejecting all systematic presuppositions on principle; this is methodical induction directed towards the processes of human lives and trying to deduce from them the essential features of life in general.

It is the strength of this philosophy of life that its direct reference to

---

[4] Maurice Maeterlinck, Belgian writer, 1862–1949.

life without metaphysical prejudice developed the powers of vision and artistic creation in these thinkers. They live in the constant effort of increasing their awareness. Just as the scholastic thinker developed the capacity to survey a long series of deductions or the inductive power to see many cases side by side, so they acquired the capacity to describe the secret ways in which the soul pursues happiness, the real connections between the desires which spring from our dark instincts, the means that come from outside to satisfy them and the intervention of memories, thoughts and fantasies. So these writers occupy a territory which technically developed philosophy always left empty.[5]

The philosophy of the authors mentioned differs from such a science [of psychology] by dealing neither with the individual relations between hidden and only occasionally surfacing tendencies and outer reality nor with the individual possibilities of life. It tries to give definitive expression to the highest value, to the good in life and to the road to happiness which lie hidden in us and appear externally as only instrumental values. If I call the causal nexus in which the values of life are produced or the relation of our satisfaction-craving self to the outer world, the significance or meaning of life, then these writers are daring to give definitive expression to this meaning or significance. But in doing so they have become the bedfellows of the metaphysicians and, in their more limited sphere, make the same claim. They, too, want to grasp something ultimate and unconditional. And their means, too, are inadequate. For the only sure test of the relations which they seek lies in the sparse moments of our life when we become aware of how what is hidden within us relates to what affects us; these are individual, bright points of light on wide, dark waters whose depth is unfathomable. Each writer talks only about himself. He interprets what he sees of life outside himself accordingly.

The intention to grasp something ultimate and conditional which is related to the strivings of the metaphysicians, leads to a characteristic mistake by the philosophers of life. What it discovers within the individual himself is, within limits, correct but it becomes false when the individual takes his own corner for the whole world. The errors which Bacon deduced from the cave of individuality[6] are fatal for this philosophy. They underestimate historical, geographical and personal relativity. History corrects them. Schopenhauer got rid of his tempestuous, anxiety-ridden self in contemplation. Carlyle concentrated on the heroic will as the highest value in the great religious personalities. Tolstoi re-enacted the leap from the natural life to self-abnegation.

---

[5] There follows a paragraph on D's own descriptive psychology which is pencilled through in the MS.   [6] What Bacon called 'the idols of the den'.

Maeterlinck's problem was life itself. He started from the stoic philosophy of life, and, like it, he undertook to link pantheism with a heightened consciousness of his own self. According to him, the spiritual personality grows through the consciousness of our relation to the infinite and invisible because the individual soul, in its unconscious depth, is linked to this universal life and can only be assured of its value by seeing itself as an expression of the ineffably divine. From this he deduced in his *The Treasure of the Humble* his ideal of a new art which places the quiet, unnoticeable, relations between the simple soul and the invisible, and the development of personality which thus occurs, in the centre of drama (in contrast to the representation of immense abnormal passions in the drama of Shakespeare). In the same way he derived the ideal of mental aliveness, which responds to the most subtle relations of the soul, from the impact of the invisible.

In *Wisdom and Destiny* he added the instruction to make every experience fruitful for the development of personality. The stoic connection between increasing our independence and submitting to the powers of life by harmonizing our nature with things as they are – the establishment, that is, of a harmony between the world and ourselves – became his fundamental conception. When the inaccessible ground of our mental life becomes stronger and more alive, when truth and justice develop in it, it enters into a harmonious relation with its fate in the outside world. In his last work, *The Buried Temple*, he goes on to show how the exercise of justice produces feelings of happiness which, to some extent, make us independent of the external world. But here comes the decisive turning-point into paradoxical one-sidedness from which none of the philosophers of life in our time has escaped. We now hear of a timeless, invisible I.

4

Nietzsche represents and articulates the final consequence to be drawn from the denial of discursive, logical knowledge. Man as a creator of culture is, for him first, the artist, then the scientific consciousness and, finally, because he despairs of that mission too, the philosopher who creates and sets values. It is characteristic of an eccentric man of feeling and imagination that he should put all his vitality into one form of existence and that, when he finds it inadequate – because no one form of life can be everything – he should reject it as radically as he accepted it before. The cultural mission of the artist presented itself to him in the form of Richard Wagner (he did not superimpose this on Wagner for he conceived himself like this) but the radical exclusiveness with which

Present-day Culture and Philosophy

he saw the artist as the only man and creator, his blindness towards the limitations of this form of life, was bound to lead to the opposite view. So, neither from the experience of this first period nor from the Socratically-orientated second period did anything positive remain for him. He disliked the positing of limits in Kant so the third point of view, the philosopher creating values, is again something unconditional and unlimited. The philosopher's job is to heighten men's feeling of the positive value of life and thus to reform them. But Trasymachus and Critias,[7] Spinoza and Hobbes, Feuerbach and Stirner had already expressed acceptance of the will and its power so strongly that history did not need Nietzsche, not to mention all those who as artists or men of action lived according to this ideal. So the concern of this value creating and value setting philosopher should have been to express what is valuable in all the varied forms which the will to live produces. To this Nietzsche's works give no answer; they tell us nothing about the method according to which this new Saggiatore[8] who leaves Galileo behind, is to proceed. 'The philosophic spirit had, in order to be possible to any extent at all, to masquerade and disguise itself as one of the previously fixed types of the contemplative man, to disguise itself as priest, wizard, soothsayer, as a religious man generally: the ascetic ideal has for a long time served the philosopher as a superficial form, as a condition which enabled him to exist. . .to be able to be a philosopher he had to exemplify the ideal: to exemplify it, he was bound to believe in it. The peculiarly etherealized abstraction of philosophers, with their negation of the world, their enmity to life. . .is the result of those enforced conditions under which philosophy came into existence and continued to exist. . .The ascetic priest has taken the repulsive and sinister form of the caterpillar, beneath which and behind which alone philosophy could live and slink about.'[9]

'The real philosophers, however, are commanders and law-givers: they say "Thus shall it be!" They determine first the Whither and Why of mankind and thereby set aside the previous labour of all philosophic workers and all subjugators of the past – they grasp at the future with creative hand and whatever is and was becomes for them thereby a means, an instrument and a hammer. Their knowing is creating, their creating is a law-giving, their will to truth is will to power' (*Beyond Good and Evil*, A (II) transl. H. Zimmern (same edition).

The philosophers, these 'Caesar-like trainers and men who impose

[7] This, no doubt, refers to the figures in Plato's dialogues.

[8] *Il Saggiatore*, meaning *The Assayer*, is the title of an essay on the new scientific method written by Galileo in 1623.

[9] *Genealogy of Morals, Ascetic Ideal*, section 10, transl. by H. B. Samuel (from *Complete Works of Nietzsche*, ed. O. Levy, London, Edinburgh, 1909–23).

culture' are more than merely discoverers, these 'most sublime type of slaves, nothing in themselves'. 'Even the great Chinaman of Königsberg, was only a critic' (*Beyond Good and Evil*, A (10), compare also *Human, all too Human* Vol. 1 A 6, 11 A 31. *The Dawn* A 41 and 62. *Gay Science* 151 *Beyond Good and Evil* A 5). The reason why the 'creation of values' thus becomes vaguer and vaguer and why the method through which the philosopher achieves it is nothing but personal intuition – just as in the artist and the French philosophers of life of the eighteenth century – and also why there is no indication as to how such a method might be developed, lies in Nietzsche's attitude towards the real sciences. From ignorance he rejected psychology as a science. This stands in quaint contradiction to his presentation of unfounded psychological hypotheses about the development of moral norms[10] as if they were scientific results. He remains a complete amateur in the use of historical facts for the understanding of functional connections within a culture; at the same time he has isolated the individual because of his original starting-point, namely the cult of genius and great men. He has divorced the purpose of the individual from the development of a culture; for to him great men are not merely the moving forces but also the essential achievements of the historical process. So the individual, divorced from the functional contexts of a culture, becomes devoid of content; formally, he loses the relation to something progressive and firm. Yet the most significant feature of the real morality of the modern age lies in the transfer of interest to this. Acceptance of life is now a personal immersion either in the eternity of knowledge and artistic apprehension or in the progress of culture itself.

So he did not succeed in his ambition to explain a significant and so far not understood aspect of philosophy in terms of the reforming elements in Socrates, Spinoza and Bruno.

A final and most extreme conception of philosophy goes even beyond Nietzsche. He had accepted value creation in the philosopher as something objective because though it could not be validly determined it could be grasped by a convincing intuition. But this, too, could be abandoned. Then the spirit, robbed of what is valid and lasting in its philosophic products, becomes a power for producing conceptual poetry. But this is self-destructive for the result is not worth the effort.

[10] *The Genealogy of Morals.*

5

The Historical Consciousness of the Nineteenth Century

According to the law of continuity, what the human mind has grasped in a final philosophical generalization as the expression of a certain stage in culture is retained. The unity of human reason in the co-operation of the sciences, the character of general validity and, based on it, the common progress of the human mind towards power over nature and society: these were the final generalizations reached by the eighteenth century.

But this rationalization of the universe also meant an impoverishment of the human mind. The complete, living individual is greater than can be methodologically conceived by this abstract procedure. We saw that the great world-views of the seventeenth and eighteenth centuries were the expressions of great personalities. World-views and ideals of life have, by continuous selection, become typical expressions of the many-sidedness of human nature; this law determines the extent to which the world-views of the seventeenth and eighteenth centuries fit into the three great forms of these views.[11] But they were expressed by means of conceptual abstractions and presupposed the rationality of the universe. Even the apprehension of value and immanent purpose within the one reality was subjected by Leibniz to the principle of sufficient reason.

It is true that, even in the seventeenth and eighteenth centuries up till the emergence of Rousseau, sceptics and mystics objected to these presuppositions and this method. Montaigne, Charron, Sanchez, Pascal and Pierre Bayle, in particular, provided a sceptical background to the seventeenth and eighteenth centuries. Pascal found in Cartesianism the basis for the most acute justification of Mysticism it had ever received. Finally, theological thought in the lower strata of culture was always predominantly founded on the inwardness of religious experience. In 1675 Spener's *Pia Desideria* appeared. This was the beginning of a return from objective dogma to Christian experience. The period when dogma was based on rationality came to an end, because it could not compete with the philosophic system of rationality. But all these movements could not impede the culturally conditioned progress of rational systems. At the beginning of the eighteenth century Leibniz' *Théodicée* and Newton's *Principia* were its scientific highlights and it achieved its highest scientific expression in Voltaire, Wolff, Mendelssohn and Lessing; it was the very soul of Frederick the Great's

[11] See 'Types of World-View', pp. 133ff.

government. The limits of every great philosophic generalization first appear in an inner decline. The minds shrink, become impoverished and uncertain of the principle which imbues them; or, because they have inherited it, its power is blunted by tradition.

There is clear evidence for this: the Scottish school[12] became superficial, French Positivism turned into a grey, sterile materialism; German Enlightenment became vulgar in Nicolai, Biester & Co. The principle of rationality had exhausted its power.

The movement which began with Rousseau and ended with Romanticism contains a system of new and related ideas. Rationalism had denied the past and rejected ages of imagination, emotion and formless subjectivity as lower stages of human development. Rousseau came and rejected even this last period of human culture and, thus, culture altogether. He did not, like the pietists, seek more lively sources of human happiness in the past. The mind of this powerful man was directed towards the future. In an environment in which absolutism, courtly regulation of life, the abstractions of mathematically based science, devastation and impoverishment were spreading, he sought a new beginning: it lay in the living totality of human nature, in its right to develop and to shape from within itself a world-view and an ideal of life. Such an attitude of mind was bound to dissolve into empty passion or become destructive by rejecting society unless it incorporated the content of the historical manifestations of the whole man. Rousseau, the man, had to recognize himself in the great poets and thinkers who created from the fullness of their being; he had to seek a more clearly defined and positive ideal in national life where free, shaping forces were still pulsatingly alive. If human nature is to achieve its full reality and power and the full richness of human existence, it can only do so in the historical consciousness; it must become conscious of, and understand, the greatest manifestations of mankind and derive concrete ideals of a more beautiful and free future from them. The totality of human nature is only to be found in history; the individual can only become conscious of it and enjoy it when he assembles the minds of the past within himself. This is why Herder, Schiller and Goethe could not be content with *Werther* or *The Robbers*. They had to go on to a concrete ideal. They first found it in the Greeks; the Romantics then went back to the original vitality of the Germanic spirit; the East, too, was brought to life.

Yet the capacity to revitalize the past seems to make the human spirit unable to shape the future by its own firm will. The Romantics

---

[12] The group of philosophers starting with T. Reid, 1710–96 and including J. Beattie, 1735–1803 and D. Stewart, 1753–1828.

abandoned themselves completely to the past; the great gain of the eighteenth century appears to have been lost. Everything historical is relative; when we assemble it in our minds it seems to work towards dissolution, scepticism and impotent subjectivity.

Thus this period poses a particular problem. What is relative must be related more profoundly with what is universally valid. The empathic understanding of the whole past must become a power for shaping the future. The human spirit must connect the heightening of its awareness achieved through true historical consciousness, with the gain of the seventeenth and eighteenth centuries. The pathfinders on this road were Hegel, Schleiermacher, Carlyle and Niebuhr.

We must first become fully conscious of what the relativity of all historical reality implies. The study of all the conditions of man on this earth, the contacts between nations, religions and concepts, inevitably increased the chaos of historical facts. Only when we have grasped all the forms of human life, from primitive peoples to the present day, does it become possible to see the generally valid in the relative, a firm future in the past, greater esteem for the individual through historical consciousness and so recognize reality as the yardstick for progress into the future; this we can then link with clear goals for the future. Historical consciousness itself must contain rules and powers to help us confront the past and turn freely and independently towards a unitary goal of human culture. A historical consciousness which is no longer abstract or conceptual and, therefore, does not dissolve into unlimited ideality, forms a basis for the unity of mankind in universally valid thought. From this arise clear goals, a common task, a sound yardstick for what is attainable and a deepened ideal of life. This determines the generalization which philosophy has to make; it would be the expression of the struggle of our whole culture to reach a stage higher than any previous one.

III. The Nature of Philosophy

Part two, Section III

Vol. v, pp. 404–16

3. The Insolubility of the Task.
The Declining Power of Metaphysics

Metaphysics has assumed innumerable forms. It moves forward restlessly from possibility to possibility, is dissatisfied with each in turn and replaces it with something new. A hidden inner contradiction, intrinsic to its nature, marks each new manifestation, forcing it to abandon that form and seek a new one. For metaphysics is a strange amphibian. Its aim is to solve the enigma of the world and of life but to do so in universally valid form. One of its faces is turned towards religion and poetry, the other towards the sciences. But it is neither a science in this sense, nor is it art or religion. It comes into existence on the basis of the presupposition that there is an aspect of the secret of life which is accessible to disciplined thought. If this exists, as Aristotle, Spinoza, Hegel and Schopenhauer[1] assumed, then philosophy is more than any religion or art and, indeed, more than any particular science. Where can we find the point at which conceptual knowledge and its object, the enigma of life, are linked? Where does the unique context of our world not only reveal a particular regularity of events but also make its own nature comprehensible? This point must lie outside the realm of the sciences and their methods. Metaphysics must rise above the reflections of common sense to discover its own subject-matter and method. Attempts to do this in the history of metaphysics have been reviewed and their insufficiencies demonstrated. There is no need here to repeat the reasons, given from the time of Voltaire,[2] Hume[3] and Kant onwards, to explain the constant change of metaphysical systems and their incapacity to meet the requirements of science. I shall only emphasize what belongs to the present context.

The different activities linked together in the structure of the mind are coming to know reality in terms of causal relations, experiencing value, meaning and significance, and willing (containing within itself its purpose and the rule which binds it). The relationship of these three in the mind is part of our experience; it is one of the ultimate facts which consciousness can reach. The subject responds to objects in these various forms of activity and we cannot go further and find a reason

---

[1] A. Schopenhauer, 1788–1860.   [2] F. M. A. Voltaire, 1694–1778.
[3] D. Hume, 1711–76.

The Nature of Philosophy

behind this fact. So the categories of being, cause, value and purpose, because they originate from these different activities, cannot be deduced from each other or from a higher principle. We can only see the world in terms of one of these basic categories. We can notice, as it were, only one side of our relationship to it – never the whole relationship as it is determined by the connection between these categories. This is the first reason why metaphysics is impossible; if it is to succeed it must either make an internal connection between them by fallacious arguments or truncate what we actually do in life. A further limitation of conceptual thought appears within each of these activities. Thought cannot add a final unconditional cause to the conditioned sequence of events; for the arrangement of a manifold consisting of elements which behave uniformly towards each other remains an enigma and an unchanging entity cannot explain change or multiplicity. We can never overcome the subjective and relative character of valuations which originate from feeling: an unconditional value is a postulate but not a concept which can be made fully meaningful. We cannot demonstrate a highest or unconditional purpose because this presupposes discovering an unconditional value; the valid principle involved in mutual obligation does not allow us to deduce the purpose of the individual or of society.

Thus no metaphysics can satisfy the demand for a scientific proof; but there remains a fixed starting-point for philosophy: man is so related to the world that each of these three activities expresses an aspect of it. Philosophy cannot apprehend the essential nature of the world through a metaphysical system and prove this knowledge validly. No single work of art gives us a total view of life but works of art taken together bring us nearer to one: in the same way each typical world-view of philosophy presents us with a world as seen by a great philosopher who subordinates two of the activities and the categories they contain to the third and its categories. So, of the immense labour of the metaphysical spirit, only the historical consciousness remains, which it applies to itself and thus experiences the inexhaustible depth of the world. The final conclusion of the mind is not that all the world-views through which it has passed are relative but that it is sovereign over them all and at the same time positively conscious of how the one reality of the world is given to us through its different activities.

It is the task of the theory of world-views to describe methodically, on the basis of an analysis of the historical development of religion, poetry and metaphysics – but in contrast to relativism – the relationship of the human mind to the enigma of the world and of life.

IV. Philosophy and science

Reflection about thought, its forms and laws, grows constantly in the demonstrations and conceptualizations of metaphysics. The following conditions of knowing are investigated: the assumption that there is a reality independent of ourselves but accessible to thought, the belief that there are other people who can be understood by us, and, finally, the presupposition that the temporal course of our mental life is real and that the experiences depicted in the mind can be validly conceptualized. Reflection on the processes through which a world-view originates and on the grounds which justify its presuppositions, accompanies the formation of such a world-view and constantly increases in the conflict of metaphysical systems.

From the essential nature of a philosophic world-view is derived its relationship to the systems of culture. Distinctions can be made in a culture according to the inner relationships between knowledge of the world, life and emotional experiences and the practical organizations through which our ideals of action are realized. Here the structure of the mind expresses itself and it also determines the philosophic world view which is thus related to all aspects of culture. Each world view strives to be valid, systematic and well grounded; it inevitably makes itself felt in every sphere of culture by making conscious what happens, demonstrating, judging critically and making connections. Then it encounters the thought which has originated in the systems of culture.

1. The Functions of Philosophy which Originate from Conceptualization in Cultural Life

Man's reflection about his doings and his striving for universally valid knowledge did not develop in world-views alone. Before philosophers emerged political activity had given rise to differentiations in the functions of the state and the classification of constitutions; the basic concepts of civil and penal law had developed in legal practice and court procedures; religion had formulated dogmas, contrasted and interrelated them; forms of artistic activity had been distinguished; for all progress towards greater complexity in purposive human activity is made under the guidance of conceptual thought.

Thus philosophy acquired the function of developing the thought that had emerged in the individual spheres of culture. There is no firm boundary between religious and philosophic metaphysics and, in the same way, technical thought continuously merges with philosophic. The philosophic spirit is always characterized by universal reflection upon itself and by the power flowing from it to shape and reform personality; it also has a strong tendency to justify and make connections. So the function of philosophy, which I have mentioned above, is, from the outset, not tied to the formation of a world-view and exists even where metaphysics is neither sought nor acknowledged.

2. *General Epistemology and the Theory of Individual Cultural Spheres*

The reflective character of philosophy gives rise to another of its aspects which has always existed side by side with the striving for a universally valid world-view in which experiences based on the different activities are combined into objective unity. When we consider what these activities are directed towards, investigate what we learn through them and examine the validity of this knowledge, we see the other side of self-reflection. Seen in this light, philosophy is the *basic discipline* of which the subject-matter is the forms, rules and relationships of all thought processes which aim at valid knowledge. In the form of logic it investigates the conditions for validity inherent in all correct thought processes whatever the sphere of thought. In the form of epistemology it traces the consciousness of the reality of experience and of the objectivity of external perception back to the justification of these presuppositions of knowledge. As such a *theory of knowledge* it is a science.

On the basis of this, its most important function, it enters into relationships to the different spheres of culture and takes over particular tasks in each of them.

When we are dealing with ideas and knowledge of the world, philosophy enters into relationships with the sciences which produce particular parts of our knowledge of the world. This fundamental accomplishment of philosophy is most closely related to logic and epistemology. It illuminates the methods of the sciences by means of general logic and relates this clarification to the methodological concepts which have originated in the sciences. Philosophy investigates the presuppositions, goals and limitations of knowledge in the sciences and applies the results thus gained to the problem of the inner structure and system in the two great groups – the sciences and human studies. None of its relationships to any system of culture is as clear and distinct and none has developed with such systematic consistency; therefore none of the one-sided definitions of philosophy is as convincing as *the theory of theories*, the justification and systematization of the sciences into knowledge of reality.

Less transparent is the relationship of philosophy to everyday *knowledge of life*.[4] Life is the inner relationship of mental processes within a person. Knowledge of life is growing awareness of, and reflection on, life. It makes us aware that what is relative, subjective, accidental and isolated in the elementary forms of purposive actions has value and purpose for us. What is the significance of the passions in the total context of our lives? What value has sacrifice in a secular life? Or glory, or external recognition? To answer such questions we need not only the individual's knowledge of life but also that acquired by society. Society is the comprehensive regulator of the life of feelings and instincts; through law and custom it sets limits, derived from the need for co-existence, to unruly passions; by division of labour, marriage and property it creates the conditions for an orderly satisfaction of instincts. So it liberates us from their dreadful domination; life finds room for the higher spiritual feelings and aspirations and these can gain control. The knowledge of life which society thus achieves produces more and more adequate definitions of the values of life and, by means of public opinion, gives them a well-defined position; thus society itself produces a graduation of values which, in turn, conditions the individual. On this social basis the individual's knowledge of life is superimposed. It originates in various ways. Its main basis is those personal experiences which reveal a value. We learn other lessons by observing human emotions – passions which may even disorganize people and consequently their relationship to others and even cause suffering. We supplement this knowledge of life by studying history which shows the broad outlines of human destiny, and poetry which reveals the painfully sweet tension and release of passion and the illusions it creates. All this combines to make man more free and capable of resignation and of happily dedicating himself to the great objectivities of life.

At first this knowledge of life is unmethodical and must, once it becomes aware of the range and limits of its method, be transformed into methodical reflection which tries to overcome the subjectivity of valuation. So it changes into philosophy. All the stages of this journey are documented by writings about characters, temperament, conduct and value of life. As poetry is an important link in the development of theories about temperament, character and conduct of life its interpretation of the human soul and its evaluation of things prepares the ground for an insatiable desire to understand and for a more conscious comprehension of the meaning of life. Homer is the teacher of reflective writers and Euripides[5] their pupil. All personal religion

---

[4] See also pp. 178–81.　　　[5] 480–406 B.C.

The Nature of Philosophy

develops on the same basis – knowledge of life and an exceptionally strong awareness of how illusory all worldly goods are – produce dedication to the transcendent world in every religious genius. Religious experience would be empty and insipid unless experience of the misery, the depravity or, at least, the pettiness of human affairs (and the separation and suffering in them) led up to a more holy life far from this circle of perdition. Buddha, Lao-tse[6] and, as several passages from the gospel reveal, Christ have trodden this journey into loneliness; so have Augustine[7] and Pascal.[8] This personal knowledge of life, together with scholarship and traditional customs, forms the true basis of philosophy. The personal element in the greatest philosophers rests on this knowledge. Its purification and justification form an essential, indeed the most effective, part of philosophic systems. This is particularly clear in Plato, the Stoa and Spinoza; to a more limited extent it can be seen in Kant, if one considers his anthropology and his earlier writings together. Thus the system of immanent values of life and that of objective, instrumental values originate in philosophy; the former belong to a state of the soul, the latter to something external which has the capacity to produce values of life.

Finally, in the cultural-historical context philosophy is related to the practical world, its ideals and customs. For it is reflection on the will, its rules, purposes and goals. It has found its expression in the spheres of custom, commerce, law, state, control of nature and morality. The nature of willing can only be explained through them; the setting of purposes, commitment and rule permeates them all. This gives rise to the most deep-seated problem of philosophy in the sphere of the will: the question whether all moral rules can be derived from purposes. The insight which Kant achieved in his categorical imperative can be developed into the idea that there is only one unconditional certainty in the moral world – that the mutual commitment of wills in an explicit contract or in the silent assumption of reciprocity is unconditionally valid for every mind; thus justice, honesty, fidelity and truthfulness form the firm scaffolding of the moral world; all purposes and all rules of life, even kindness and the striving for perfection are subordinated to it; there is a hierarchy of obligation which descends from duty to the moral demand of kindness, devotion to others and personal improvement. The philosophical analysis of moral consciousness determines the conditions under which systems of purposes develop in society by ascertaining the sphere of validity of moral ideals and distinguishing the obligation of duty from the flexibility of purpose. Philosophy

[6] About 600 B.C. [7] 354–430.
[8] 1620–87.

127

makes the spheres of customs which the human studies describe and analyse comprehensible in terms of the structures of individuals and society; from their teleological character it deduces how customs developed according to the laws of formation and places all these under the highest law, that of obligation; it thus becomes an inner power which strives for the improvement of man and the further development of his customs, but at the same time provides firm standards in the form of a moral rule and elucidation of the realities of life.

At this point we can look back once more to the philosophic world-views. Now we can see the extent of their foundations. The significance which the knowledge of life has for the development of a world view, emerges. Finally it is clear that problems which have their own significance and can be discussed independently of their place in world-views can arise in the large spheres conditioned by mental activity.

The relationships of philosophy to the different spheres of human life establishes its right to justify and combine knowledge about these spheres with the sciences in which this knowledge has been systematized and to explore these spheres in particular philosophic disciplines such as the philosophy of law, religion or art. It is scarcely controversial that each of these theories must be derived from the historical and social facts which constitute the sphere of art or religion, of law or state; thus the work of these disciplines coincides with that of the sciences. It is also clear that any philosophical theory which, instead of drawing on the subject-matter itself, clings to what is offered by the sciences and only re-examines it here and there, has no right to exist. But, because of the limitations of human power, the specialized scientist will only rarely have an assured command of logic, epistemology and psychology so that a philosophic theory by using them is likely to add something new. But such a separate philosophic theory can only be justified as something provisional which springs from the insufficiencies of the present situation. On the other hand, the task of examining the inner mutual relationships of the sciences, on which the logical structure of each of them depends, will remain an increasingly important part of the functions of philosophy.

3. *The Philosophic Spirit in the Sciences and Literature*

The influence of metaphysics is constantly decreasing but the function of philosophy to justify and systematize the thought which has developed in particular spheres of culture is constantly becoming more important. The significance of the positivist philosophy of D'Alembert,[9] Comte,[10] Mill[11] and Mach[12] lies in the fact that it starts from within the sciences, goes on with their procedures and applies the yardstick of their universally valid knowledge everywhere. In another sphere, the philosophic thinking of Carlyle[13] or Nietzsche is positivistic because it strives to generalize and justify the way we experience life and how this is developed by poets and writers. It is natural that in this undogmatic way philosophy should influence the whole intellectual life of modern times. The methodical, generalizing spirit which inter-related the sciences played a decisive role in Galileo's, Kepler's and Newton's research; it then penetrated into French science through the positivism of D'Alembert and Lagrange[14] and continued to make its impact through Ernst von Baer,[15] Robert Mayer,[16] Helmholtz[17] and Hertz[18] who based themselves on the philosophy of nature and Kant's critical philosophy. This same philosophic spirit became prominent in the particular disciplines of society and history, especially after the work of the great socialist theoreticians. So it is characteristic of the present state of philosophy that its strongest influence does not come from the systems but from this undogmatic philosophic thought which permeates the sciences and the whole of literature. In the latter sphere writers like Tolstoi and Maeterlinck exercise a considerable philosophic influence.[19] Strong philosophic impulses come from drama, the novel and even from lyrical poetry.

The philosophic spirit exists wherever a thinker, free from the forms of systematic philosophy, examines the obscure phenomena of instinct, authority and faith which are unique to each individual. It is also present whenever scientists provide an ultimate, methodological justification for their science or reach generalizations which link and justify several sciences. Again, it is seen wherever values of life and ideals are freshly examined. Thought must reconcile chaotic or warring elements in an age or a man's heart; it must illuminate what is obscure and relate and combine what is separate. This spirit leaves no valuations and aspirations unexamined and no piece of knowledge isolated; it seeks grounds for the validity of whatever is valid. In this sense the eighteenth century rightly described itself as the philosophi-

[9] J. D'Alembert, 1717–83.   [10] A. Comte, 1798–1857.
[11] J. S. Mill, 1806–73.   [12] E. Mach, 1836–1916.
[13] T. Carlyle, 1795–1881.
[14] T. Lagrange, French mathematician and astronomer, 1736–1813.
[15] K. E. Baer, German biologist, 1792–1878.
[16] J. R. Mayer, German scientist, 1814–78.
[17] H. Helmholtz, German scientist, 1821–94.
[18] H. R. Hertz, German scientist, 1857–94.
[19] See pp. 114–16.

cal century because then reason gained dominance over the dark, instinctive processes within us and every historical formation was traced back to its origin and justification.

V. The concept of the nature of philosophy: a survey of its history and systematic characteristics

Philosophy has proved to be the quintessence of very different functions joined together by knowledge of their inevitable connection. A function always relates to a teleological context and refers to acts which belong together and are performed within it. The concept is not taken from the analogy with organic life nor does it describe natural capacity or original power. The functions of philosophy are related to the teleological structures of both the philosophizing subject and of society. They are acts in which a person looks into himself and yet affects his environment; he does the same in religion and poetry. So philosophy is an activity which springs from the need of the individual man to reflect on what he does, to shape and regulate his actions inwardly and to form a stable relationship to the whole of human society; at the same time it is a function based on the structure of society and needed for its perfect life, a function, therefore, which is carried on in the same way in many minds and links them together in a social and historical bond. In this latter respect it is a cultural system. For the characteristics of such a system are that the activities of the individuals which belong to it are similar and that there is a bond between the individuals in which the activity takes place. If this bond assumes fixed forms organizations originate within a cultural system. Art and philosophy, among purposive systems, link the individuals to each other least for the function of the artist or philosopher is not conditioned by any organization; they operate in the sphere where the spirit of freedom is greatest. Even if belonging to such an organization as a university or academy increases the philosopher's contribution to society, he is only in his element when he has freedom of thought; this must never be limited, for not only his philosophical character but also confidence in his unconditional truthfulness and, therefore, his impact depends on it.

The general characteristics of all the functions of philosophy are based on the nature of the apprehension of objects and of conceptual thought. From this point of view philosophy is simply the strongest, most consistent and comprehensive form of thought; no firm frontier divides it from empirical consciousness. Conceptual thought has a tendency of its own; judgment proceeds towards the highest generalizations, conceptualization and classification towards a hierarchical arrangement, systematization towards a complete system and justification towards a final principle. In these activities thought is being directed to the world which is the common subject-matter of all the thinking of different people and the system of perceptions into which all things in space and the variety of their changes and movements in time are arranged. All feeling and acts of will are given their place in the world because the bodies to which they belong and the elements of perception interwoven in them are pinpointed in space. All the values, purposes and goals posited in these feelings or acts of will are part of the world which embraces all human life. Thought tries to express and unify all the ideas, impressions, values and purposes given in empirical consciousness, experience and the empirical sciences; it moves from the pattern of things and changes in the world towards a conception of the world; it seeks a principle or cause which accounts for the world; it strives to determine the value, meaning and significance of the world and asks about its purpose. Wherever the inherent tendency of thought divorces generalization, systematization and justification from a specialized interest it engenders philosophy. Whenever the subject reflects on the actions by which he affects the world, this reflection becomes philosophical. The basic characteristic of all functions of philosophy is, therefore, the tendency of the mind to transcend commitment to any definite, finite and limited interest and to subordinate any theory originating from a limited need to a conclusive idea. This tendency is based on the laws of thought and corresponds to certain needs of human nature, which cannot be fully analysed – the joy of knowledge, the need to stabilize man's position in the world and the striving to overcome the limiting conditions of life. Every mental activity seeks firm basis for thought which is not subject to relativity.

This general function of philosophy appears in all the philosophies which have been attempted under different historical conditions. Special and dynamic functions also develop from the manifold conditions of life – to make world-views generally valid, to reflect on knowledge, to relate theories formed in the particular purposive systems to the context of all knowledge, to examine the whole of culture critically, to systematize and justify everything. They are all particular activities based on the unitary nature of philosophy. For it adapts itself to every stage in the development of culture and all historical conditions. This explains the constant differentiation of its activities, the flexibility and agility with which it unfolds into whole systems or concentrates all its power on a particular problem transferring its energy to one new task after another.

We have reached the point at which a description of the nature of philosophy throws light back on its history and forward on its systematic context. If the system of philosophic functions could explain the order in which culturally conditioned problems occur simultaneously, or one after the other, and the way in which they are solved, their history would become comprehensible. We need to describe the main stages of progressive reflection about knowledge. We must trace historically how the philosophic spirit relates theories, emerging from the purposive systems of culture, to the system of knowledge and thereby develops them, and how it creates new disciplines in the human studies which then pass into the hands of specialists. We must show how the great types of philosophic world-views progress steadily but assume particular forms according to the thinking of an Age and national characteristics. Thus the history of philosophy passes three problems on to systematic philosophy: it must provide a basis, a justification and systematization for the sciences and come to grips with the never ending desire for ultimate reflection on being, ground, value, purpose and their relationships in a world view – whatever form or direction this takes.

The Types of World-view and their Development in the Metaphysical Systems

Introduction

Vol. VIII, pp. 75–118

The conflict of the systems

I

The anarchy of the philosophic systems is one of the most effective reasons for continually renewed scepticism. Historical consciousness of the limitless variety of philosophic systems contradicts the claim each of them makes to universal validity and this supports the sceptical spirit much more powerfully than any systematic argument. An infinite, chaotic variety of philosophic systems lies behind us and spreads around us. Ever since they have existed they have excluded and fought each other and there is no hope of making a decision in favour of any one of them.

The history of philosophy confirms this effect of the conflict between philosophic systems, religious views and moral principles on the increase of scepticism. The struggle between the older Greek explanations of the world encouraged the philosophy of doubt in the age of Greek Enlightenment. When Alexander's campaigns and the combination of different nations into larger empires brought the differences of customs, religions, life and world-views to the notice of the Greeks the sceptical schools formed and extended their subversive operations to the problems of theology (evil and theodicy, the conflict between God's personality and his infinity and perfection) and to the assumptions about man's moral goal. The systems of faith and philosophic dogmas of the newer European nations were shaken in their universal validity once Mohammedans and Christians compared their convictions at the court of Frederick the Second of Hohenstaufen[1] and once the philosophy of Averroës and Aristotle became known to the scholastic thinkers. Once antiquity had been revived and Greek and Roman authors were genuinely understood, and once the age of

---

[1] King of Sicily and German Emperor, 1195–1250.

133

discovery had taught us about the variety of climates, peoples, ways and thought on our planet, men completely lost their assurance about hitherto firmly defined convictions. Today, travellers record carefully the most varied kinds of faith; we note and analyse the great and powerful phenomena of religious and metaphysical convictions among the priesthoods of the East, in the Greek cities or among the Arabs. We look back on an immense field of ruined religious traditions, metaphysical claims and demonstrated systems; for many centuries the human spirit has tried out and examined various ways of explaining the pattern of things scientifically, describing it poetically or proclaiming it religiously. Methodical, critical, historical research examines every fragment, every remnant of this long labour of our race. One system excludes the other; one disproves the other; none can demonstrate its own truth; we find nothing of the peaceful discourse of Raphael's *School of Athens*, which was the expression of the eclectic tendency of that time, in the sources of history. So the contradiction between the increasing, historical consciousness and philosophy's claim to universal validity has hardened. More and more people watch new philosophic systems with amused curiosity wondering what audiences they will gather and how long they will keep them.

2

But the doubts aroused by the progressive development of historical consciousness reach much deeper than the sceptical conclusions based on the contradictions of human opinions. The historical thinking of the Greeks and Romans mainly presupposes a definite human species equipped with definite characteristics. The Christian doctrine of the first and second Adam and of the Son of Man presupposed the same. The natural system of the sixteenth century was still sustained by the same presupposition. In Christianity it discovered an abstract, permanent paradigm of religion, natural theology; it abstracted the doctrine of natural law from Roman jurisprudence, and a model of taste from Greek artistic activity. According to this natural system all historical differences contained basic constant and universal forms of social and legal arrangements, of religious faith and of morality. This method of deducing common features from the comparison of historical forms of life and by using the idea of supreme types, abstracting natural law, natural theology and rational morality from the varied customs, laws and theologies, still dominated the century of constructive philosophy. This procedure was developed by Hippias[2] and passed via the Stoa into

[2] Hippias of Elis, Greek sophist, fifth century B.C.

Roman thought. The dissolution of this natural system was sparked off by the analytical spirit of the eighteenth century. It started in England where the most unbiased survey of primitive and foreign peoples – their ways of living and thinking and their customs – joined forces with empiricist theories and the application of the analytical method to epistemology, ethics and aesthetics. Voltaire and Montesquieu[3] introduced this spirit into France. Hume and D'Alembert, Condillac[4] and Destutt[5] regarded man as a bundle of instincts and associations almost infinitely capable of being moulded into various forms by different climates, customs and education. The classical expressions of this historical point of view were Hume's *The Natural History of Religion* and *Dialogues Concerning Natural Religion*. The idea of development which was to dominate the nineteenth century had already emerged in the works of the eighteenth. Knowledge of how the earth evolved and of how different forms of life followed each other grew during the period between Buffon[6] and Kant and Lamarck.[7] On the other hand the study of civilized nations was developed in germinal works in which Winckelmann,[8] Lessing and Herder started to apply the ideas of development.

Finally, the study of primitive peoples provided the link between the theory of natural evolution and the insights of developmental history based on national politics, religion, law, customs, language, poetry and literature. So the point of view of developmental history could be applied to the study of the whole natural and historical development of man and man as a type dissolved in this process.

The evolutionary theory which thus originated is necessarily linked to the knowledge of the relativity of every historical form of life. In the vision which encompasses the earth and its whole past the absolute validity of any individual form of life, constitution, religion or philosophy vanishes. So, more drastically than awareness of conflicting systems, the development of historical consciousness destroys faith in the universal validity of any philosophy which attempts to express world order cogently through a system of concepts. Philosophy must seek its inner coherence not in the world but in man. To understand life as it is lived by man is the will of contemporary man. The variety of systems which tried to grasp the order of the world is clearly related to life; this variety is one of life's most important and illuminating

[3] French man of letters, 1689–1755.
[4] E. B. Condillac, French philosopher, 1750–80.
[5] A. L. C. Destutt de Tracy, French philosopher, 1754–1836.
[6] Georges-Louis-Leclere, Comte de Buffon, French naturalist, 1707–88.
[7] J. B. Lamarck, French naturalist, 1744–1829.
[8] J. J. Winckelmann, German archaeologist and art-historian, 1717–68.

creations; so the same development of historical consciousness which did such a destructive job on the great systems must help us to eliminate the hard contradiction between the claim to universal validity in every philosophical system and the historical anarchy of these systems.

I. Life and world view

[I have omitted sections 1 and 2, called Life and Knowledge of Life, because they overlap with passages from Volume VII.]

3. The Enigma of Life

If, from our varied experiences, we try to understand life as a whole it appears to contain contradictory elements; creative, though controlled by natural laws, rational yet arbitrary, it continually reveals new aspects; so it is clear in detail but enigmatic as a whole. The mind tries to unify life's relationships and the experiences based on them and fails. At the centre of incomprehensibility are procreation, birth, development and death. The living know about death and yet cannot comprehend it. From the first glimpse of a corpse death is incomprehensible to life; this is the primary basis for our attitude to the world as something other, alien and terrible. The fact of death drives us to fantasies designed to make it comprehensible. Worship of the dead, veneration of ancestors and the cult of the departed produce the basic ideas of religious faith and metaphysics. The strangeness of life increases when, in society and nature, man observes constant struggle, constant annihilation of one creature by another, the cruelty of the forces of nature. Knowledge of life makes us increasingly aware of strange, irreconcilable contradictions – the general ephemeralness and our will for something permanent, the power of nature and the independence of our will, the temporal and spatial limitations of everything and our power to transcend every limit. These enigmas occupied the Egyptian and Babylonian priests as well as they do today's Christian clergymen in their sermons, Heracleitus[9] as well as Hegel, and the Prometheus of Aeschylus[10] as well as Goethe's Faust.

4. The Law of Formation of World Views

Every great impression shows man a particular side of life; the world appears in a new light; our attitudes towards life develop as such experiences are repeated and combine. From one of life's relationships the whole of life is coloured and interpreted in sensitive and thoughtful

[9] 576–480 B.C.   [10] 525–456 B.C.

minds; thus universal attitudes develop. They change as life reveals ever new sides to man; but, individuals adopt different basic attitudes according to their make-up. Some cling to the down-to-earth, tangible things and live in the enjoyment of the day; others, in spite of chance and fate, pursue great purposes which give their existence enduring significance: there are grave natures which cannot bear the ephemeralness of what they love and own; to them life seems valueless, as if woven from vanity and dreams, and they seek something abiding beyond the earth. Among the major attitudes to life the most comprehensive are optimism and pessimism. But they occur in various nuances. Thus, to the spectator, the world appears strange, a colourful, fleeting spectacle: but, to the one who directs his life to an orderly plan, the world is familiar and homely: he stands on firm feet and belongs in it.

Such attitudes towards life, the innumerable nuances of responses to the world, form the lower stratum for the formation of world-views. These try to solve the enigma of life on the basis of the experiences in which the individual's varied relationships of life are reflected. In the higher forms of world-views one procedure is particularly prominent – understanding something which cannot be grasped as it is given to us by means of something more distinct. What is distinct becomes a means of understanding or basis for explanation of the incomprehensible. Science analyses and develops the general relationships of homogenous facts which it has thus isolated; religion, poetry and spontaneous metaphysics articulate the meaning and sense of the whole. The one knows, the other understands. Such an interpretation of the world, which clarifies its manifold nature by simplification, begins in language and develops in metaphor which is representation of one idea by another related to it and which, in some sense, illuminates it. The same is true of personification which humanizes and thus makes comprehensible, and of analogical inference from the known to the related unknown which approximates to scientific thinking. Wherever religion, myth, poetry or spontaneous metaphysics seek to illuminate and to impress they do so by these same procedures.

5. The Structure of World-Views

All world-views, if they seek a complete solution of the enigma of life, invariably contain the same structure. This structure always takes the form of a system in which questions about the meaning and significance of the world are answered in terms of a conception of the world. From this an ideal, a highest good and supreme principles of conduct are deduced. This structure is determined by the following mental laws; in a lifetime the apprehension of reality becomes the basis for evaluating circumstances and objects in terms of pleasure and displeasure, like and dislike, approval and disapproval; this valuation, in turn, becomes the lower stratum for determining the will. Our conduct regularly passes through these three states of consciousness and it is characteristic of mental life that, in such a system of interactions, the lower active stratum persists and the relations embedded in these ways of behaving – judging objects, enjoying them and wanting to do something about them – determine the arrangement of these strata above each other; thus they constitute the structure of the formations in which the mind's system of interactions expresses itself. A lyrical poem shows these connections in their simplest form – a situation, a sequence of feelings and, often, arising from them, desires, strivings or actions. Every one of life's relationships develops into a formation in which these ways of behaving are structurally linked. Therefore the world-views are also regular formations in which this structure of mental life is expressed. They are always based on a conception of the world which springs from the order in which we come to understand it. We observe inner processes and outer objects. We elucidate the resulting observations using elementary acts of thought to clarify the basic relationships of reality; if the observations are transitory they can be depicted and arranged in our imagination and this enables us to overcome the accidental nature of observations; the growing definiteness and freedom of the mind and its dominance over reality is completed in the region of judgments and concepts, where the pattern and nature of reality is validly grasped. Any fully developed worldview must start with these regular stages of knowing reality. From these another typical form of behaviour develops in analogous, regular stages. We enjoy the value of our existence in awareness of ourselves; we ascribe to things and people around us an instrumental value because they heighten and extend our existence; we determine these values according to how much these objects can help or harm us; we evaluate them and seek an unconditional yardstick for these valuations. So circumstances, people and things receive a meaning in relation to the whole of reality and this whole itself acquires significance. As we pass through these stages in the growth of our emotional attitudes a second level of the structure of the world-view develops; the conception of the world becomes the basis for the evaluation of life and the understanding of the world. According to the same law of mental life evaluation of life and understanding of the world give rise to the highest level of consciousness – the ideals, the highest good and the supreme principles through which the world-view receives its practical energy – the point, as it were, with which it penetrates human life, the outer world and the depth of the soul itself. The world-view becomes formative, it shapes and remoulds! Even this highest level of world-view develops through different stages. From intention, striving or a tendency permanent purposes develop. They are directed towards the realization of an idea, the relationship of ends and means, the choice between ends, the selection of means and, finally, the combination of purposes into the highest order of our practical conduct – an embracing plan of life, a highest good, supreme norms of action, an ideal to shape personal life and society.

This is the structure of a world-view. Here what the enigma of life contains as a bundle of tasks is elevated into a conscious, necessary system of problems and solutions; this progress takes place in orderly, internally determined stages; it follows that every world-view develops and in doing so achieves an explanation of what is contained in it; thus, gradually, in the course of time, it achieves permanence, definiteness and power: it is a product of history.

6. The Variety of World-Views

World-views develop under different conditions. Climate, race and nationality, determined by history, and the development of states, the temporal delimitation into epochs and Ages in which nations co-operate, combine to produce the special conditions which influence the rise of differences in world-views. The life which originates under such specialized conditions is very varied and so are the men who apprehend it. These typical differences are joined by those of individuals, their environment and experience. Just as the earth is covered by innumerable forms of living creatures who constantly fight for existence and the room to expand, the forms of world-view develop in the human world and struggle for power over the mind.

The mind, oppressed by the restless change of impressions and destinies and by the power of the external world, is compelled to seek inner strength to resist it all; so it is led by change and instability, by its continuously changing moods and its views of life, towards permanent evaluations of life and firm goals. The world-views which further the understanding of life and lead to useful goals survive and replace the lesser ones. A selection takes place between them. In the sequence of generations the world-views which are viable are constantly perfected. World-views are shaped by the same process that creates the variety of organic creatures.

The deepest secret of their specific character lies in the pattern which the teleological structure of mental life impresses upon the particular forms of world-view.

In the midst of the apparently accidental nature of these forms there exists a purposiveness which springs from the mutual dependence of the questions contained in the enigma of life, and also from the unvarying relationship between conception of the world, evaluation of life and goals of the will. A common human nature and the arrangements by which individuality is produced[11] are vitally related to reality which is always and everywhere the same; life always shows the same sides.

Incalculable factors intrude into this regular structure of world-views and their differentiation into individual forms[12] – the variations of life, the succession of historical periods, alterations in the state of science, the genius of nations and individuals; as a result the interest in problems and the power of certain ideas which grow from historical life and dominate it, change constantly; ever new combinations of knowledge of life, attitudes and thoughts emerge in world-views according to the place they occupy in history; there is something haphazard about the strength and significance of their constituents. Yet, because of the regularity in the depth of their structure and logical order they are not aggregates but formations.

Comparative procedures show that these formations fall into related groups. The comparative method can reveal types, lines of development and rules of transformation in world views just as it can in languages, religions and states. The types revealed pervade the historically determined individuality of particular formations. They are always conditioned by the particular sphere in which they originate. But to deduce the types from the latter would be a grave error of the constructive method. Only the comparative, historical, procedure can approximate to the formation of such types, their variations, developments and combinations. Here research must always keep open the possibility of developing its results. Every formulation is only provisional. It is, and remains, an aid to deeper historical insight. The comparative, historical, procedure always combines with preparatory, systematic reflection by which the historical material is interpreted. Even this psychological and systematically historical interpretation of the material is exposed to the mistakes of constructive thought which seeks to impose a simple arrangement, a pre-formed inner tendency in every sphere.

[11] This is what Schopenhauer called the 'principium individuationis'. Dilthey was greatly interested in it, and indeed saw it as a focal point of many of his studies.

[12] See preceding footnote.

The Types of World-View

I shall summarize what we have discovered so far in a general principle which comparative, historical procedure confirms at every point. World-views are not products of thought. They do not originate from the mere will to know. The comprehension of reality is an important factor in their formation, but only one. They emerge from our attitude to, and knowledge of, life and from our whole mental structure. The elevation of life to consciousness through knowledge of reality, evaluation of life and achievement of will is the slow, heavy work which mankind has accomplished in the development of views of life.

Looking at the course of history as a whole confirms this principle of the theory of world-views and also one of its important consequences which takes us back to the starting-point of this essay. The formation of world-views is determined by the will to stabilize the conception of the world, the evaluation of life and the guidance of the will and arises from the basic stages of psychological development as I have described them. Both religion and philosophy seek stability, effectiveness, domination and universal validity. But mankind has not advanced a single step on this path. The struggle of world-views among themselves has not decided any essential point. History selects among them but their great types persist side by side autonomous, unprovable and indestructible. They cannot owe their origin to any demonstration because they cannot be dissolved by any demonstration. Individual stages and special formulations of a type can be disproved, but its root in life persists and has its effect in bringing forth new formulations.

II. The types of world-view in religion, poetry and metaphysics

[The introduction and sections one and two on religion and poetry are omitted.]

3. The types of world-view in metaphysics

All the threads converge into a theory of the structure, types and development of world-views in metaphysics. I shall summarize the decisive circumstances.

I

The whole development and stabilization of world-views is directed towards their becoming valid knowledge. To poets of great intellectual power, also, strong impressions seem to illuminate life afresh; but the tendency towards stability goes beyond them. In the core of the world religions there remains something bizarre and extreme which derives from heightened religious experience and from the focusing of the mind, by religious techniques, on the invisible; which is inaccessible to reason. Orthodoxy insists upon it rigidly; mysticism and spiritualism seek to re-translate it into experience; rationalism seeks to grasp it and inevitably dissects it; thus the will of the main religions of the world to dominate, based on the inner experience of the faithful, on tradition and authority, is replaced by the claim of reason to transform the world-view and give it rational validity. Once a world view is elevated into a scientifically justified conceptual scheme which lays claim to universal validity, metaphysics comes into being. History proves that, wherever it occurs, metaphysics has been anticipated by a religious development, influenced by poetry and affected by national conditions, attitudes and ideals. The will to valid knowledge gives this new form of world view a structure of its own.

Who could say at what point the striving for knowledge, which is active in all social purposes, becomes scientific? Only in the Ionian colonies[13] was the mathematical and astronomical knowledge of the Babylonians and Egyptians divorced from practical tasks and involvement with the priesthood and so made independent. When research was directed towards the whole of the world, emerging philosophy and the developing sciences drew close together. Mathematics, astronomy and geography became means of knowing the world. The old problem of solving the enigma of life occupied the Pythagoreans[14] and Heracleitus as much as it did the priests of the East. Though in the colonies the advancing power of the sciences placed the problem of explaining nature in the centre of philosophy, during its later development all the great questions contained in the enigma of life were discussed in the philosophic schools: indeed they focused on the inner relationship between knowledge of reality, orientation of life and guidance of the will in the individual and society, in short, on the development of a world-view.

At first the structure of world-views in metaphysics was determined by their connection with science. The conception of the world based on the senses was transformed into an astronomical one; the world of feeling and acts of will was objectified in concepts of values, goods, purposes and rules: the searchers into the enigma of life were led by the requirements of conceptual form and demonstration to logic and epistemology as primary foundations: work on the solution itself

[13] Dilthey refers to the Ionic school of Thales, Anaximander, Anaximenes in the sixth century B.C.

[14] The followers of Pythagoras, sixth century B.C.

passed from conditioned and limited data to being in general, a first cause, a highest good, a final purpose; metaphysics became a system and, from working with insufficient ideas and concepts developed in life and science, progressed to instrumental concepts which transcended all experiences.

The relationship of metaphysics to science was joined by the relationship to worldly culture. As philosophy enters the spirit of all cultural purposes it gains new strength and, at the same time, transmits to them the energy of its main thought. It ascertains the procedures and cognitive value of the sciences: unmethodical knowledge of life and the literature about it are developed into a general evaluation of life; the basic concepts of law as they had emerged from legal practice are systematized; conclusions about the functions of the state and constitutional forms and changes, which have sprung from the techniques of political life, are related to the highest tasks of human society. Philosophy undertakes the proof of dogmas or, where their dark kernel is inaccessible to conceptual thought, demolishes them; it rationalizes the forms and rules of artistic activity in terms of the purpose of art; thus philosophy tries to establish the direction of society by thought.

Finally, every one of these metaphysical systems is conditioned by the place it occupies in the history of philosophy; it is dependent on the nature of the problems and determined by the concepts which emerge from that nature.

This is the origin of the structure of metaphysical systems with their logical coherence and their variously conditioned irregularity – their representative features, which express a particular state of scientific thought in particular systems, and their uniqueness.

So each great metaphysical system, by its many-sidedness, becomes capable of illuminating every part of the life to which it belongs.

The trend of this whole great movement is towards a single, universally valid system of metaphysics. Its adherents saw the differentiation of metaphysics which springs from the depths of life as an accidental and subjective addition which had to be eliminated. So the immense labour, directed towards the creation of a uniform, demonstrable system of concepts through which the enigma of life is methodically solved, acquires independent significance; in the progress towards this goal every system acquires its place according to the state of conceptualization it has reached. Among the civilized countries of Europe the Mediterranean states were the first to undertake this conceptualization; after the Renaissance they were followed by the Germanic and Romanic states – particularly by the upper class which was only occasionally influenced by the dominant religion and sought increasingly to free itself from its influence.

II

In this context differences based on the rational character of metaphysical work arise among the systems. Some of these, such as dogmatism and critical philosophy, indicate stages in the development of the systems. Other differences pervade the whole development; they spring from the attempt of metaphysics to give a coherent account of what is involved in the apprehension of reality, the evaluation of life and the setting of purposes; they are concerned with the possible ways of solving these central problems. If we focus on the demonstrations of metaphysics we are confronted by the contrasts between empiricism and rationalism, between realism and idealism. The given reality is interpreted in terms of the opposite concepts of one and many, becoming and being, causality and teleology and with corresponding differences in the systems. The different points of view from which the relationship between the Ground of the world[15] and the world and between the soul and the body is conceived are expressed in the points of view of theism and pantheism, materialism and spiritualism. The problems of practical philosophy give rise to other differences from which I should like to single out eudaemonism[16] and its development into utilitarianism and the doctrine of an unconditional rule of the moral world.[17] All these differences have their place in the branches of metaphysics and indicate some of the possibilities of analysing these spheres rationally in terms of opposite concepts. These can be conceived as systematically evolved hypotheses by means of which the metaphysical spirit gets nearer to achieving a universally valid system.

Finally there emerged attempts to classify the metaphysical systems from this point of view. In a way characteristic of metaphysical conceptualization, contrasting concepts mark the differences between systems by, for example, opposing realism to idealism.

Who could miss the significance of philosophic conceptualization for the most varied spheres? It lays the foundations for the independent sciences and relates them to each other as I have argued earlier in detail. But what distinguishes the achievements of metaphysics from the work of the sciences is the will to submit the pattern of the universe and of life itself to the scientific methods which have been developed in

[15] By 'Ground of the world' or 'World ground' is meant the source of the world conceived by different philosophers to be God, matter or spirit.
[16] A moral philosophy which treats 'happiness' as its focal concept.
[17] Dilthey no doubt here has in mind Kant's theory of the categorical imperative.

special spheres of knowledge. By drawing conclusions about the unconditional they move beyond the limits of the methods of the individual sciences.

III

At this point I can make clear the basic idea which inspired this attempt at a theory of world-views and is applied in this work. *Historical consciousness* takes us behind the tendency of metaphysicians to form a uniform, universally valid system, behind the differences conditioned by this tendency, which divide the thinkers and, finally, behind the summarizing of these differences in terms of classifications. It is concerned with the actual, existing conflict of systems, rooted in their general nature, and relates this general nature to the development of religion and poetry. It shows how all metaphysical conceptualization failed to advance a single step towards a unified system. So we can see that the conflict of metaphysical systems is ultimately *rooted in life itself*, in the knowledge of life and one's attitudes to its problems. These attitudes provide the basis both for the variety of systems and for the possibility of distinguishing certain types. Each of these types covers *knowledge of reality, evaluation of life and setting of purposes*. They are independent of the antithetic points of view from which fundamental problems are solved.

The nature of these types emerges quite clearly when one looks at the great metaphysical geniuses, each of whom has expressed his personal way of life in a conceptual system which claims to be valid. His typical outlook on life is one with his character and expresses itself in how he arranges his life. It permeates all his actions; it is expressed in his style. Though these systems are, of course, conditioned by the current state of concepts, their concepts are, from the historical point of view, only means for the construction and demonstration of their world view.

Spinoza[18] began his tract *On the Improvement of the Understanding* with consideration of the futility we experience in our everyday sufferings and joys, fears and hopes. He resolved to seek the true good which brings eternal joy and solved this task in his *Ethic*. Man is liberated from the bondage of the passions by knowing God as the immanent ground of all that is transitory and by the infinite, intellectual love which follows from this knowledge; through this God, the Infinite, loves himself in the finite human spirit. Fichte's whole development typifies an attitude of mind – man's moral independence

---

[18] 1632–77.

of nature and the whole course of the world; his stormy life, which was a continuous effort of will, culminated in his formulating the ideal of the heroic man in whom the highest achievement of human nature – acted out in history which is the stage of moral life – links him to the super-terrestrial order of things. The immense, historical effect of Epicurus[19] who, intellectually, fell far short of the greatest thinkers, is due to the pure clarity with which he expressed a typical state of mind – the calm, serene submission of man to the laws of nature and the sensuous, yet prudent, enjoyment of its gifts.

Thus every genuine world-view is an intuition which springs from our involvement in life. Hegel's early notes deriving from the effect which his religio-metaphysical experiences and his interpretation of early Christian documents had on each other, are examples of such intuitions.[20] This involvement in life is brought about by our attitudes and personal relationships. This is the underlying meaning of the extravagant saying that the poet is the true human being. These attitudes to life disclose certain aspects of the world. I do not dare to go further. We do not know by what law the differentiation of the metaphysical systems emerges from life. If we want to get a better understanding of the types of world-views we must turn to history. Essentially it teaches us to grasp the connection between life and metaphysics, to enter life which is the centre of these systems, and to be conscious of their continuity (in which typical attitudes persist) however we may delimit and classify them. What matters is deeper insight from the point of view of life and tracing the central aims of metaphysics.

From this point of view I shall distinguish three main types of world-views. *Historical comparison* is the only way to make this distinction. To start with, every metaphysician, confronted with the enigma of life, begins disentangling the skein, as it were, from a particular point; this point is determined by his attitude to life itself and determines the particular structure of his system. We can group the various systems according to their dependence, relatedness, mutual attraction or repulsion. But here there is a further difficulty which affects all historical comparison. When selecting the features of what is compared a presupposed yardstick must be applied and this yardstick determines what follows. What I am saying has, therefore, a provisional character. Its hard core can only be the intuition which has developed from long preoccupation with metaphysical systems. Even thinking of them in terms of historical formulations can only be

---

[19] 341–270 B.C.
[20] Dilthey had developed this theory (*The Young Hegel*, Vol. IV of *Collected Works*).

subjective. Different logical arrangements, for example (combining the two forms of idealism or objective idealism and naturalism and similar possibilities), are open to any one. This differentiation of types is only intended to help us to see, from the point of view of life, deeper into history.

III. Naturalism

I

Man constantly finds himself determined by nature. This includes his body as well as the external world. The state of his own body and the powerful animal instincts which pervade it determine his feelings about life. To see and deal with life as fulfilling its cycle through the satisfaction of the animal instincts and through our servitude to the external world from which we get out nourishment, is as old as mankind. In hunger and sexual desire, in ageing and death, man sees himself subject to the daemonic forces of nature. He is part of nature. Heraclitus and the apostle Paul in similar words scornfully describe this as the view of life of the sensuous multitude. It is permanent; there was no age in which it did not dominate part of mankind. Even when an Eastern priesthood exerted the most rigid rule the sensuous man's philosophy of life existed; even when Catholicism suppressed every theoretical expression of this point of view there was much talk about 'Epicureans'; what it was not permitted to express in philosophic principles sounded forth in the songs of the Provence, in many a German courtly poem, in the French and German epics of Tristan. Plato described the Epicureanism of the nobles and the rich which we meet again as the philosophy of life of men of the world in the eighteenth century. The satisfaction of man's animal nature is joined by a factor in which man is most dependent on his environment: pleasure in status and honour. This view of the world is always based on the same behaviour – subordination of the will to the body's animal instincts and their relationship to the external world; thought and purposeful activity serve this animal nature and their sole function is to satisfy it.

This attitude to life is expressed in much of the literature of all nations – sometimes as the unbroken force of animal nature more often in conflict with the religious view of the world. Its battle-cry is the emancipation of the flesh. This resistance is relatively justified in history as the reaction of an ever newly born affirmation of natural life against the necessary but terrible discipline of mankind by religion. When this affirmation becomes philosophy it gives rise to naturalism which gives theoretical expression to what animates it; the process of nature is the sole and entire reality; there is nothing else; mental life is only formally distinguished from physical nature by the characteristics of consciousness which, having no content of its own, is causally determined by physical reality.

The structure of naturalism is the same from Democritus[21] to Hobbes[22] and to 'the system of Nature'. This consists of sensualism as its theory of knowledge, materialism as its metaphysics and a double-sided practical attitude – the will towards enjoyment and the recon-ciliation with the overpowering and alien course of the world by submitting oneself to it through reflection.

The philosophic justification of naturalism rests on two basic properties of the physical world. How overwhelming in our experience of reality are the extent and power of physical matter! Infinitely and continuously it extends to envelop the sparse manifestations of the mind; so these appear like interpolations in the great text of the physical order. Thus natural man, when he reflects on these condi-tions, must find himself entirely subject to the physical order. Secondly, nature is the original source of all our knowledge of uniformities. Experience of daily life teaches us about these unifor-mities and how to reckon with them; the sciences of the physical world, by studying these uniformities, gradually gain knowledge of how they are systematically connected; thus they achieve an ideal of knowledge which is unattainable by the human studies, based on personal experience and understanding.

But there are difficulties contained in this point of view which drive naturalism, in a restless dialectic, to ever new formulations of its attitude to the world and to life. The matter from which it starts is something which appears to consciousness; so it becomes subject to a circle – to deduce consciousness itself from what is only given as phenomenon to that consciousness. It is also impossible to derive feelings and thoughts from movement, which is a given phenomenon of consciousness. The incommensurability of these two facts leads – once the most varied attempts from classical materialism to *The system of Nature* have shown that the problem is insoluble – to the positivist correlation of the physical and the mental. This, too, is subject to grave objections. Finally, the morality of original naturalism proves insufficient to account for the development of society.

[2, 3 and 4 are omitted. They contain further historical accounts of naturalism.]

---

[21] *Fl.* fifth century B.C.   [22] T. Hobbes, 1588–1679.

The Types of World-View

IV. Idealism of freedom

[Introductory passage and section 1 omitted. It is a historical introduction to the subject.]

2

The representatives of the idealism of freedom are linked by their consciousness of belonging together and of differing from objective idealism and naturalism; this corresponds to the actual relationships between the different systems of this type. There is a bond which holds together the world-view, method and metaphysics in these systems – it is the mental attitude which asserts the mind's sovereign independence from all given facts; the mind knows itself to be differentiated from all physical causality. With profound ethical insight Fichte saw the connection between the personal characters of a group of thinkers and the idealism of freedom, a connection unlike that in any system based on nature. This sovereign independence then finds itself tied – not physically but by moral norms and obligations – when other people are involved; this gives rise to the concept of a commonwealth of men in which individuals are joined together by norms and yet inwardly free. Invariably linked to these premises is the idea that the free and responsible individuals, governed by an inner law and the commonwealth of men, are related to an absolute, personal and free cause. This is based on a way of life: spontaneous, free vitality finds that it is a force which influences the freedom of other people and is, in turn, influenced by them. This vital way of determining and being determined by will becomes the pattern of the world order on which it is, as it were, projected; it is rediscovered in every relationship, even the most comprehensive, in which the systematic thinker finds himself.

The Divinity is separate from the physical, causal order and conceived of as governing in opposition to it – a projection of purposive reason independent of the given facts. Anaxagoras[23] and Aristotle[24] have, with philosophic accuracy, expressed this conception of the divine in the relationship between God and matter. In the Christian conception of the Creation out of nothing, out of non-being, the idea of a personal God receives its most radical metaphysical formulation: for this suggests that God transcends the causal law which governs the natural world according to the principle that nothing comes out of nothing. Kant justified critically the fact that God lies beyond the knowledge of the world, which links its insights according to the principle of causality; God is only there for the will which postulates him because it is free.

[23] *Fl.* mid-fifth century B.C.   [24] 385–322 B.C.

3

This is the origin of the structure common to all systems of this type of world-view. Epistemologically, as soon as it becomes philosophically conscious of its presuppositions, it is based on the facts of consciousness. In metaphysics this world view passes through different forms. It occurs first in Attic philosophy as the conception of formative reason which shapes matter into the world. The great discovery that conceptual thought and moral will is independent of nature and related to a spiritual order is the starting-point of Plato's conception and remains the basis in Aristotle. The second conception, the doctrine of creation, anticipated by the Roman concept of will and the view of the divine governance of the world, was developed in Christianity. It constructs a transcendent world from the relationships experienced in acts of will. The particular Christian concepts of God are the relationship of a father to his children, contact with God, providence as the symbol of how the world is governed, justice and mercy. A long road has been traversed from there to the highest purification of this consciousness of God in German transcendental philosophy. Here the idealism of freedom, seen most perfectly in Schiller,[25] constructs the supersensuous world of heroic greatness which is only there for the will because it is posited by its ideal of infinite striving.

4

The facts of consciousness provide this world-view with a universally valid basis. Being the metaphysical consciousness of the heroic man it is indestructible; it will renew itself in every great and active personality.

But it cannot define and demonstrate its principle scientifically and validly. Here, too, a restless dialectic begins, passing from possibility to possibility, but is unable to achieve a solution of its problem. The purposive will, active in family, law and state, was developed by the Romans in concepts of life which were ultimately derived from their inborn practical capacity for living it. This rested on something inaccessible and undemonstrable. In a circular argument the regularity in the ways of living was based on presupposed, innate features, which could only be deduced from these ways and the agreement of nations. This was the way in which the Roman philosophy of life justified its idealism of personality. Christian consciousness, thereupon, stipulated the transcendence of the spirit, its independence from all natural orders, as the principle of this point of view. But this

[25] F. Schiller, 1766–1824.

is only a symbolic expression of the experience of choosing – self-sacrifice (the giving up of one's life in defiance of the natural combination of motives for survival) – and of the power to live for the realization of an invisible order. The ideal of the saint is its own proof but cannot be demonstrated logically. Later Kant and transcendental philosophy undertook to define and give universally valid grounds for this ideal will. Something unconditional in the form of a highest norm and highest value was contrasted with the course of the world. The attempt failed. But it was renewed in the French idealism of the person, from Maine de Biran[26] to Bergson,[27] in the idealistic forms of pragmatism as it appeared in James[28] and related thinkers, and in the great German movement of transcendental philosophy. Its power is indestructible and only its forms and proofs change. This power rests on a way of life which takes its impetus from active men and demands firm rules for the setting of purposes.

[A Schiller quotation follows.]

V. Objective idealism

[Some introductory remarks and section 1 are omitted because they mainly provide historical illustrations and discuss metaphysics generally.]

2

The epistemological, methodological approach of consciousness towards the enigma of life was, in the first of the three world views, the step from knowledge of uniformities in the physical world to generalizations which made it possible to subject even mental facts to outer, mechanical regularity. The idealism of freedom found firm ground for a valid solution of the enigma of life in the facts of consciousness; it postulated the existence and ascertainability of general, not further analysable, characteristics of consciousness which, with spontaneous power, shape life and a world view from the material of outer reality. The third type of epistemological, methodological approach is quite different from these. It can be observed in Heracleitus as well as the Stoa, in Giordano Bruno[29] and Spinoza and in Shaftesbury,[30] Schelling, Hegel, Schopenhauer and Schleiermacher, for it is based on their attitude to life. We call an attitude contemplative, reflective, aesthetic or artistic when the subject rests, as it were, from the labour of scientific knowledge and from the actions which realize the purposes arising from our needs. In this contemplative attitude our emotional life, in

---

[26] M. F. P. Maine de Biran, 1766–1824.   [27] H. Bergson, 1859–1941.
[28] W. James, 1842–1910.   [29] 1550–1600.
[30] Anthony Ashley Cooper, third earl of Shaftesbury, 1671–1713.

which abundance of life, value and the happiness of existence are experienced personally, expands into a kind of universal sympathy. Through this expansion of ourselves in universal sympathy we fill and animate the whole of reality with the values which we feel, the activities in which we express ourselves and with the highest ideas of beauty, goodness and truth. We rediscover in reality the moods which it evokes in us. As we expand our sense of life into sympathy with the whole world and experience our kinship with all the phenomena of reality, our joy in life and consciousness of our own power increases. This is the frame of mind in which the individual feels himself one with divine reality and kin to every part of it. No one has expressed this frame of mind more beautifully than Goethe. He praises the happiness of 'feeling and enjoying' nature. 'You allow me not only a coldly curious visit but grant me to look into its heart as into that of a friend.' 'You parade the ranks of the living before me and teach me to know my brothers in the bush, in the air and in the water.'

For this frame of mind all the discords of life are dissolved in a universal harmony. The tragic sense of the contradictions of existence, the pessimistic mood and humour which realistically grasps the limitation and oppressive narrowness of phenomena but finds the ideal victorious in the depths of reality, are only stages which lead upwards towards awareness of a universal context of existence and value.

The way of apprehending is always the same in this objective idealism: seeing parts together in a whole and elevating the context of life into that of the world rather than classifying cases according to their similarity or uniformity.

The first thinker of this type to reflect on his philosophic procedure was, as far as we know, Heracleitus. By profound thought he made the contemplative attitude conscious and contrasted it with the personifying thought of faith, with sense-perception, which he despised because of its isolation, and with scientific knowledge of the world. The philosopher takes as the subject of his reflection whatever surrounds him closely, constantly and daily and remains recognizably the same. Being the witness of what is happening to us is an inspired description of the deep reflectiveness in which the phenomena of the world which the multitude take for granted, become objects of surprise and thought to the true philosopher. By means of this contemplative attitude Heracleitus came to understand that the course of the world is always the same – a constant flow and decay of all things yet permeated by intellectual order. This consciousness of the permanent laws of the universe underlying flux helps him to overcome the tragic sense of the restless progression of time in which the present always is and is no longer.

The Types of World-View

In Stoicism there prevailed the same conception of the universe as a whole of which the individual objects are parts and in which they are held together by a uniform force. It abandoned the subordination of facts to abstract conceptual units which predominated in Plato and Aristotle: the logical relation between the particular and the general was replaced in their system by the organic relation of a whole to its parts: this gave rise to the form of apprehension which Kant called the intuition of immanent teleology of the organic and which he related closely to aesthetic intuition.[31]

After the decline of scholasticism which, in the service of Christian theology, had used the substantial forms to justify a transcendental world, the same categories for viewing the world (that of the whole and its parts and of the individuality of these parts even the very smallest) re-emerged in the transition period from the Middle Ages to modern times.[32] This refined aesthetic conception of the universe, according to which each individual thing, being a microcosm, mirrors the universe from its own position, had already emerged in Nicholas of Cusa.[33] Spinoza is the representative of the doctrine of *one* universe and even the world view of Leibniz, in spite of his conception of God justified in his *Monadology* and connected with his theological orientation, was a product of this attitude. Full epistemological consciousness of this contemplative attitude arose in Schelling, Schopenhauer and Schleiermacher. The different sides of the attitude, characteristic of this type of world-view, received varied expressions; Schelling's intellectual intuition, Schopenhauer's aesthetic contemplation in which the mind, freed from the will, no longer traces the causal relations of things but abstracts the essence of the phenomena and, finally, the religion of Schleiermacher's addresses which embodies an empathic intuition of the universe.

3

The common metaphysical formula of this whole class of systems results from this attitude. All phenomena of the universe are two-sided; seen from one side, by outer perception, they are given as sense-objects and stand as such in physical contexts, but at the same time they contain, seen from within, as it were, connections of life which we ourselves can experience inwardly. This principle can also be expressed as the kinship of all parts of the universe with the divine foundation and with each other. A universally-sympathetic frame of mind, which experiences the presence of God in spatially appearing reality, corresponds to this principle. This consciousness of kinship is

[31] In the *Critique of Judgment.*
[32] See 'The Great Poetry of Imagination', pp. 79ff.   [33] 1401–64.

the common, basic, metaphysical feature in the religion of the Hindus, Greeks and Germans; in metaphysics it gives rise to the view that all things, being part of a whole, are inherent in a unitary world-ground and all values immanent in a context of meaning which makes up the significance of the world. Through contemplation and intuition the individual relives in his life (however he may interpret it) the life of the universe and experiences in the outwardly-given phenomena an inwardly-alive, divine order. Finally, a deterministic conception usually springs from this same attitude, for the particular is here determined by the whole and the pattern of phenomena is conceived as inwardly determined whatever other characteristics it may also possess.

4

What this formulation of objective idealism specifically asserts about the nature of the world is expressed symbolically only – by religion, poetry and metaphysics. It is essentially unknowable. Metaphysics only distinguishes individual sides of the subject's pattern of life and projects them into infinity as the pattern of the world. Here a new, restless, dialectic springs up pressing on from system to system until, after exhausting all possibilities, the insolubility of the problem is recognized.

Is this world-ground reason or will? If we define it as thought will is still necessary for anything to originate. If we think of it as will purposive thought is pre-supposed. But will and thought cannot be reduced to each other. Here logical thought about the world-ground comes to an end; all that remains is the reflection of its vitality in mysticism. If one thinks of the world-ground as a person the metaphor requires that it should have concrete, limiting characteristics. But if one applies the idea of the infinite all its characteristics vanish and only the inexhaustible and incomprehensible – the darkness of mysticism – remain. If it is conscious, the contrast between subject and object applies to it but, if it is unconscious, we cannot comprehend how out of itself it could produce consciousness, which is something higher; once more we are faced by something incomprehensible. We cannot think how world unity can give rise to multiplicity, the eternal to change; logically this is incomprehensible. The relationship of being and thought, of extension and thinking, does not become more comprehensible through the magic word identity. So these metaphysical systems, too, leave only a frame of mind and a world-view behind them.

[A concluding quotation from Goethe omitted.]

IV

Dilthey's Epistemology
and Methodology

An Introduction to the Human Studies

EDITOR'S INTRODUCTION

First published in 1883 this work is a massive attack on the problem which occupied Dilthey all his life – laying solid theoretical foundations for the human studies. The work remained a fragment and little wonder if one considers the scale of the programme set out in the preface which I have given here. What there is of the *Introduction* (Vols. I and II of the *Collected Works*) is substantial but is confined entirely to the historical approach. The systematic part of the work was never written. The fragments collected in Vol. VII are, in a sense, the continuation and missing counterpart of Dilthey's reflections on the epistemology and methodology of the human studies.[1] To the latter, widely considered Dilthey's most important writing, I have given considerable space. The *Introduction,* on the other hand, is only represented by two short extracts, which help us to see Dilthey's continuous preoccupation with these problems in proper perspective. But a detailed history of ideas cannot be represented fairly by short extracts and so none of this material is reproduced.

One of the main theses which the historical material served to demonstrate was this: the germs of both the sciences and the human studies had emerged and developed under the tutelage of metaphysics. In the period from the sixteenth to the eighteenth century the sciences became independent of metaphysics, through an epistemological clarification of their foundations and the development of their methodology. The human studies did not share in this emancipation. Instead they merely exchanged subjection to science which came to be accepted as the model of all knowledge for subjection to metaphysics. Dilthey considered that only by developing a methodology of their own could the human studies achieve their independence.

Dilthey sympathized with, and was inspired by, the desire of such men as Comte and Mill, to make the human studies into rigorous, empirical and 'scientific' disciplines. But he was profoundly opposed to what he considered their narrow conception of experience and their belief that to be scientific they must follow exactly the methods of physics or chemistry. He believed that the so-called historical school provided an essential corrective to this tendency. Here Dilthey was referring to groups of scholars, many of them Germans, who shared his belief in the importance and superior value of explanations in terms of historical developments. They had originally reacted against what Dilthey calls the system of nature or natural system. This maintains that the nature of things is immutable and accessible to reason and that there is a common human nature which is only superficially affected by social and historical factors. It also claimed that the basis of actual codes of law was natural law and the rational core of all religions natural religion. The historical school rejected all these views and maintained that everything including laws, religions and even human nature was a product of history and subject to historical change. So

[1] See pp. 170–245.

every phenomenon could only be understood in terms of its historical setting. Dilthey saw himself as the philosophic spokesman of this school. He agreed with their aims and line of approach but thought that they needed philosophic justification. This he sought, as is briefly indicated in the 'Preface' in a modification of Kant's epistemology.

The epistemological points of view, to which he refers in the passage I have included, always remained central to Dilthey's thinking. It is the assumption that we can only evaluate and justify our knowledge of the world by considering the active mental processes by which we acquire it. But to Dilthey the knowing subject was not a pure consciousness or transcendental ego but the human being shaped by historical conditions.

The second section chosen from Vol. I illustrates Dilthey's treatment of the relationship between body and mind on which he bases his conception of the interdependence of the sciences and the human studies.

An Introduction to the
Human Studies

PREFACE

Vol. 1, pp. xv–xix

This is the first half of a work which combines a historical with a systematic approach for the purpose of solving, as convincingly as I can, the problem of the philosophic foundations of the human studies. In the historical approach I shall outline the struggle philosophy had to establish these foundations; I shall seek to determine the historical place of individual theories within this development and try to assess their historically determined value. By immersing myself into this development I hope to arrive at a judgment of the goals of contemporary scholarship. The historical description prepares the ground for the epistemological justification with which the other half of this work will deal.

As the historical and systematic accounts are intended to supplement each other it may make reading the historical part easier if I indicate the basic ideas of the latter.

The emancipation of the individual sciences began at the end of the Middle Ages, even though for a long time – indeed, far into the last century – the study of society and history remained in the old bondage to metaphysics. But the growing power of science led to a new bondage which was no less oppressive than the old. It was the historical school – using the term in its broadest sense – which brought about the emancipation of historical consciousness and historical scholarship. At the time when, in France, the system of social ideals (which in the seventeenth and eighteenth centuries had produced natural law, natural religion, abstract, political theory and abstract economics) produced the Revolution and when the armies of this revolution occupied and destroyed the ramshackle, 1,000-year-old, edifice of the German Empire a new view developed in our country. Treating historical growth as the source of all mind-constructed facts proved the falsehood of that whole system of social ideals. This view was held by Winckelmann, Herder, the Romantic School, Niebuhr,[1] Jakob Grimm,[2] Savigny[3] and Böckh.[4] It was strengthened by the reaction

---

[1] Niebuhr, German historian, 1733–1815.   [2] 1785–1863.
[3] F. C. Savigny, founder of modern legal studies, 1778–1861.
[4] A. Böckh, German philologist, 1785–1867.

against the revolution. In England it was promoted by Burke,[5] in France by Guizot[6] and Tocqueville.[7] In the conflicts which tore European society it clashed with the ideas of the eighteenth century about law, politics and religion. This school of thought was animated by a purely empirical approach and a loving absorption in the uniqueness of the empirical process; aiming at a universal vision of history it tried to determine the value of particular circumstances from the context of their development; its historical approach to social theory sought an explanation and a model for contemporary life in the study of the past; it saw all mental life as historical. From that school a stream of new ideas flowed through innumerable channels into the particular disciplines.

But the historical school has not, up till now, broken the inner barrier which inevitably inhibited its theoretical development and practical influence. It lacked philosophic foundations because its study and evaluation of historical phenomena was not linked to an analysis of the facts of consciousness and, therefore, not based on the only kind of knowledge which is ultimately certain. A healthy relationship to epistemology and psychology is missing. This is why it has not yet achieved an explanatory method; by themselves historical vision and comparative method cannot produce an independent system of the human studies nor exercise any practical influence. Unable to develop and justify its vital and profound views the historical school could only protest ineffectually against the more arid and superficial, but competently argued, theories of Comte, Mill and Buckle,[8] who tried to solve the enigma of the historical world by applying scientific principles and methods to it. The strong hatred and awkward language with which Carlyle and other vital spirits opposed exact science were symptomatic of the situation. Uncertain about the foundations of the human studies some individual scholars retreated into mere descriptions; others were satisfied with acute, subjective, accounts; a third group returned to metaphysics which offers principles capable of transforming daily life to those who trust it.

My awareness of the state of the human studies prompted me to attempt a philosophic justification of the principles guiding the historical school and of the specific research inspired by it; this should settle the controversy between the historical school and the abstract theories. While I was doing my research I was plagued by questions which, no doubt, occupy any thoughtful historian, lawyer or politician. So I came to need and to plan a foundation for the human studies.

[5] E. Burke, 1728–97.
[6] F. Guizot, French historian and statesman, 1787–1874.
[7] A. C. de Tocqueville, 1805–59.
[8] H. T. Buckle, English historian, 1821–62.

Introduction to the Human Studies

What is the system of presuppositions which justifies the judgments of historians, the conclusions of economists and the concepts of lawyers and provides criteria for establishing that they are true? Is this system based on metaphysics? Is there a philosophy of history or a law of nature which is sustained by metaphysical concepts? Where, if such ideas have to be rejected, is there a firm foundation for the system of presuppositions which interrelates the individual disciplines and provides them with certainty?

The answers which Comte and the Positivists, Stuart Mill and the Empiricists, gave to these questions seem to truncate historical reality in order to assimilate it to the concepts and methods of science. On the other hand, the reaction against them, an inspired example of which is Lotze's[9] *Microcosmos*, seems to sacrifice the justifiable independence of the particular disciplines and the fruitful power of their empirical methods to a sentimental mood which nostalgically seeks to recall, through science, a mental satisfaction which has gone for ever. Only in inner experience, in the facts of consciousness, did I find firm anchorage for my thoughts and I am confident that readers will be convinced by my proof of this. All science and scholarship is empirical but all experience is originally connected, and given validity, by our consciousness (within which it occurs), indeed by our whole nature. We call this point of view which consistently recognizes that it is impossible to go beyond consciousness, to see, as it were, without eyes or to direct a cognitive gaze behind the eye itself, epistemological; modern scholarship cannot acknowledge any other. Now I could see that, from this point of view, the independence of the human studies could be given the kind of justification required by the historical school. From this point of view our picture of the whole of nature stands revealed as a shadow cast by a hidden reality; undistorted reality only exists for us in the facts of consciousness given by inner experience. The analysis of these facts is the core of the human studies; knowledge of the principles of the world of mind remains, as the historical school assumed, within the sphere of the human studies which, therefore, form an autonomous system.

On these points I agreed in many ways with the epistemological school of Locke,[10] Hume and Kant. But I had to differ from this school in the way I conceived the connection between the facts of consciousness, which we all recognize as the basis of philosophy. Apart from a few beginnings (which were not scientifically developed) like those of Herder and Wilhelm von Humboldt,[11] epistemology (that of the

---

[9] R. M. Lotze, German philosopher and physiologist, 1817–81.
[10] 1632–1704. [11] 1767–1835.

Empiricists and of Kant) has, up till now, explained experience and cognition merely from the facts of apprehension. No real blood flows in the veins of the knowing subject constructed by Locke, Hume and Kant; it is only the diluted juice of reason, a mere process of thought. Cognition seems to develop concepts such as the external world, time, substance and cause from perception, imagination and thought. However, my historical and psychological studies of man as a whole led me to explain cognition and its concepts in terms of the powers of man as a willing, feeling and imagining being. So I have used the following method: I have related every constituent of present-day, abstract scientific thought to the whole of human nature (as experience and the study of language and history reveal it) and sought to connect them. As a result the most important constituents of my picture and knowledge of reality – personal individuality, external world, other persons, their temporal life and interaction – can be explained in terms of the whole of human nature in which willing, feeling and thinking are only different aspects of the real process of life. The questions we all ask of philosophy cannot be answered by rigid *a priori* conditions of knowledge but only by a history which starts from the totality of our nature and sketches its development.

This solves the most obstinate problem of this approach, the questions about the origin and justification of our convictions about the reality of the external world. To the perceiving mind the external world remains only a phenomenon but to the whole human being who wills, feels and imagines this external reality (whatever its special characteristics) is something independent and as immediately given and certain as his own self – it is part of life, not a mere idea. We do not know of this external world through an inference from effects to causes or some corresponding process; the ideas of cause and effect are only abstractions from the life of the will. Thus the horizon of experience widens: at first it only seems to tell us about our own inner states but in knowing myself I also know about the external world and other people. How far I can demonstrate this and how far it is possible to develop a securely based system of social and historical knowledge from the point of view indicated must be left to the reader's judgment.

I have not shrunk from being somewhat circumstantial because I wanted to link the main thought and the main principles of this epistemological foundation of the human studies to different aspects of modern scholarship and so give it a broader basis. In book one I shall start with a survey of the particular human studies which provide the material and impulse for this work and from this material draw inferences about these disciplines. In book two of the present volume I shall trace the history of epistemology during the period in which the fate of metaphysical explanations was decided. I shall try to prove that the metaphysics generally accepted then was based on a stage of scientific development which we have left behind. This is why any metaphysical justification of the human studies is a thing of the past. In books four and five I shall attempt my own epistemological justification of the human studies. The detailed historical part is due not only to the practical requirements of an introduction but also to my conviction that historical reflection is as valuable as epistemological. For some generations this same conviction has been expressed by a preference for the history of philosophy and by Hegel's, Comte's and Schelling's attempts (in his later works) to justify their systems historically. From the evolutionary point of view this conviction can be even more convincingly justified. For the history of intellectual development shows – in the bright light of the sun – the growth of the tree whose roots epistemology must seek beneath the earth.

[There follows a final paragraph which contains some apologies, hopes and a cross-reference to Dilthey's Schleiermacher biography.]

III. The Relationship of the Human Studies to the Sciences

Vol. 1, pp. 14–21

The human studies embrace many physical facts and are based on knowledge of the physical world. If one could imagine purely mental beings in a community which only consisted of such beings then their emergence, preservation, development and extinction would be dependent on purely mental conditions (whatever idea we may form of the background from which they emerged and into which they receded); their welfare would be based on their relation to a world of mind, their contact with each other and their interactions would be purely mental and would result in purely mental consequences; even their eclipse from the realm of such beings would have its cause in the mental sphere. A society of such individuals would be known by pure 'Geisteswissenschaften'. In fact, an individual like any other animal originates, survives and develops through the functioning of his body and its relation to his physical environment; his sense of life is, at least partly, based on this functioning; his impressions are conditioned by his sense-organs and the way they are affected by the environment; the wealth and flexibility of his ideas and the strength and direction of his acts of will are, in many ways, dependent on changes in his nervous system. His acts of will contract muscles and so his impact on the outer world is tied to the molecular movements of his body; the permanent effects of his acts of will only persist as changes in the material world. If we want to separate out man's mental life it must be abstracted from the psycho-physical unit which is the whole man. Organized into society men form the reality which is the subject-matter of the historical-social disciplines.

Whatever the metaphysical facts may be, man as a whole may be regarded from two points of view; seen from within he is a system of mental facts but to the senses he is a physical whole. Introspection and perception are separate acts so we can never grasp what goes on in a man's mind at the same time as we observe his body. So a scientific approach which tries to find out the relationship between the mental and the physical expressed in the unity of body and mind is compelled to adopt two irreducible points of view. If I start from inner experience I find that the whole external world is given in my consciousness and that all the laws of nature are subject to the conditions of my consciousness and therefore depend on them. This is the point of view which German philosophy at the turn of the eighteenth century described as transcendental philosophy. But if I start from the physical world as I see it, I notice that mental facts have their place in the temporal and spatial arrangements of the external world and that changes in mental life result from interference – natural or experimental – with the nervous system. Observation of human growth and of the effects of illness extend these impressions into a comprehensive picture of how the mind depends on the body. This is the origin of the scientific approach which proceeds from the external to the internal, from material to mental changes. The antagonism between the philosopher and the scientist is conditioned by the contrast in their starting-points.

My starting-point is the scientific approach. As long as it remains conscious of its limitations its results are incontestable. But their value as knowledge is more precisely defined from the point of view of inner experience. Science dissects the causal order of nature. Where this dissection reaches the point at which a material fact or change is regularly related to a mental fact or change without a further intermediary link being discoverable, we can only note this regular connection but cannot apply the relation of cause and effect to it. We find uniformities in one sphere regularly linked to those in the other, a relationship which is expressed by the mathematical concept of function. To think of the parallel courses of mental and physical changes as comparable to two synchronized clocks tallies with experi-

Introduction to the Human Studies

ence just as well as an explanation in terms of one clock;[12] stripped of the metaphor this means treating both spheres of experience as different appearances of one thing. The mind is dependent on the natural world because natural processes affect the particular material facts and changes which are regularly, and apparently directly, linked to mental facts and changes. Science observes the chain of causes reaching to the psycho-physical life; there a change in which the relationship between the material and the mental eludes a causal explanation, in turn, evokes one in the material world. In this context the physiologist's experiments disclose the significance of the structure of the nervous system. By analysing how the confusing phenomena of life depend on each other we can trace the sequence of natural changes which reach man, enter his nervous system through the senses, and give rise to sensations, ideas, feelings and desires which, in turn, affect the course of nature. The living being, filled with an immediate sense of his undivided existence, is analysed into an empirically observable system of relationships between conscious states and the structure and functions of the nervous system. Every mental action reveals its relationship to a change in our body through the nervous system and a physical change is accompanied by a change in our mental state only via the nervous system.

From this analysis of psycho-physical units we derive a clearer idea of their dependence on the context of nature in which they occur, which they affect and from which they retire; this also throws light on how historical and social studies depend on science. From this we can ascertain how far the theories of Comte and Herbert Spencer[13] about the position of these disciplines in the hierarchy of science are justified. This work will try to account for the relative independence of the human studies; it must, therefore, equally explain – to show the opposite side of the coin – the systematic way in which they depend on the sciences and thus form the last and highest link in a construction which starts from mathematical foundations. The facts of mind are the upper limits of the facts of nature which, in turn, are the underlying conditions of mental life. The human world, that is human society and history, is the highest phenomenon of the empirical world. Therefore, to understand this human world, we must know about the system of physical conditions which constantly determines its development.

Man, because of his position in the causal context of nature, is conditioned by a *double relationship* to it.

[12] This is a rather elliptical reference to debates in the history of philosophy: Malebranche held the former view, Spinoza the latter.
[13] 1820–1903.

Dilthey's Epistemology and Methodology

As we saw, the psycho-physical unit is, through its nervous system, constantly affected by the general course of nature which it, in turn, affects. Where man affects nature he does so characteristically in the form of actions guided by purposes. On the one hand, the course of nature with its specific characteristics can influence man's purposes; on the other, it helps to determine the means for the achievement of these ends. And so, even when we affect nature, because we are creatures of will reflecting on our purposes and not blind forces, we are still dependent on nature. So man is doubly dependent on nature. As a causal chain starting from the position of the earth in the cosmos it determines social-historical reality; hence, for the empirical researcher, the great problem of the relation between the order of nature and freedom subdivides into innumerable specific questions about relations between specific facts of the mind and the influences of nature. On the other hand the purposes of the human world react on nature and on the earth which man, in this sense, considers his abode and where he is busily making himself comfortable; these reactions, too, are dependent on using the laws of nature. All purposes lie within man's mental sphere for only there is anything real to him, but the purpose seeks its means in nature. The change in the external world which the creative power of mind has produced is often insignificant; and yet, only through it does the value thus created exist for other people. So a few pages, the material remains of deep thought in which ancient thinkers moved towards the assumption that the earth moved, fell into the hands of Copernicus and precipitated a revolution in our world view.

Here we can see how relative the delimitation of the two classes of disciplines is. Controversies, like those about the position of general linguistics, are sterile. At the two points of transition between the study of nature and that of the mind – where nature affects the development of mind and where it is affected by mind or forms the bridge for affecting other minds – knowledge of both the sciences and the human studies mingles. This knowledge of how nature shapes human beings is combined with insight into how it provides us with material for action because these are the two ways in which nature affects human life. An important part of grammar and musical theory derives from our knowledge of the natural laws about sound formation and the genius of language or music is tied to these laws; the study of their achievements is, therefore, based on understanding this dependence.

At this point we can see that knowledge of the conditions which are part of nature and the subject-matter of the sciences, forms the basis for the study of mental facts. The spread of mankind over the whole of the earth and man's destiny in history is, like the development of the individual, conditioned by the whole cosmic process. For example, wars are one of the main ingredients of history; they are the result of political decisions but they are fought and won with weapons. So the theory of war depends, primarily, on knowledge of the physical conditions which are the basis and means for the conflict of wills. Our aim in fighting is to impose our will on the enemy by means of physical force. Theoretically, the aim is to reduce the enemy to complete helplessness; in practice, it is a matter of bringing him to the point where his position is more disadvantageous than the sacrifice demanded from him and can only be exchanged for something worse. In making such calculations the physical conditions and means are most important and, therefore, of the greatest interest to the investigator, while there is little to say about the mental factors.

The Construction of the Historical World
in the Human Studies

EDITOR'S INTRODUCTION

Under this general title B. Groethuysen, the editor of Vol. VII of Dilthey's *Collected Works*, has put together various sketches and unfinished drafts for a systematic treatment of the foundations of the human studies which Dilthey intended to form the second part of his Introduction to the Human Studies. Only two sections, less than a third of the text, were published in Dilthey's lifetime (*Proceedings of the Prussian Academy of Science*, 1906 and 1910). The rest comes from MSS of the same period.

In spite of its fragmentary nature this volume is Dilthey's most original and exciting work, containing the fullest account of his epistemology and methodology of the human studies. This is why I have given more space to it than to other aspects of Dilthey's work and reproduced substantial portions from it. Having discussed the gist of Dilthey's theories in my general introduction I shall now list some of the main themes of the passages selected.

1. The distinction between the sciences and the human studies is spelled out in terms of their subject-matter but it is made clear that this is not based on a dualistic ontology. The outer and the inner worlds, matter and mind, need not be considered as two distinct parts of ultimate reality. They are the products of looking at reality with different interests and using different methods. If we consider speech as a movement of physical organs we are dealing with matter; if we are listening to what is said we are giving our attention to mind.

2. Knowledge of the human world develops, first of all, in everyday life. We come to know something of ourselves, the world and other people because we are involved with our environment. We do not just see a brick wall but something which obstructs our view or protects our property; we see not only a tall, fat man but a friend or a rival.

We acquire knowledge of life from our encounters with things and people. This knowledge possessed by all of us (though in a more developed form by men of affairs, experienced politicians or businessmen) and reflected in public opinion and popular wisdom is an original, but unsystematic and uncritical, organization of the lessons we learn in life. It is the basis on which the human studies build systematic knowledge.

Because the human studies are directly rooted in practical concerns they are exposed to the danger of bias. We can correct this by recognizing that the entities we are studying (a person, or a nation for example) are not merely subjects seen from our point of view but have their own points of view, philosophies, values and interests.

3. The process by which we come to know what people think, feel or value is understanding. Dilthey's approach pivots on his theory of understanding. This covers the distinction between elementary and complex acts of understanding and complementary theories about meaning and expressions.

4. Hermeneutics, the methodology of studying the objectifications of mind, such as laws or literary works, is singled out as the key-discipline of all the human studies. This makes it clear that Dilthey's approach was *not* a form of psychologism, because it did not make psychology the basic clue to all the studies concerned with mind. This rejection of psychologism can be seen in Dilthey's earlier works, even – though not without ambiguity – in his *Ideas for a Descriptive Psychology*.

5. The analysis of the social-historical world requires the use of a range of concepts which Dilthey defines and discusses. Among these are nations, Ages, cultural systems, contexts of meaning, systems of interaction and development.

6. Vol. VII also contains Dilthey's most sustained attempt at a 'Critique of Historical Reason'. Though not fully worked out and containing some loose ends and obscurities, it contains the most stimulating and fruitful suggestions for completing such an undertaking.

At the core of Dilthey's theory of knowledge is his account of the categories of life which, like Kant's theory of the categories, is linked to a discussion of time. This section is both important and difficult so I have given it in full.

The Construction of the Historical World in the Human Studies

Vol. VII, pp. 79–88

I. The delimitation of the human studies

I

I shall start from the whole range of facts which forms the firm basis for any reasoning about the human studies. Side by side with the sciences a group of studies, linked by their common subject-matter, has grown naturally from the problems of life itself. These include history, economics, jurisprudence, politics, the study of religion, literature, poetry, architecture, music, and of philosophic world views and systems, and, finally, psychology. All these studies refer to the same great fact: mankind – which they describe, recount and judge and about which they form concepts and theories.

What is usually separated into physical and mental is vitally linked in mankind. For we, ourselves, are part of nature and nature is active in our obscure and unconscious instincts; states of mind are constantly expressed in gestures, facial changes and words and have an objective existence in institutions, states, churches and seats of learning; these provide the contexts of history.

This does not preclude the human studies from distinguishing, where required, the physical from the mental. But we must remember that they work with abstractions, not with entities, and that these abstractions are only valid within the limits imposed by the point of view from which they arose. I shall now describe the point of view according to which I distinguish the mental from the physical and determine the meaning I give these expressions in what follows. What comes first are experiences. As I have tried to prove earlier, these occur in a context which, in the midst of change remains the same throughout life. On the basis of this context, what I have earlier called the acquired structure of mental life develops. It includes our ideas, valuations and purposes and exists as a link between them. In each of them the acquired structure exists in particular combinations, in relationships between ideas, evaluations and goal preferences. This structure constantly affects our actions, colouring our ideas and states,

organizing our impressions and regulating our emotions; it is constantly present and constantly active, without our being aware of it. I
see no objection to our abstracting this structure of experiences from
the pattern of a man's life, calling it the mental and making it the
subject of judgments and theoretical discussions. We are justified in
forming this concept because what we have thus singled out as the
logical subject makes possible the judgments and theories required in
the human studies. The concept of the physical is equally legitimate.
Impressions and images are part of experience. To make them
comprehensible we must in practice treat them as emanating from
physical objects. Both concepts can only be used when we remember
that they are abstracted from the fact – man; they do not denote full
realities but only legitimately formed abstractions.

In the studies listed the subjects of assertions vary in comprehensive-
ness from individuals, families, more complex associations, nations,
Ages, historical movements or evolutionary series, social organizations,
systems of culture and other sections of the whole of humanity, to
humanity itself. These can be talked about and described and theories
can be developed about them, but they always refer to the same fact,
humanity or human – social – historical reality. So it is possible to
define this group of disciplines in terms of its common reference to the
same face – humanity – and thus to distinguish them from the sciences.
In addition, because of this common reference, assertions about
the logical subjects comprised in the fact, humanity, support each
other. The two great classes of the disciplines listed, the study of history
(including the description of the contemporary state of society) and the
systematic human studies are, throughout, dependent on each other
and form a solid whole.

II

This definition of the human studies, though true as far as it goes, is not
exhaustive. We must discover *how* the human studies are related to
the fact of humanity. Only then can we define their subject-matter
precisely. For clearly it cannot be logically correct to distinguish the
human studies from sciences on the grounds that they cover different
ranges of facts. After all, physiology deals with an aspect of man and is
a science. The basis for distinguishing the two classes of disciplines
cannot lie in the facts *per se*. The human studies must be related
differently to the mental and the physical aspects of man. And this,
indeed, is the case.

In these studies a tendency inherent in the subject-matter itself is at work. The study of language embraces the physiology of the speech-organs as well as the semantics of words and sentences. The chemical effects of gunpowder are as much part of the course of modern war as the moral qualities of the soldiers who stand in its smoke. But, in the nature of the group of disciplines with which we are dealing there is a tendency, which grows stronger and stronger as they develop, to relegate the physical side of events to the role of conditions and means of comprehension. This is the turn towards reflection, the movement of understanding from the external to the internal. This tendency makes use of every expression of life in order to understand the mental content from which it arises. In history we read of economic activities, settlements, wars and the creating of states. They fill our souls with great images and tell us about the historical world which surrounds us: but what moves us, above all, in these accounts is what is inaccessible to the senses and can only be experienced inwardly; this is inherent in the outer events which originate from it and, in its turn, is affected by them. The tendency I am speaking of does not depend on looking at life from the outside but is based on life itself. For all that is valuable in life is contained in what can be experienced and the whole outer clamour of history revolves round it: goals unknown to nature arise within it. The will strives to achieve development and organization. Only in the world of the mind which creatively, responsibly and autonomously, stirs within us, has life its value, its goal and its meaning.

One can say that in all scholarly work two tendencies assert themselves.

Man finds himself determined by nature, which embraces the sparse, sporadic mental processes. Seen in this way they appear to be interpolations in the great text of the physical world. At the same time our conception of a spatial world is the original basis for our knowledge of uniformities on which we must rely from the outset. We are able to control the physical world by studying its laws. These can only be discovered if the way we experience nature, our involvement in it, and the living feeling with which we enjoy it, recedes behind the abstract apprehension of the world in terms of space, time, mass and motion. All these factors combine to make man efface himself so that, from his impressions, he can map out this great object, nature, as a structure governed by laws. Thus it becomes the centre of reality for man.

But that same man then turns back to life, to himself. To return to experience, through which alone we have access to nature and to life, the only source of meaning, value and purpose is the other great tendency which determines scholarly work. From this a second centre comes into being. It gives unity to all that happens to man, what he creates and does, the systems of purposes through which he lives and the outer organization of society in which individuals congregate. Here understanding penetrates the observable facts of human history to reach what is not accessible to the senses and yet affects external facts and expresses itself through them.

The first tendency aims at grasping mental contexts in the language, concepts and methods of science and so it alienates itself. The other tendency is to seek out, and reflect upon, the unobservable content which manifests itself in the observable outer course of human events. History shows that, through the human studies, man is getting nearer and nearer to his distant goal – self-knowledge.

This second tendency is also directed towards interpreting not only the human world but also nature (which can only be explained but never understood) in mental terms. Men like Fichte, Schelling, Hegel, Schopenhauer, Fechner,[1] Lotze and their successors tried to do this and to eavesdrop on the hidden meaning of nature.

At this point the meaning of the concepts inner and outer and the justification for using them become clear. They designate the relationship which exists in the understanding between the outer phenomena of life and what produces them and is expressed in them. The relationship between inner and outer exists only for understanding, just as the relationship between phenomena and that by which they are explained exists only for scientific cognition.

III

At this point the nature and relationship of the group of disciplines we started with can be determined more precisely.

We have already distinguished humanity from organic nature, which is most closely related to it, as well as from inorganic nature. This meant making a distinction between parts of the world. These parts form stages and mankind can be distinguished from the animal world because it has reached the stage in which concepts, valuations, realization of purposes, responsibility and consciousness of the meaning of life occur. We have already described the most general, common characteristic of our group of disciplines as its reference to man and mankind. This forms the bond between the disciplines. When we examine the special nature of this relationship between man and the human studies we find that it is not enough to describe man as their common subject-matter. Indeed, that subject-matter only comes into being through a particular attitude to humanity which is not imported

[1] G. T. Fechner, German philosopher and psychologist, 1801–87.

from outside but based on man's nature. When we have to deal with states, churches, institutions, customs, books and works of art we find that, like man himself, they always contain a relationship between what is outside and perceived by the senses and something they cannot reach which is inside.

We must now determine what this inner side is. It is a common error to identify our knowledge of it with psychology. I shall try to eliminate this error by making the following points.

The apparatus of law-books, judges, litigants, defendants, at a particular time and place is, first of all, the expression of a purposive system of laws which makes this apparatus effective. This purposive system is directed towards an unambiguous, external regulation of individual wills; it creates the conditions for the perfect life, as far as they can be realized by compulsion, and delimits the power spheres of individuals in relation to each other, to things and to the general will. The law must, therefore, take the form of imperatives backed by the power of a community to enforce them. Thus historical understanding of the law in force in a certain community at a given time can be achieved by going back from the outer apparatus to what it manifests, the intellectual system of legal imperatives produced by the collective will and enforced by it. Ihering[2] discusses the spirit of Roman law in this way. His understanding of this spirit is not psychological insight. It is achieved by going back to a mind-created structure with a pattern and law of its own. Jurisprudence, from the interpretation of a passage in the Corpus Juris to the understanding of the whole Roman law and thence to the comparison of legal systems, is based on this. Hence its subject-matter is not identical with the outer facts and occurrences through, and in, which the law takes its course. These facts are the concern of jurisprudence only in so far as they embody the law. The actual capture of the criminal, the illness of witnesses, or the apparatus of execution belong to pathology and technology.

It is the same with aesthetics. The work of a poet lies in front of me. It consists of letters, is put together by compositors and printed by machines. But literary history and criticism are only concerned with what the pattern of words refers to, not – and this is decisive – with the processes in the poet's mind but with a structure created by these processes yet separable from them. The structure of a drama lies in its particular combination of subject, poetic mood, plot and means of presentation. Each contributes to the structure of the work according to a law intrinsic to poetry. Thus the primary subject-matter of literary history or criticism is wholly distinct from the mental processes of the

[2] R. V. Ihering, German authority on Roman law, 1818–92.

poet or his reader. A mind-created structure comes into being and enters the world of the senses; we can understand it only by penetrating that world.

These illustrations throw light on the subject-matter of the disciplines under consideration, their nature and their difference from the sciences. Their subject-matter, too, is not impressions as they are experienced, but objects created by cognition in order to organize them.[3] In both cases the object is created according to the law imposed by the facts. In this both groups of disciplines agree. But they differ in the way in which their subject-matter is formed, that is, in the procedure which constitutes these disciplines. In the one a mental object emerges in the understanding; in the other a physical object in knowledge.

Now we may pronounce the word 'Geisteswissenschaften', for its meaning is clear. In the eighteenth century, when the need to find a common name for this group of disciplines arose, they were called the moral sciences, Geisteswissenschaften, or even the cultural sciences. The change of name alone shows that none of them is quite appropriate for what is to be referred to. So I want to indicate here the sense in which I use the word. It is the sense in which Montesquieu spoke of the spirit of the laws. Hegel of the objective mind, or Ihering of the spirit of the Roman law. To compare the usefulness of this expression with that of others used now will be possible later.

IV

Now we can meet the final requirement for a definition of the human studies. We can distinguish the human studies from the sciences by certain, clear, characteristics. These are to be found in the attitude of mind, already described, which moulds the subject-matter of the human studies quite differently from that of scientific knowledge. Humanity seen through the senses is just a physical fact which can only be explained scientifically. It only becomes the subject-matter of the human studies when we experience human states, give expressions to them and understand these expressions. The interrelation of life, expression and understanding, embraces gestures, facial expressions and words, all of which men use to communicate with each other; it also includes permanent mental creations which reveal their author's deeper meaning, and lasting objectifications of the mind in social structures where common human nature is surely, and for ever,

[3] Dilthey here assumes the Kantian – as against the empiricist – account of such cases as 'seeing a table'.

manifest. The psycho-physical unit, man, knows even himself through the same mutual relationship of expression and understanding; he becomes aware of himself in the present; he recognizes himself in memory as something that once was; but, when he tries to hold fast and grasp his states of mind by turning his attention upon himself, the narrow limits of such an introspective method of self-knowledge show themselves; only his actions and creations and the effect they have on others teach man about himself. So he only gains self-knowledge by the circuitous route of understanding. We learn what we once were and how we became what we are by looking at the way we acted in the past, the plans we once made for our lives, and the professional career we pursued. We have to consult old, forgotten letters and the judgments made about us long ago. In short, we can only know ourselves thoroughly through understanding; but we cannot understand ourselves and others except by projecting what we have actually experienced into every expression of our own and others' lives. So man becomes the subject-matter of the human studies only when we relate experience, expression and understanding to each other. They are based on this connection, which is their distinguishing characteristic. A discipline only belongs to the human studies when we can approach its subject-matter through the connection between life, expression and understanding.

All the properties which have been singled out as constituting the character of the human studies, the cultural sciences and history, follow from this common characteristic. The special relationship in which the unique and individual stands to general uniformities is one example. The connection between factual assertions, valuations and concepts of ends is another. It also follows that 'the apprehension of the unique and individual is as much a final goal in these disciplines as the development of abstract uniformities'.[4] There are further consequences; all the basic concepts with which this group of disciplines operates are different from the corresponding ones in the sphere of science.

We are justified in describing disciplines as human studies when they endeavour to trace what is creative, valuable and active in man and the objective mind he has produced.

[4] Vol. I, p. 33.

Construction of the Historical World

The structure of the human studies

Vol. vii, pp. 130–66

The special structure of the human studies is the product of the conditions under which they apprehend objects; particular problems arise from the forms and general processes of thought and are solved by a particular combination of methods.

In the development of these procedures the human studies have always been influenced by the physical sciences. Their methods, having developed earlier, were extensively adapted to the problems of the human studies. This is especially clear in two cases. The comparative methods increasingly applied in the systematic human studies were first evolved in biology, and experimental methods developed in astronomy and physiology were transferred to psychology, aesthetics and educational theory. Even today a psychologist, educationalist, philologist or art-critic will often ask himself when tackling individual problems if the techniques and methods for the solution of analogous problems in the physical sciences could be fruitfully applied in his own field.

But in spite of such individual points of contact, the methodology of the human studies is, from its starting-point onwards, different from that of the physical sciences.

Life and the human studies

Here I am only concerned with the general principles which are decisive for insight into the human studies as a whole: the description of methods belongs to the exposition of the construction of the human studies. I shall prefix two explanations of terms. By 'persons' I understand the constituents of the social-historical world. By 'mental structure' I refer to the inter-relationship between various processes within the person.

1. Life

The human studies rest on the relationship between experience, expression and understanding. So their development depends as much on the depth of experience as on the increasing revelation of its content; it is also conditioned by the spread of understanding over all objective manifestations of mind and by the increasingly complete and methodical extraction of the mental content from different expressions.

What we grasp through experience and understanding is life as the interweaving of all mankind. When we first confront this vast fact, which is our starting-point not only for the human studies but also for philosophy, we must try to get behind its scientific elaboration and grasp life in its raw state.

The distinctive facts of the life of mankind present themselves to us as the special characteristics of individual persons, as their relations, attitudes, conduct, their effect on things and people, and what they suffer from them. This permanent basis, from which differentiated processes arise, contains nothing which is not vitally related to an I. As everything is related to it the state of the I changes constantly according to how things and people respond to it. There is not a person or a thing which is merely an object to me, which does not represent pressure or furtherance, the goal of some striving or a restriction on my will; every object is important, worthy of consideration, close or distant, resistant or strange. Through this vital relationship, either transitory or permanent, these people and things bring me happiness, expend my existence and heighten my powers; or they confine the scope of my life, bring pressure to bear on me and drain my strength. Changes in me correspond to the characteristics which things acquire through this vital relationship. From this basis of life, objective cognition, valuation and the setting of purposes emerge as types of conduct with countless nuances in a state of flux. In the course of a life they are internally interwoven and themselves embrace and determine all activity and development.

We can illustrate this by the way in which the lyrical poet expresses an experience; he starts from a situation and shows men and things in a vital relationship to an ideal I in which his own existence and, within it, his experiences, are imaginatively heightened; this vital relationship determines what the genuine lyrical poet sees and expresses about men, things and himself. Similarly the epic poet must only say what stands out in the vital relationship he has described. The historian, describing historical situations and characters, will give a stronger impression of real life the more he reveals of these vital relationships. He must accentuate those characteristics of men and things which are prominent and active in these relationships – he must, I would say, give the characters, things and events the form and colour of the perceptions and memories to which they gave rise in these vital relationships.

2. *Knowledge of life*

The cognition of objects is a temporal process and, therefore, contains memory pictures. As, with the progress of time, experience accumulates and constantly recedes, we come to remember our passage through life. In the same way understanding of other people produces memories of their circumstances and images of different situations. All these memories of external facts, events and persons are invariably combined with a sense of the context to which they belong. The individual's knowledge of life springs from the generalization of what has thus accumulated. It arises through procedure which are equivalent to induction. The number of cases on which the induction is based constantly increases in the course of a lifetime and the generalizations formed are constantly corrected. The certainty attributable to personal knowledge of life is different from scientific validity, for these generalizations are not methodically made and cannot be formalized.

The individual slant which colours the personal knowledge of life is corrected and enlarged by the common experience. By this I mean the shared beliefs emerging in any coherent circle of people. These are assertions about the passage of life, judgments of value, rules of conduct, definitions of goals and of what is good. It is characteristic of them that they are the products of the common life. They apply as much to the life of individuals as to that of communities. As custom, tradition and public opinion they influence individuals and their experience; because the community has the weight of numbers behind it and outlasts the individual, this power usually proves superior to his will. The certainty of this common knowledge of life is greater than that of individuals because, in common knowledge, individual points of view cancel each other out and the number of cases on which the induction rests is much greater. On the other hand, in the case of common knowledge, we know less where it comes from than in the case of individuals.

3. *Differences of conduct and classes of statements in the knowledge of life*

The knowledge of life contains classes of statements based on differences of conduct.[5] For life is not only the source of the empirical content of knowledge; the typical classes of assertions are also conditioned by typical forms of human conduct. Now I merely want to affirm the existence of this relationship between the differences of conduct and the assertions of the knowledge of life.

From individual factual relations between the I and things and men, individual situations of life arise: differentiated states of the self, feelings of pressure or exhilaration, desire for an object, fear or hope.

---

[5] Dilthey here means thinking, willing, feeling and the like.

In so far as things or people which make a demand on the self come to occupy a place in its existence, become sources of help or hindrance, objects of desire, striving or recoil, they acquire, through these vital relationships, a meaning over and above our factual comprehension of them. All these characterizations of self, things or people, because they arise from these vital relationships, become conscious and are expressed in language. Therefore it contains distinctions between factual assertion, wish, exclamation and command. A survey of the expressions used for the behaviour and the attitudes of the self towards men and things shows that they fall into certain main classes. They assert a fact or a value, affirm a purpose, formulate a rule, or express the significance of a fact in the wider context into which it is interwoven. There are also relationships between the various kinds of assertions contained in the knowledge of life. Factual assertions form a layer on which valuations rest; the layer of valuations, in turn, serves as a basis for the setting of purposes.

The various forms of conduct and their products are objectified in statements which assert that they are facts. The resulting observations of people and things then become independent of the vital relationships from which they emerge. The facts are raised to a general knowledge of life by a procedure equivalent to induction. This is the origin of the many kinds of statements which emerged in generalized folk-wisdom and literature as proverbs, maxims and reflections about passions, characters and values of life. In them the differences which we noticed in the expressions of attitudes or forms of conduct recur.

There are further differences in the way our knowledge of life is formulated. In life itself cognition, valuation, the giving of rules and setting of purposes occurs at different levels which mutually presuppose each other. We have already pointed to such levels in the cognition of objects: they exist in the other forms of conduct. Thus, estimating the practical value of things or people presupposes that we have ascertained their capacity to help or harm; a decision only becomes possible when we have considered the relation between goals and reality and how the latter contains the means for achieving the former.

4. Ideal units as the basis of life and our knowledge of it

The lives of individuals are infinitely enriched through their relationships to their environment, to other people and to things. But every individual is also a point where webs of relationships intersect; these relationships go through individuals, exist within them, but also reach

beyond their life and possess an independent existence and development of their own through the content, value and purpose which they
realize. Thus they are subjects of an ideal kind. Some kind of
knowledge of reality is inherent in them; standpoints for valuation
develop within them; purposes are realized in them; they have a
meaning which they sustain in the context of the mind-constructed
world.

This is already the case in some of the systems of culture, for
instance, art and philosophy, where there is no organization to link
their parts. But organized associations also develop. Economic life
produces its own associations, science its own research centres,
religions develop the strongest of all cultural organizations. The
highest development of common goals within a community is found
in the family and the state and in the different intermediate forms
between them.

Every organized unit in a state acquires a knowledge of itself, of the
rules on which its existence is founded and of its place in the whole. It
enjoys what has become valuable within it and realizes the intrinsic
purposes which maintain and further its existence. Being itself a value
of mankind it realizes values. It has a meaning of its own in the context
of mankind.

At this point society and history unfold before us. But it would be
wrong to confine history to the co-operation of human beings for
common purposes. The individual person in his independent existence is a historical being. He is determined by his position in time and
space and in the interaction of cultural systems and communities. The
historian has, therefore, to understand the whole life of an individual
as it reveals itself at a certain time and place. It is the whole web of
relationships which stretches from individuals furthering their own
existence to the cultural systems and communities and, finally, to the
whole of mankind, which makes up the character of society and
history. Individuals, as much as communities and contexts, are the
logical subjects of history.

5. *The emergence of the human studies from the life of individuals and communities*

Life, knowledge of life and the human studies are, thus, internally
related and constantly interact. The basis of the human studies is not
conceptualization but total awareness of a mental state and its
reconstruction based on empathy. Here life grasps life and the power
with which these two basic processes of the human studies are

accomplished is a necessary precondition if all their branches are to be adequate.

Here we notice a decisive difference between the physical sciences and the human studies. In the former scientific thinking has become remote from our day-to-day contact with the external world and its original achievements are esoteric, but in the human studies a connection between life and science is retained, so that thought arising from daily life remains the foundation of scholarly activity. In certain circumstances life itself succeeds in penetrating its own depth to an extent which surpasses the power of a Carlyle and achieves a highly developed understanding of others which even Ranke[6] cannot equal. Great religious personalities, like Augustine and Pascal, provide the external examples of knowledge based on personal experience; the court and politics give training in the art of understanding other people which looks behind outward appearances; a man of action like Bismarck,[7] who is naturally aware of his goals whenever he writes a letter or conducts a conversation, cannot be equalled in the art of reading intentions behind expressions by any interpreter of political papers or critic of historical accounts. Often there is nothing to chose between a poetically sensitive listener's comprehension of a play and the most excellent literary-historical analysis. Even conceptualization in the historical and social studies is constantly determined by life itself. I am referring to the connection which frequently leads from life, from conceptualization about fate, characters, passions, values or purposes of existence, to history as a science. When, in France, political activity and one's position at court was based more on understanding people and leading personalities than on a scientific study of law, economics and politics, literary memoirs and studies of character and passions reached a height they have never achieved since; they were produced by people who were very little influenced by the scientific study of psychology and history. There is a link between these observations of high society and the writers and poets who learn from them and the systematic philosophers and scientific historians who are educated by poetry and literature. We see in the beginnings of political science among the Greeks how concepts of constitutions and their accomplishments originate from political life itself so that new creations in it lead to new theories. This whole relation is clearest in the earlier stages of jurisprudence among the Romans and Teutons.

[6] Leopold von Ranke, 1795–1886.   [7] 1815–98.

Construction of the Historical World

6. *The relationship to life of the human studies*
and the task of making them valid

Life as a starting-point and abiding context provides the first basic feature of the structure of the human studies; for they rest on experience, understanding and knowledge of life. This direct relationship between life and the human studies leads, in the latter, to a conflict between the tendencies of life and the goal of science. Because historians, economists, teachers of law and students of religion are involved in life they want to influence it. They subject historical personages, mass movements and trends to their judgment, which is conditioned by their individuality, the nation to which they belong and the age in which they live. Even when they think they are being objective they are determined by their horizon, for every analysis of the concepts of a former generation reveals constituents in them which derive from the presuppositions of that generation. Yet every science implies a claim to validity. If there are to be strictly scientific human studies they must aim more consciously and critically at validity.

Many of the scientific divergences which have recently appeared in the logic of the human studies stem from the conflict between these two tendencies. Because this appears most strongly in history I have made it the focal point of this discussion. Only in the actual construction of the human studies is this conflict settled, but the general statements which follow about the connections between the human studies already contain the principle for this settlement. We can stick to the results we have reached. Life and knowledge of it are the ever freshly-flowing sources of the understanding of the social-historical world, starting from life, understanding penetrates into ever new depths; only by reacting to life and society do the human studies achieve their highest significance, a significance which is constantly increasing. But the road to such effectiveness must pass through the objectivity of scientific knowledge. Men were already aware of this in the great creative periods of the human studies. After many distractions due to our national development and to the application of a one-sided ideal of culture since Jakob Burckhardt,[8] we are today filled with the desire to develop this objectivity of the human studies with an open mind, critically and stringently. I find the principle for the settlement of the conflict within these studies in the understanding of the historical world as a system of interactions centred on itself; each individual system of interactions contained in it has, through the positing of values and their realization, its centre within itself, but all are

[8] 1818–97.

183

structurally linked into a whole in which the meaning of the whole web of the social-historical world arises from the significance of the individual parts; thus every value-judgment and every purpose projected into the future must be based exclusively on these structural relationships. We are approaching this ideal principle in the subsequent, general, statements about the connections between the human studies.

The procedures through which the mind-constructed world is given

The connections among the human studies are determined by their being based on experience and understanding, both of which have characteristics that distinguish the human studies radically from the sciences and give the construction of the human studies a character of its own.

1. *How experience gives rise to ideas*

Every visual image differs from others referring to the same object according to the standpoint and conditions of perception. The various forms of the cognition of objects link these images into a system of inner relations. The total conception which arises from the series of images according to the basic factual conditions is something added by thought. In contrast, a person's experiences are related in time, each of them has a place in a sequence the parts of which are linked by memory. So far I am not concerned with the problem of the reality of those experiences or with the difficulty of taking them in, but merely with the difference between having an experience and being confronted with an image.[9] Consciousness of experience is one with its content just as subjectivity is one with its subject; the experience is not an object which confronts the person who has it, its existence for me cannot be distinguished from *what* is presented to me. Here there are no different positions in space from which to observe what is there. Different points of view from which to conceive it can only arise afterwards in reflection and do not affect its character as an experience. It is exempted from the relativity of sense-impressions where images of objects are affected by the observer, his position and the obstacles in his line of vision. Thus a direct sequence of ideas leads from experience to

[9] I.e. walking round a house we receive in temporal sequence images of front, side and back walls, just as we might have a sequence of images in a dream; seeing a house, by contrast, means grasping these images as related outside that time sequence. This is, of course, Kant's famous argument in the 'Analogies of Experience' (*Critique of Pure Reason*, B223–B248).

the order of concepts in which it is grasped by thought. First of all it is illuminated by the elementary acts of thought; here memories, which retain it, have a special significance. And what happens when this experience becomes the object of my reflections? I lie awake at night worrying whether I shall be able, in old age, to complete works I have already begun; I consider what is still to be done. The consciousness contained in this experience is structured; a cognition of objective facts forms its basis; on it rests an attitude of care and sorrow about these facts and of striving to get beyond them. All this is before me as a structured whole. I become conscious of distinctions within the situation. I abstract and isolate the structural connections. All that I thus abstract is contained in the experience itself and is only being clarified. Elements in my awareness of the experience draw me on to elements of others which, in the course of my life – though separated by long stretches of time – were structurally connected with them; previous reviews have made me familiar with my works; linked to them in the far distant past are the events through which they originated. Another element leads into the future: work in progress still demands incalculable labour; I worry about it and prepare myself inwardly for the task. All this 'about', 'from' and 'towards', all these relations to what has been lived and remembered or still lies in the future, carry me along backwards and forwards. Because living through an experience calls for ever-new links, we are carried along in this way. Interest, originating in the emotional power of the experience, may also play its part. This is a being carried along, not a volition, least of all an abstract will to knowledge, which it has been called since Schleiermacher's *Dialectic*. In the sequence which then arises, the past, as well as the possible future, is transcendent to the moment filled with experience. But both past and future elements are related to the experience in a sequence which, through these relationships, is welded into a whole. Because remembering involves recognition everything past is a repro-duction, structurally related to a former experience. Future possi-bilities are also linked to the sequence because of the range of potentialities mapped out by it. Thus, in this process, there arises a view of the continuity of mental life in time which constitutes the course of a life. In it every single experience is related to the whole. This continuity of life is not a sum or quintessence of successive moments but a unity constituted by relationships which link all the parts. From the present we run through a series of memories back to the point where our small, malleable and unformed self is lost in the twilight and we press forward from the present to possibilities, which are grounded in it, but, at the same time, assume vague and vast dimensions.

This has an important consequence for the mutual relations of the human studies. Life itself contains the constituents, regularities and relationships which constitute awareness of the course of a life; knowledge of the passage of one's life is as real as experience itself.

2. *Interdependence of the processes in understanding*

Though experience presents us with the reality of life in its many ramifications we, only, seem to know one particular thing, namely our own life. It remains knowledge of something unique and no logical aid can overcome this limitation, which is rooted in the way it is experienced. Understanding alone surmounts the limitation of the individual experience and, at the same time, lends to personal experiences the character of knowledge of life. Extending over several people, mental creations and communities, it widens the horizon of the individual life and, in the human studies, opens up the path which leads from the common to the general.

Mutual understanding assures us of what individuals have in common. They are connected with each other by common, i.e. similar or identical, features. This same relation permeates the whole of the human world. These common bonds are expressed in identity of reason, in sympathy on the emotional plane and in the mutual commitments of right and duty accompanied by consciousness of obligation.

What persons have in common is the starting-point for all the relations between the particular and the general in the human studies. A basic experience of what men have in common permeates the whole conception of the mind-constructed world; through it consciousness of a unitary self and similarity with others, identity of human nature and individuality are linked. This is the presupposition for understanding. From an elementary interpretation which only requires knowledge of the meaning of words and the rules according to which they are linked into meaningful sentences – i.e. language and thought held in common – the circle of common conditions for understanding widens to the extent to which we are concerned with higher combinations of expressions.

A second basic relationship, decisive for the structure of the human studies, emerges from the analysis of understanding. We have seen how the truths of the human studies rest on experience and understanding: but, on the other hand, understanding presupposes the use of the truths of the human studies. I will illustrate this by an example. Suppose we are trying to understand Bismarck. Our material consists of an extraordinary wealth of letters, documents, anecdotes and reports about him. All this refers to his life. To understand what influenced this great statesman and what he achieved, the historian must extend the range of his material. As long as the process of understanding goes on the collection of material has not been concluded. Recognizing the relevance of people, events and circumstances presupposes some generalizations. Therefore the understanding of Bismarck is based on them. These generalizations range from the common characteristics of man to those of particular classes. From the point of view of the psychology of individuals the historian will place Bismarck among the men of action and trace in him their characteristic combination of traits. From another point of view he will recognize in the independence of his nature, in his habit of dominating and leading, and in his strong will the characteristics of the Prussian landed aristocracy. As his long life occupies a specific place in the course of Prussian history another group of general statements must determine the features common to people of that Age. The enormous pressures which the circumstances of his country exerted on its political self-confidence naturally evoked the most varied reactions. To understand this requires general statements about the pressure which a situation exerts on a political whole and its parts and about their reaction. The degree of methodological certainty achieved by understanding depends on the development of the general truths on which the understanding of this relationship is based. It now becomes clear that this great man of action, whose roots lay in Prussia and its monarchy, must have experienced the external pressures exerted on Prussia in a particular way. He, therefore, of necessity judged the internal question of the constitution of the state mainly from the point of view of the power of the state. Because common factors like the state, religion, the law of the land, meet in him and because, as a historical personality, he was a force determined and moved to a considerable degree by these common factors, while, at the same time, affecting them, the historian needs a general knowledge of them. Put briefly, his understanding will only be ultimately perfected through reference to the essence of all the human studies. Every relationship which must be elaborated in presenting this historic personality reaches the highest achievable certainty and clarity only when determined by scientific concepts about the individual spheres. The relation between these spheres is founded ultimately on a total conception of the historical world.

Thus our example illustrates the double relationship involved in understanding. Understanding presupposes experience and experience only becomes knowledge of life if understanding leads us from the narrowness and subjectivity of experience to the whole and the general. Moreover, the understanding of an individual personality, to be complete, requires systematic knowledge, while systematic knowledge is equally dependent on the vivid grasping of the individual person. Knowledge of inorganic nature proceeds through a hierarchy of sciences in which the lower stratum is always independent of the one for which it lays the foundations; in the human studies everything from the process of understanding onwards is determined by the relationship of *mutual dependence.*

The history of these disciplines shows a corresponding development. Historiography is always conditioned by the knowledge of the systematic rélationships interwoven into history and exploring them more deeply determines the progress of historical understanding. Thucydides[10] relied on the political knowledge which had grown from the practice of the independent Greek states and on the political theories developed in the period of the Sophists. Polybius[11] combined in himself the whole political wisdom of the Roman aristocracy at the peak of its social and intellectual development with the study of Greek political literature from Plato to the Stoa. The combination of Florentine and Venetian statesmanship – developed in a sophisticated upper class given to lively political debate – with the renewal and development of classical theories made Machiavelli's[12] and Guicciardini's[13] historiography possible. The ecclesiastical history written by Eusebius[14] and the history written by the supporters and opponents of the Reformation, such as Neander[15] and Ritschl,[16] were full of systematic concepts about religion and Church law. Finally, the development of modern historiography is based, in the case of the historical school, on the combination of the new jurisprudence and the experiences of a revolutionary age and, in the case of Hegel, on the systematization of the newly developed human studies. Though Ranke seems to confront things with a naive joy in narration, his historiography can, nevertheless, only be understood by tracing the various sources of systematic thought which converged in his education. As we get towards the present this mutual dependence of the historical and systematic increases.

Even the great seminal achievements of historical criticism have always been dependent not only on the formal development of its

---

[10] 460–395 B.C.   [11] About 207–125 B.C.
[12] 1469–1527.   [13] F. Guicciardini, 1483–1540.
[14] Ecclesiastical historian, 256–340.
[15] J. Neander, German theologian, 1789–1850.
[16] A. B. Ritschl, German theologian, 1822–1889.

method but also on a deeper comprehension of systematic contexts: on the progress of grammar, the study of linguistic connections developed by Rhetoric, the new conception of poetry (familiar to us from Wolf's[17] predecessors who used a new Poetics to draw conclusions about Homer), Fr. A. Wolf's own new aesthetic culture, Niebuhr's economic, juridical and political insights, Schleiermacher's new Platonic philosophy and on Baur's[18] understanding, pioneered by Schleiermacher and Hegel, of the process in which the dogmas originated.

On the other hand, the progress of the systematic human studies has always been conditioned by experience penetrating new depths, the extension of understanding to a wider range of expressions of historical life, by the disclosure of hitherto unknown historical sources and by the emergence of great masses of experience in new historical situations. This is already shown by the development of the first outline of a political science in the age of the Sophists, Plato and Aristotle, as well as the emergence of Rhetoric and Poetics as a theory of mental creation, at the same time.

So the interaction of experience and understanding of individuals or collectives as super-individual subjects determined the great progress of the human studies. Though the great geniuses of narrative art like Thucydides, Guicciardini, Gibbon,[19] Macaulay[20] or Ranke produced timeless historical works in spite of limitations, the human studies as a whole had to advance gradually. Historical consciousness gradually gained insight into the systematic interactions of history, historiography penetrated the interconnections which constituted a nation, an Age, a line of historical development; the resulting understanding of the depths of life, as they existed at particular points of history, transcends all that has gone before. How could we compare anything understood in the past to the understanding of a contemporary historian, artist, poet or writer?

3. The gradual elucidation of expressions through the constant interaction of the two types of discipline

The fundamental relation between experience and understanding at which we now arrive is that of mutual dependence. More closely defined, it is one of gradual elucidation through the constant interaction of the two classes of truth. The obscurity of experience is illuminated, the mistakes which arise from narrow comprehension of

---

[17] T. A. Wolf, German philosopher and classical scholar, 1759–1824.
[18] F. C. Baur, German historian of Christianity, 1792–1860.
[19] 1737–96.   [20] 1800–59.

the subject are corrected, experience itself is widened and completed, by our understanding other people – just as other people are understood through our own experience. Understanding constantly widens the range of historical knowledge by the more intensive use of sources, by insight into a hitherto uncomprehended past and, finally, by the progress of history itself which produces new events and thus widens the very subject of understanding. This progressive widening-out requires ever new general truths for the comprehension of this world of specific events. At the same time, the extension of the historical horizon makes the formation of ever more general and fruitful concepts possible. Thus at every point and at every time in the work of the human studies experience, understanding and representation of the mind-constructed world in general concepts interact. Every stage of this work has an inner, unified conception of the mind-constructed world. For historical knowledge of specific events and general truths develop in interaction with each other and are part of the same integral point view. At every stage understanding of the mind-constructed world, from the general idea of it to methods of criticism and individual investigations, is uniform or homogenous.

Here we might look back, once more, to the time in which modern historical consciousness originated. This occurred when the conceptualizations of the systematic disciplines came to be consciously based on the study of historical life and when the knowledge of the particular was consciously affected by the systematic disciplines of economics, law, politics and religion. At this point the connection between the human studies could be methodologically grasped. The same mind-constructed world becomes – when there is a difference of approach – the object of two classes of disciplines. Universal history with the unique story of mankind as its subject-matter and the system of the independently constituted human studies of man (such as those of language, economics, politics, law, religion and art) supplement each other. They are distinguished by their goals and the methods determined by them, but, at the same time, constantly co-operate in building up our knowledge of the mind-constructed world. Experience, empathy and general truths are linked from the outset by the basic act of understanding. Conceptualization is not based on norms and values which transcend the cognition of objects but originates from the tendency, dominating all conceptual thought, to lift what is firm and permanent from the flux of events. Thus the method works in a dual direction. Directed towards the particular it moves from the part to the whole and back from it to the part; directed towards the general the same interaction between it and the particular holds.

Construction of the Historical World

The objectifications of life

I

The totality of understanding reveals – in contrast with the subjectivity of experience – the objectifications of life. A realization of the objectivity of life, i.e. of its externalizations in many kinds of structural systems, becomes an additional basis for the human studies. The individual, the communities and the works into which life and mind have entered, form the outer realm of the mind. These manifestations of life, as they present themselves to understanding in the external world, are, as it were, embedded in the context of nature. The great outer reality of mind always surrounds us. It is a manifestation of the mind in the world of the senses – from a fleeting expression to the century-long rule of a constitution or code of law. *Every single expression represents a common feature* in the realm of this objective mind. Every word, every sentence, every gesture or polite formula, every work of art and every political deed is intelligible because the people who expressed themselves through them and those who understood them have something in common; the individual always experiences, thinks and acts in a common sphere and only there does he understand. Everything that is understood carries, as it were, the hallmark of familiarity derived from such common features. We live in this atmosphere, it surrounds us constantly. We are immersed in it. We are at home everywhere in this historical and understood world; we understand the sense and meaning of it all; we ourselves are woven into this common sphere.

The change of expressions which affect us challenges us constantly to new understanding, but, because every expression and the understanding of it is, at the same time, connected with others, our understanding carries us along naturally from the given particular to the whole. As the relations between what is alike increase, the possibilities of generalization, already contained in the common features of what is understood, grow.

Understanding highlights a further characteristic of the objectification of life which determines both classification and generalization. The objectification of life contains in itself many differentiated systems. From the distinctions of race down to the difference of expressions and customs of a people or, indeed, a country town, there exist natural divisions based on mental differences. Differentiations of another kind arise in the cultural systems; yet others distinguish Ages from each other; in short, many lines, which mark out areas of related life from some point of view or other, traverse the world of objective mind and cross in it. The fullness of life expresses itself in innumerable nuances and can only be understood through the recurrence of these differences.

Only through the idea of the objectification of life do we gain insight into the nature of the historical. Here everything arose from mental activity and therefore bears the hallmark of historicity. It is interwoven into the world of the senses as a product of history. From the distribution of trees in a park, the arrangement of houses in a street, the functional tool of an artisan, to the sentence pronounced in the courtroom, we are hourly surrounded by the products of history. Whatever characteristics of its own the mind puts into expressions today, are, tomorrow, if they persist, history. With the passage of time we are surrounded by Roman ruins, cathedrals and the summer castles of autocrats. History is not something separated from life or remote in time from the present.

To summarize. The human studies have as their comprehensive subject-matter the objectification of life. But, in so far as this becomes something we understand, it contains the relation of inner to outer throughout. Accordingly this objectification is always related, in understanding, to experience in which the person becomes aware of his own inner life and capable of interpreting that of others. If the facts of the human studies are contained in this then everything inflexible and everything alien, because it belongs to the images of the physical world, must be removed from the idea of these facts. Every fact is man-made and, therefore, historical; it is understood and, therefore, contains common features; it is known because understood, and it contains a classification of the manifold because every interpretation of an expression by the higher understanding rests on such a classification. The classifying of expressions is already rooted in the facts of the human studies.

Here the concepts of the human studies is completed. Their range is identical with that of understanding and understanding consistently has the objectification of life as its subject-matter. Thus the range of the human studies is determined by the objectification of life in the external world. Mind can only understand what it has created. Nature, the subject-matter of the physical sciences, embraces the reality which has arisen independently of the activity of mind. Everything on which man has actively impressed his stamp forms the subject-matter of the human studies.[21] Up till now I have also called the objectification of life 'objective mind'. The term is a profound and fortunate creation of

[21] [Five lines omitted because they contain a terminological explanation irrelevant to the translation.]

Hegel's. However, I must distinguish precisely and clearly the sense in which I use it from that which Hegel gave it. This difference applies as much to the place of the concept in the system as to its function and denotation.

In Hegel's system the word designates a stage in the development of the mind. He places this stage between the subjective and the absolute mind. Accordingly, the concept of the objective mind has for him a place in the ideal construction of the development of mind which, though it is based on and tries to explain speculatively, historical reality and the relations prevailing in it, for this very reason leaves the temporal, empirical and historical relations behind. The idea which, in nature, externalizes itself into otherness, and thus steps outside itself, returns on the basis of this characteristic to itself in the mind. The world-spirit regains its pure ideality. It realizes its freedom in its development.

As subjective mind it is the manifold of individual minds. Once the individual mind develops a will on the basis of coming to know the rational purpose unfolding in the world, it makes a transition into freedom. This provides the basis for the philosophy of objective mind which shows how the free, rational, and, therefore, universal will becomes objective in a moral world: 'freedom, which has freedom for its content and purpose, is, in the first instance, merely a concept, a principle of the mind and heart destined to develop into objectivity, into a legal, moral, religious and scientific reality' (*Philosophy of Mind*). This posits the development from the objective to the absolute mind: 'the objective mind is the absolute idea, but only in itself; in so far as it stands on the ground of finitude, its real rationality retains the aspect of outward appearance'.

The objectification of mind occurs in law, morality and ethics. Ethics actualizes the general rational will in the family, civil society and the state. And the state actualizes its nature as the outer reality of the ethical idea in world history.

With this the ideal construction of the historical world reached the point where the two stages of the mind, the general rational will of the individual, and its objectification in the ethical world as its higher unity, make the last and highest stage possible – the mind's knowledge about itself as the creative power of all reality in art, religion and philosophy. The subjective and objective mind are to be considered as the road on which the highest reality of mind, the absolute mind, develops.

What was the historical position and content of this concept of objective mind discovered by Hegel? The much misunderstood German Enlightenment had recognized the significance of the state as the all-embracing community through which the morality inherent in individuals becomes actual. Since the days of the Greeks and Romans no one has expressed an understanding of state and law more powerfully and profoundly than such leading officials of Frederick's state, as Carmer, Svarez, Klein, Zedlitz and Herzberg. Hegel combined this conception of the nature and value of the state with the ideas of antiquity about morality and the state and with his own realization of their effectiveness. Common features became significant in history. The historical school reached simultaneously – through historical research – the same discovery of a collective mind which Hegel had gained through a peculiar kind of metaphysical-historical intuition. It, too, came to understand – better than the Greek idealist philosophers – the nature of the common roots which could not be derived from the interaction of individuals in morals, state, law and faith. This historical consciousness emerged in Germany.

Hegel has summarized the result of this whole movement in one concept – that of objective mind.

Today we can no longer retain the presuppositions on which Hegel based this concept. He constructed communities from the universal, rational will. Today we must start from the reality of life; life contains the sum of all mental activities. Hegel constructed metaphysically; we analyse the given. The contemporary analysis of human existence fills us all with a sense of fragility, of the power of dark instincts, of the suffering from ignorance and illusion and of how ephemeral life is, even where the highest creations of communal life arise from it. Thus we cannot understand the objective mind through reason but must go back to the structural connections of persons, and by extension, of communities. We cannot assign the objective mind a place in an ideal construction, but must start with its historical reality. This we try to understand and describe in adequate concepts. Once the objective mind is divorced from its one-sided foundation on a universal reason (which expresses the nature of the world-spirit) and from any ideal construction, a new conception of it becomes possible; the objective mind embraces language, custom and every form or style of life as well as the family, society, the state and the law. Consequently, what Hegel distinguished from objective mind as absolute mind, namely art, religion and philosophy also falls under this same concept. These, because they reflect the common factors expressed by creative individuals, are powerful objectifications of mind which thus becomes accessible to knowledge.

This objective mind is differentiated into structures from mankind down to the most narrowly defined types. This differentiation gives rise to individuality. If we can understand individual human expressions on the basis, and by means of, the universally human, we re-experience the inner connections which lead from the latter to the former. Once this process is comprehended individual psychology can explain theoretically how individuality arises.

The same combination of fundamental regularities and the resultant differentiation into individuals (and, therefore, the combination of general theory and comparative procedure) forms the basis of the systematic human studies. Their generalizations about moral life or poetry thus become the foundation for insight into the differences between various moral ideals or poetic activities.

In the objective mind, past ages, in which the great, total forces of history have taken shape, are contemporary reality. The individual, as bearer and representative of the general feature interwoven in him, enjoys and grasps the history in which they arose. He understands history because he himself is a historical being.

In one final point the concept of objective mind here developed diverges from that of Hegel. Once we replace Hegel's reason by life in its totality (experience, understanding, historical context and power of the irrational) the problem of how scientific history is possible arises. For Hegel this problem did not exist. His metaphysic (in which the world-spirit with nature as its manifestation, the objective mind as its actualization and the absolute mind, culminating in philosophy, as the realization of the knowledge of it, are in themselves identical) has left this problem behind. But, today, the task is the reverse – to recognize the actual historical expressions as the true foundation of historical knowledge and to find a method of answering the question how universally valid knowledge of the historical world can be based on what is thus given.

The mind-constructed world as a system of interactions

Experience and understanding of the objectifications of life disclose the mind-constructed world. We must now define more closely the nature of this world (the historical and social world) as the object of the human studies.

Let us first summarize the results of the preceding investigations about the interrelatedness of the human studies. This rests on the relationship between experience and understanding from which three main principles have emerged. Our knowledge of what is given in experience is extended through the interpretation of the objectifications of life and this interpretation, in turn, is only made possible by plumbing the depths of subjective experience. Similarly, understanding of the particular depends on knowledge of the general which, in turn, presupposes understanding. Finally, a part of the historical course of events can only be understood completely in terms of its relation to the whole and a universal-historical survey of the whole presupposes the understanding of the parts united in it.

As a result, the comprehensions of every particular state of affairs of the human studies within its common historical whole and the comprehension of the conceptual representation of this whole in the systematic human studies are mutually interdependent. In the progress of the human studies the interaction of experience and understanding in the comprehension of the mind-constructed world, the mutual dependence of general and particular knowledge and, finally, the gradual illumination of the mind-constructed world, are everywhere present. Therefore, we find them again in all the operations of the human studies whose structure is universally based on them. So we shall have to recognize the interdependence of interpretation, criticism, linking of sources, and synthesis in a historical whole. The concepts of such subjects as economics, law, philosophy, art and religion which refer to the interactions of different persons in a common task, originate in a similar way. In scientific thought a concept can only be formed when we have ascertained the facts which are to be subsumed under it; but to ascertain and select these facts we must be able to recognize them as coming under this concept. To define the concept of poetry I must abstract it from all the facts which constitute its denotation and to ascertain which works belong to poetry. I must already know how to recognize a work as poetical.

This relation is, therefore, the most general feature of the structure of the human studies.

1. *The general character of the system of interaction of the mind-constructed world*

Thus we learn to comprehend the mind-constructed world as a system of interactions or as an inter-relationship contained in its enduring creations. This system of interactions and its creations is the subject-matter of the human studies. They analyse either that system of interactions or the logical, aesthetic or religious structure characteristic of a sub-system, or that of a constitution or code (which points back to the system of interactions from which it originated).

This system of interactions is distinguished from the causal order of nature by the fact that, in accordance with the structure of mental life, it creates objects of value and realizes *purposes*: and this, not occasionally, not here and there, but as a result of the mind's dynamic structure to do this once it understands. I call this the immanent teleological character of the mind's system of interaction. By this I mean a combination of creative acts based on the structure of a system of interactions. Historical life is productive. It constantly creates goods and things of value and all concepts about them are reflections of this activity.

Objects of value and goods in the mind-constructed world are created by individuals, communities and cultural systems in which the individuals co-operate. This co-operation is determined by the fact that, in order to realize objects of value, individuals subject themselves to rules and set themselves purposes. Every kind of co-operation contains a vital relationship – basic to human nature and linking individuals – a core, as it were, which cannot be grasped psychologically but is revealed in every such system of relations. Any achievement is determined by the structural connections between comprehension and the mental states expressed in valuation and the positing of purposes, goods and norms. Such a system of interactions operates primarily in individuals. They are thus the crossing points of systems of relations, each of which is a continual source of activity. Consequently, in each system, common values and orderly procedures for realizing them are established and accepted as unconditionally valid. So in every permanent relationship between individuals values, rules and purposes are developed, made conscious and consolidated by reflection. This creative activity, under the natural conditions which constantly provide material and stimulation for it, occurs in individuals, communities, cultural systems and nations and becomes conscious of itself in the human studies.

In accordance with the structural system, every mental unit has its centre within itself. Like the individual every cultural system, every community has its own focal point. In it, a conception of reality, valuation and the attainment of goals are linked into a whole.

A fundamental relation in the system of interactions, the subject-matter of the human studies, now stands revealed. The different units from which creative activity proceeds are woven into wider social-historical contexts; these are nations, Ages, historical periods. In this way complex forms of historical connections develop. The historian must bring together the values, purposes and commitments sustained by individuals, communities and systems of relations which occur in them. He compares them, emphasizes what is common to them and synthesizes the various systems of interactions; a different form of unity arises from the fact that every historical unit has its own centre. Individuals, cultural systems or communities which are contemporaneous and constantly interacting, communicate with each other and thus supplement their own lives with that of others; nations are often relatively self-contained and, because of this, have their own horizons; but, if I now consider the period of the Middle Ages, I find its horizon to be different from that of previous periods. Even where the results of these periods persist they are assimilated into the system of the medieval world which has a *closed horizon*. Thus an *epoch* is *centred on itself in a new sense*. The common practices of an epoch become the norm for the activities of individuals who live in it. The society of an epoch has a pattern of interactions which has uniform features. There is an inner affinity in the comprehension of objects. The ways of feeling, the emotions and the impulses which arise from them, are similar to each other. The will, too, choses uniform goals, strives for related goods, and finds itself committed in a similar way. It is the task of historical analysis to discover the consensus which governs the concrete purposes, values and ways of thought of a period. Even the prevailing contrasts are determined by this common background. Thus, every action, every thought, every common activity, in short, every part of this historical whole, has its significance through its relationship to the whole of the epoch or Age. The historian's judgment ascertains what the individual has achieved within this context and how far his vision and activity may have extended beyond it.

The system of the human studies to which we aspire must, therefore, be thought of in terms of the following points of view. We must see the historical world as a whole, this whole as a system of interactions, and this system of interactions as a source of objects of value and purposes (that is as creative). We must understand this whole from within itself and its values and purposes as centred in Ages or epochs of universal history. So the direct relationship between life with its values and purposes and history is replaced by scholarly concern with general validity. We must seek the inherent relationship between productive power, values, purpose, meaning and significance within the historical system of interactions. Only on the basis of such objective history do these questions arise: is prediction of the future possible and, if so, how far? and can our lives be subordinated to the common goals of mankind?

The system of interactions is primarily comprehended by the experiencing subject for whom the sequence of inner events unfolds in structural relations. These connections are then rediscovered in other individuals through understanding. Thus the fundamental form of the connections arises in the individual who combines present, past and possibilities of the future in the course of his life. This also has its place in the historical process in which the person belongs. When the wider context of an event is observed by a spectator or reported in an account, the conception of historical events arises; and, as the individual events occupy a position in time – presupposing causes in the past and consequences in the future – every event requires a sequel and the present leads into the future.

Another kind of connection prevails in works which, separated from their authors, have their own life and are a law unto themselves. Before we arrive at the system of interactions in which they originated we must grasp the connections which are there in the completed work. The logical connections which link legal principles into a code of law emerge in understanding. If we read one of Shakespeare's comedies we find the component parts of an event not only temporally and causally linked but elevated into unity according to the laws of poetical composition; this unity lifts the beginning and the end out of the causal chain and links its parts into a whole.

2. The system of interactions as a fundamental concept of the human studies

In the human studies we grasp the mind-constructed world in the form of systems of interactions produced in the course of time. Activity, energy, passage of time, happenings are, therefore, the characteristic conceptualizations of the human studies. Contents of this kind are quite independent of the functional need of a concept within the thought-structure of the human studies to have a well-defined and constant meaning in all judgments. The characteristics which combine to give a concept its meaning have to meet the same requirements. And the propositions into which concepts are linked must not contain contradictions either within or among themselves. This timeless validity which exists in thought and determines the form of concepts, has nothing to do with the fact that the content of concepts in the human studies can represent the passage of time, activity, energy and happenings.[22]

We see in the structure of the individual a tendency or urge which communicates itself to all composite forms of the mind-constructed world. In that world total forces emerge which affect the historical

---

[22] I.e. the term 'decline' conveys change but it can only be used meaningfully to the extent to which it has an unchanging meaning.

Dilthey's Epistemology and Methodology

context in a particular direction. All the concepts of the human studies in so far as they represent a part of the system of interactions, contain the idea of something going on, happening or being active. Even when we analyse objectifications of mental life as something complete and, as it were, at rest, we still need to grasp the system of interactions from which these objectifications originated. So, to a large extent, the concepts of the human studies are fixed representations of something going on, a pinning down in thought of what is itself an occurrence or trend. The systematic human studies also must form concepts which express the fact that life has an inherent direction, is changeable and restless, but, above all, that it sets itself purposes. In addition the historical and systematic human studies must develop corresponding relations between concepts.

It was to Hegel's credit that in his logic he tried to express the restless stream of events. But he was mistaken when he thought that this could not be reconciled with the principle of contradiction; insoluble contradictions only arise if one wants *to explain* the fact that life flows. It was and is equally mistaken to reject, on the same presupposition, the formation of systematic concepts in the historical sphere. So the many-sidedness of historical life congeals in Hegel's dialectical method while it drowns in unfathomable depths among the opponents of systematic conceptualization in the historical sphere.

Here one can understand Fichte's deepest intention. The I intensely absorbed in itself, discovers itself to be not substance, being or fact, but life, activity and energy. So he has already developed the concept of energy in the historical world.

3. *The procedure for identifying individual systems of interaction*

A system of interaction as such is always complex. Identification starts from a single effect the cause of which we can trace by going back step by step. Only a few of many factors can be ascertained and are relevant to the effect. If, for example, we are looking for the interrelated causes which changed our literature so that the Enlightenment was superseded, we must classify and weigh the relevant factors; somewhere, too, we must set a limit to the infinite causal nexus in the light of the significance of these factors and our purpose. So we abstract a system of interactions to explain the change in question. Methodical analysis, from different points of view, singles out individual connections from the concrete system of interactions and this analysis makes genuine progress in the systematic human studies and in history possible.

Construction of the Historical World

Our knowledge of the system of interaction grows through inductively ascertaining facts and causal connections, synthesizing them into causal chains, isolating individual links, comparing them and similar procedures. We use the same method when we study the permanent creations which have emerged from this system of interactions – pictures, statues, plays, philosophic systems, religious writings, and legal books. Their structure varies according to their character, but here, too, analysis of the complete work interlocks with the reconstruction of the whole, both of which are based on induction and reference to general truths. But thought in the human studies is concerned not only with connections but also with the search for regularities in the systems of interactions which pass from the particular to the general and back. Here procedures are most comprehensively interrelated. Generalizations help to form connections and the analysis of the concrete and universal system of connections into individual connections is the most fruitful way for discovering general truths.

But when we look at the procedure for singling out systems of interactions in the human studies we see the great difference from that which enabled the sciences to be so enormously successful. The sciences are based on the spatial relationships of phenomena. The discovery of exact general laws becomes possible because what extends or moves in space can be counted or measured. But the inner system of interactions is superimposed by thought and its basic elements cannot be observed. On the other hand, the basic units of the historical world are, as we have seen, given to us in experience and understanding. Their unitary character is based on the structural system in which cognition of objects, values and purposes are related to each other. What is characteristic of a person is to be found in this – only what is posited by his will can be a purpose, only what has proved itself in his thoughts is true and only what is positively related to his feelings is valuable to him. The counterpart of this person is a body, moving and activated by inner impulse. The human-social-historical world consists of these psycho-physical persons. This, analysis shows with certainty. The system of interactions of these units exhibits particular characteristics which are not exhausted by the relations of unity and multiplicity, whole and part, synthesis and interaction.

We can further conclude that the person is a system of interactions which has the advantage over nature, of being experienced. The intensity of its active parts cannot be measured, only estimated, and its individuality cannot be divorced from the universally human, so that humanity is only an indeterminate type. Therefore every individual

201

mental state represents a new attitude, a new relation of the whole person to things and people and, as every communal or cultural expression is the product of co-operating persons, the constituents of such composite structures as communities or cultural systems, have a corresponding character. However strongly every mental process may be determined by the purpose of the composite structure to which it belongs, it is never entirely determined by it. The individual in which it occurs takes part as a person in the system of interactions and what he expresses is the product of the person as a whole. Nature is separated into different, homogeneous systems by the differentiation of the senses, each of which has its own sphere. The same object, a bell, is hard, bronze-coloured and capable of producing a range of sounds when struck; each of its characteristics assumes a place in one of the systems of sense impressions; but we are not presented with an inner link between these characteristics. However, when I have an experience I am presented to myself as an inter-connected system. Every change of situation changes life as a whole. Similarly the whole of life is active in any expression which we comprehend. This is why neither experience nor understanding present us with homogeneous systems in which laws of change can be discovered. Understanding reveals common features and resemblances as well as innumerable nuances of differentiation from the great differences between races, tribes and nations to the infinite variety of individuals. This is why, in the mind-constructed world, we are predominantly concerned with the comprehension of individuality – from that of the individual person to mankind as an entity – and with the comparative method which gives conceptual order to individual variety (while in the sciences laws of change predominate).

These conditions define the limits of the human studies, of both psychology and the systematic disciplines – methodology will have to deal with them in detail. Speaking generally, it is clear that psychology and the individual, systematic disciplines will have a predominantly descriptive and analytical character. Here my earlier accounts about the analytical method in psychology and the systematic human studies are relevant and I refer to them as a whole.

4. *History and its understanding by means of the systematic human studies*

Knowledge in the human studies occurs, as we saw, through the interdependence of history and the systematic disciplines: and as the intention to understand always precedes conceptualization we will start with the general characteristics of historical knowledge.

Construction of the Historical World

Historical knowledge

The comprehension of the historical system of interactions grows first of all from individual points at which related remnants of the past are linked in understanding by their relation to experience: what is around us helps us to understand what is distant and past. The condition needed for this interpretation of historical remnants is that what we put into them must be permanently and universally valid for man. On the basis of the connections which the historian has experienced within himself he transfers his knowledge of customs, habits, political circumstances and religious processes (to these remnants). The germinal cell of the historical world is the experience in which the subject discovers himself in a dynamic relationship with his environment. The environment acts on the subject and is acted upon by him. It is composed of the physical and cultural surroundings. In every part of the historical world there exists, therefore, the same dynamic connection between a sequence of mental events and an environment. This is why the influence both nature and his cultural environment have on man must be ascertained and evaluated.

Just as raw materials in industry are subjected to various forms of processing so the remnants of the past are made fully, historically understandable through various procedures. Criticism, interpretation and synthesis of the understanding of a historical process interlock. But here, too, it is characteristic that one operation is not simply based on another; criticism, interpretation and intellectual synthesis differ in their tasks; but each of them can only succeed with the help of insights gained by the others.

It follows from this relationship that the explanation of historical connections is always dependent on an interrelation of mental acts which cannot be completely justified logically and cannot, therefore, be defended against historical scepticism by uncontestable proofs. We have only to think of Niebuhr's great discoveries about older Roman history. His criticism is inseparable from his reconstruction of the true course of events. He had to ascertain how the existing tradition of older Roman history arose and what conclusions about its historical value could be drawn from its origin. At the same time he had to try to deduce the real, historical course of events from what could be argued from the facts. Measured by the rules of strict demonstration this methodical procedure moves, no doubt, in a circle. And when Niebuhr availed himself, at the same time, of an analogical argument from similar developments, the knowledge of these related developments was subject to the same circle and the analogical argument, which made use of this knowledge, produced no compelling certainty.

Even in the accounts of contemporaries we must first examine the point of view of the reporter, his reliability and his relation to the event. And the further removed from the time of the events the accounts are, the less their credibility, unless the elements of such an account can be checked by reference to older, contemporary reports. The political history of the ancient world is reliable where documents exist and that of the modern one where the papers which shaped the course of a historical event are preserved. Therefore, reliable knowledge of political history only began with the methodical and critical collections of documents and free access to archives for historians. This know-ledge can, as far as the facts are concerned, stand up to historical scepticism and, on such secure foundations, a historically probable reconstruction (to which only clever but unscientific minds can deny usefulness) can be built up by analysing the sources of the accounts and examining the points of view of the reporters. This reconstruction provides reliable knowledge of actions and events, if not of the motives of the actors, and the errors about individual facts to which we remain exposed do not cast doubt on the whole.

Historiography, where it deals with mass-phenomena or, above all, with artistic or scientific works which stand up to analysis, is much more favourably placed than when it tries to comprehend the course of political events.

Stages of historical comprehension

The mastering of historical material takes place in various stages which gradually penetrate into the depths of history.

Manifold interests lead, first of all, to narration of what has occurred. This mainly satisfies a very basic need – curiosity about human affairs, particularly about those of one's native land. In addition national or civic pride asserts itself. This was the origin of narrative art, the model of which for all ages was Herodotus.[23] Then concern with explanation stepped into the foreground. The Athenian culture of the time of Thucydides first provided the right conditions for this. Acute observa-tion traced actions back to their psychological motives; the course and outcome of the power struggles between states were explained in terms of their military and political strength; the effects of constitutions were studied. As a great political thinker such as Thucydides elucidates the past through the sober study of the dynamic interactions in it, we discover that history also illuminates the future. When a former course of interactions is known and when the first stages of another sequence

---

[23] 484–425 B.C.

resemble it, the occurrence of a similar sequel can be anticipated by arguing on the basis of analogy. This conclusion, on which Thucydides based his belief that history had lessons for the future is, indeed, of decisive significance for political thought. As in the sciences, so also in history, a regularity in the pattern of interactions makes prediction and intervention based on knowledge possible. The contemporaries of the Sophists had already studied constitutions as political forces; then Polybius confronted us with historiography in which the *methodical application* of *the systematic* human studies to the *explanation* of the historical system of interactions makes it possible to introduce the effect of permanent forces such as the constitution, military organization and fiscal system, into the explanatory procedure. Polybius' subject-matter was the interaction of states which, from the beginning of the struggle between Rome and Carthage to the destruction of Carthage and Corinth, formed the historical world of the European mind. Polybius undertook to deduce individual political events from the study of permanent forces in these states. Thus his point of view became that of universal history because he combined within himself Greek theoretical culture, study of cunning political machinations and warfare in his native land with a knowledge of Rome which only intercourse with leading statesmen of the new, universal state could provide. Manifold cultural forces, above all the infinite deepening of self-knowledge and the simultaneous widening of the historical horizon became active in the period from Polybius to Machiavelli and Guicciardini; but the methods of the two great Italian historians remain strongly similar to those of Polybius.

Only in the eighteenth century was a new stage of historiography reached. Two great principles were then introduced successively; the concrete pattern of interactions lifted by the historian as his subject-matter from the general stream of history was *divided up* into individual systems – like those of law, religion or poetry – embraced by the unity of an Age. This presupposes that the historian looks beyond political history to that of culture that the function of each cultural sphere has been recognized by the systematic human studies, and that an understanding of the co-operation of such cultural systems has developed. The new historiography began in the age of Voltaire. With Winkelmann, Justus Möser[24] and Herder a second principle was added – that of development. This attributes a new fundamental characteristic to the historical system of interactions, namely that it traverses, according to its inner nature, a series of changes each of which is only possible on the basis of the previous one.

[24] German statesman and publicist, 1720–94.

Dilthey's Epistemology and Methodology

These different stages mark elements which, once grasped, have remained alive in historiography. Joyful narrative art, penetrating explanation, application of systematic knowledge, dissection into individual systems of interactions and the principle of development were combined and strengthened each other.

Isolating a system of interactions in terms of the historical subject-matter

The significance of analysing the concrete system of interactions and scientifically synthesizing its individual systems has emerged more and more clearly.

The historian can not follow the nexus of events in all directions from one point into infinity; the problem of grasping the subject-matter which forms the historian's unitary theme provides a principle of selection. Not only does the treatment of a historical subject require that it should be singled out from the breadth of the concrete system of interactions, the subject also contains a principle of selection. To study the fall of Rome, the liberation of the Netherlands or the French Revolution we must select those events and contexts which either wholly or partially caused them, i.e. the forces which, stage by stage, brought them about. The historian who deals with systems of interactions must select and combine in such a way that those familiar with the details miss nothing because each of them is represented by significant features of the total system of interactions. This, the source of his descriptive art, is also a product of a special way of seeing. When we examine these marked, pervasive links we see once more how insight into them springs from the combination of progressive historical understanding of sources and ever deeper comprehension of the web of mental life. If, then, we look more closely at the system of interactions encountered in the greatest events of history, the development of Christianity, the Reformation, the French Revolution, the national wars of liberation, we can consider it as the formation of a total force which, moving in a single direction, overthrows all resistance. We shall always find two kinds of forces co-operating. Some are tensions which derive from the sense of urgent, unfulfilled needs, from the desires of all kinds prompted by them, from an increase of frictions and struggles and, also, from the consciousness of insufficient power to defend the *status quo*. Others arise from dynamic energies – positive will, potency and faith. They rest on the vigorous instincts of the many but are illuminated and heightened by the experiences of great personalities. And, as these positive tendencies grow from the past and direct themselves towards the future, they are creative. They contain ideals clothed in an enthusiasm which has a special way of communicating and spreading itself.

From this we deduce the general principle that in the patterns of great world events the conditions of pressure and tension and dissatisfaction with the existing state of affairs – that is negative emotions of rejection – form the basis for the action which is sustained by positive valuations, goals we strive for and purposes. The great changes of the world originate from the co-operation of these two. The real agents in the system of interactions are the mental states which find expression in terms of value, good and purpose; among these states not only cultural aspirations but also the will to power, culminating in the inclination to subjugate others, must be considered as active forces. [In the following twenty-odd pages, Dilthey analyses three types of concepts used in the analysis of historical processes: the cultural systems, political organizations, including that of the nation, and periods or epochs in history.]

Drafts for a critique of historical reason
First Part: Experience, expression and understanding

1. Experience and autobiography

(1) The task of a critique of historical reason
Vol. VII, pp. 189–200

The whole context of the mind-constructed world emerges in the subject; it is the mind's effort to determine the meaningful pattern of that world which links the individual, logical processes involved. On the one hand, the knowing subject creates this mind-constructed world and, on the other, strives to know it objectively. How, then, does the mental construction of the mind-constructed world make knowledge of mind-constructed reality possible? This is the problem of what I have called a Critique of Historical Reason. It can only be solved if the individual processes which combine in the creation of this system can be sorted out and it can be shown what part each of them plays, both in the construction of the historical course of events in the mind-constructed world and in the discovery of its systematic nature. How far the difficulties inherent in the mutual dependence of specific truths can be dissolved and how the real basis of knowledge in the human studies can be gradually inferred from experience remains to be seen.

Understanding is a rediscovery of the I in the Thou: the mind rediscovers itself at ever higher levels of complex involvement: this identity of the mind in the I and the Thou, in every subject of a community, in every system of a culture and finally, in the totality of mind and universal history, makes successful co-operation between different processes in the human studies possible. The knowing subject is, here, one with its object, which is the same at all stages of its objectification. If, in this way, we know the mind-constructed world objectively we may ask how much this contributes to solving the general problem of epistemology. Kant tackled it by starting from formal logic and mathematics. Formal logic, in the time of Kant, treated the final logical abstractions, the laws and forms of thought, as the ultimate logical justification of all scientific statements. The laws and forms of thought, above all judgment, from which he derived the categories, contained for Kant the conditions of knowledge. To them he added those which, according to him, made mathematics possible. The magnitude of his achievement lay in his complete analysis of mathematical and scientific knowledge. The question, however, is, if an epistemology of history, which he himself did not provide, is possible within the framework of his concepts.

(2) *Awareness, reality: time*

I am presupposing what I have said before about life and experience. We must now demonstrate the reality of what is apprehended in experience: as we are concerned here with the objective value of the categories of the mind-constructed world which emerge from experience, I shall first indicate the sense in which the term 'category' is to be used. The predicates which we attribute to objects contain forms of apprehension. The concepts which designate such forms I call categories. Each form contains one rule of the relationship. The categories are systematically related to each other and the highest categories represent the highest points of view for apprehending reality. Each category designates its own universe of predications. The formal categories are forms of all factual assertions. Among the real categories there are those which originate in the apprehension of the mind-constructed world even though they are then transferred to apply to the whole of reality. General predicates about a particular individual's pattern of experience arise in that experience. Once they are applied to the understanding of the objectifications of life and all the subjects dealt with by the human studies the range of their validity is increased until it becomes clear that the life of the mind can be characterized in terms of systems of interactions, power, value, etc. Thus these general predicates achieve the dignity of categories of the mind-constructed world.

The categorial characterization of life is temporality which forms the basis for all the others. The expression 'passage of life' indicates this already. Time is there for us through the synthesizing unity of consciousness. Life, and the outer objects cropping up in it share the conditions of simultaneity, sequence, interval, duration and change. The mathematical sciences derived from them the abstract relationships on which Kant based his doctrine of the phenomenal nature of time.

This framework of relationships embraces, but does not exhaust, the experience of time through which the concept of time receives its ultimate meaning. Here time is experienced as the restless progression, in which the present constantly becomes the past and the future the present. The present is the filling of a moment of time with reality; it is experience, in contrast to memory or ideas of the future occurring in wishes, expectations, hopes, fears and strivings. This filling with reality constantly exists while the content of experience constantly changes. Ideas, through which we know the past and the future, exist only for those who are alive in the present. The present is always there and nothing exists except what emerges in it. The ship of our life is, as it were, carried forward on a constantly moving stream, and the present is always wherever we are on these waves – suffering, remembering or hoping, in short, living in the fullness of our reality. But we constantly sail along this stream and the moment the future becomes the present it is already sinking into the past. So the parts of filled time are not only qualitatively different from each other but, quite apart from their content, have a different character according to whether we look from the present back to the past or forward to the future. Looking back we have a series of memory pictures graded according to their value for our consciousness and feelings; like a row of houses or trees receding into the distance and becoming smaller the line of memories becomes fainter until the images are lost in the darkness of the horizon. And the more links, such as moods, outer events, means and goals, there are between the filled present and a moment of the future the greater is the number of possible outcomes, the more indefinite and nebulous the picture of the future becomes. When we look back at the past we are passive; it cannot be changed; in vain does the man already determined by it batter it with dreams of how it could have been different. In our attitude to the future we are active and free. Here the category of reality which emerges from the present is joined by that of possibility.

Dilthey's Epistemology and Methodology

We feel that we have infinite possibilities. Thus the experience of time in all its dimensions determines the content of our lives. This is why the doctrine that time is merely ideal is meaningless in the human studies. We recollect past events because of time and temporality; we turn, demanding, active and free, towards the future. We despair of the inevitable, strive, work and plan for the future, mature and develop in the course of time. All this makes up life, but, according to the doctrine of the ideality of time, it is based on a shadowy realm of timelessness, something which is not experienced. But it is in the life actually lived that the reality known in the human studies lies.

The antinomies which thought discovers in the experience of time spring from its cognitive impenetrability. Even the smallest part of temporal progress involves the passing of time. There never *is* a present; what we experience as present always contains memory of what has just been present. In other cases the past has a direct affect on, and meaning for, the present and this gives to memories a peculiar character of being present through which they become included in the present. Whatever presents itself as a unit in the flow of time because it has a unitary meaning, is the smallest unit which can be called an experience. Any more comprehensive unit which is made up of parts of a life, linked by a common meaning, is also called an experience, even where the parts are separated by interrupting events.

Experience is a temporal flow in which every state changes before it is clearly objectified because the subsequent moment always builds on the previous one and each is past before it is grasped. It then appears as a memory which is free to expand. But observation destroys the experience. So there is nothing more peculiar than the form of composition which we know as a part of a life; the only thing that remains invariable is that the structural relationship is its form.

We can try to envisage the flow of life in terms of the changing environment or see it, with Heracleitus, as seeming, but not being, the same, as seeming both many and one. But, however much we try – by some special effort – to experience the flow and strengthen our awareness of it, we are subject to the law of life itself according to which every observed moment of life is a remembered moment and not a flow; *it is fixed by attention which arrests what is essentially flow.* So we cannot grasp the essence of this life. What the youth of Sais unveils is form and not life.[25] We must be aware of this if we are to grasp the categories which emerge in life itself.

Because of this characteristic of real time, temporal succession

[25] Sais is the name of an ancient Egyptian city. The reference is to a poem by Schiller about a youth there who unveiled the statue of truth.

cannot, strictly speaking, be experienced. The recalling of the past replaces immediate experience. When we want to observe time the very observation destroys it because it fixes our attention; it halts the flow and stays what is in the process of becoming. We experience changes of what has just been and the fact that these changes have occurred. But we do not experience the flow itself. We experience persistence when we return to what we have just seen or heard and find it still there. We experience change when particular qualities of the composite whole have been replaced. The same applies when we look into ourselves, become aware of the self which experiences duration and change, and observe our inner life.

Life consists of parts, of experiences which are inwardly related to each other. Every particular experience refers to a self of which it is a part; it is structurally interrelated to other parts. Everything which pertains to mind is interrelated: interconnectedness is, therefore, a category originating from life. We apprehend connectedness through the unity of consciousness which is the condition of all apprehension. However, connectedness clearly does not follow from the fact of a manifold of experiences being presented to a unitary consciousness. Only because life is itself a structural connection of experiences – i.e. experienceable relations – is the connectedness of life given. This connectedness is apprehended in terms of a more comprehensive category which is a form of judgment about all reality – the relation between whole and part.

The life of the mind is based on the physical and represents the highest evolutionary stage on earth. Science, by discovering the laws of physical phenomena, unravels the conditions under which mind occurs. Among observable bodies we find that of man: experience is related to man in a way which cannot be further explained. But with experience we step from the world of physical phenomena into the realm of mental reality. This is the subject-matter of the human studies on which we must reflect: the value of knowledge in them is quite independent of the study of their physical conditions.

Knowledge of the mind-constructed world originates from the interaction between experience, understanding of other people, the historical comprehension of communities as the subject of historical activity and insight into objective mind. All this ultimately presupposes experience, so we must ask what it can achieve.

Experience includes elementary acts of thought. I have described this as its intellectuality. These acts occur when consciousness is intensified. A change in a stage of mind thus becomes conscious of itself. We grasp an isolated aspect of what changes. Experience is followed by judgments about what has been experienced in which this becomes objectified. It is hardly necessary to describe how our knowledge of every mental fact derives entirely from experience. We cannot recognize in another person a feeling we have not experienced. But for the development of the human studies it is decisive that we attribute general predicates, derived from experience and providing the point of departure for the categories of the human studies, to the subject who contains the possibilities of experience in the confines of his body. The formal categories spring, as we saw, from the elementary acts of thought. They are concepts which stand for what becomes comprehensible through these acts of thought. Such concepts are unity, multiplicity, identity, difference, grade and relation. They are attributes of the whole of reality.

(3) *The connectedness of life*

We can now discern a new feature of life; it is conditioned by the character of its temporality, which I have already described, but goes beyond it. We approach life, ours as well as that of others, with understanding. This occurs through particular categories which are alien to the knowledge of nature as such. If the science of nature requires the concept of purpose for the organic stages which lead up to human life, it takes this category over from human life.

The formal categories are abstract expressions for the logical acts of distinguishing, identifying, grading, combining and dividing. They are, as it were, a higher awareness which ascertains, but does not construct a priority. They occur in our primary thinking and reappear – on a higher stage – in our discursive, symbolic thinking. They are the formal conditions for understanding, as well as for knowledge, for the human studies, as well as for the sciences.

But nowhere are the real categories the same in the human studies and the sciences. I shall not enter into the problems concerning the origin of these categories. Only their validity is at issue. No real category can claim validity in the human studies as it does in science. The transfer of the procedure abstractly expressed in it to the human studies is a trespassing by scientific thought as objectionable as the introduction into the context of science of mental connections within nature which gave rise to Schelling's and Hegel's Philosophy of Nature. In the historical world there is no scientific causality, for cause, in this sense, implies that a regular effect is necessarily produced; history only knows of the relations of striving and suffering, action and reaction.

Conceptualizations of scientific knowledge – however future science may transform the concepts of substance and force which sustain and produce events – are irrelevant to the human studies. The subjects of historical assertions – ranging from individual lives to that of mankind – refer to special kinds of limited contexts. Though the formal category of the relation between whole and part is shared with all temporally and spatially organized units it acquires, in the human studies, a specific meaning from the nature of life and the process of understanding appropriate to it. It is that of a context linking the parts. Here, organic life must, according to the evolutionary character of all known reality, be viewed as an intermediary link between inorganic nature and the historical world and thus a preliminary stage of the latter.

What, then, is this specific sense in which the parts of the life of mankind are linked into a whole? What are the categories through which we come to understand this whole?

Autobiographies are the most direct expression of reflection about life. Those of Augustine, Rousseau and Goethe are typical examples. How, then, did these writers understand the continuity between the different parts of their lives? Augustine is exclusively orientated towards the dependence of his life on God. His work is, at one and the same time, religious meditation, prayer and narrative. His story culminated in his conversion, and every previous event is only a milestone on the road to this consummation in which the purpose of providence with this particular man is fulfilled. Sensual enjoyment, philosophic delight, the rhetorician's pleasure in scintillating speech, the circumstances of life have no intrinsic value for him. He feels the content of all these strangely mixed with longing for that transcendental relationship; they are all transitory and only in his conversion does an eternal relationship, untainted by suffering, come into being. Thus, to understand his life, we must relate its parts to the realization of an absolute value, an unconditional highest good. Looking back, we see the meaning of all the earlier features of his life in terms of this relationship: we find not development but preparation for the turning away from all that is transitory. As for Rousseau: the way he related himself to his life in the *Confessions* can only be appreciated in the same categories of meaning, values, significance and purpose. All France swarmed with rumours about his marriage, and his past. Misanthropic to the point of persecution mania and in dreadful loneliness he contemplated the incessant intrigues of his enemies against him. When he looked back in memory he saw himself driven from his Calvinistically strict home, struggling upwards from an obscure life of adventure towards a confirmation of his greatness, soiled on the way by the dirt of the streets, forced to put up with bad food of all descriptions and impotent in the face of the domination of the elegant world and the leading intellectuals around him. But, whatever he had done and suffered and whatever was corrupt in him, he saw himself, and this, after all, was the ideal of his age, as a noble, generous soul who felt for humanity. This he wanted to show the world; he wanted to justify his spiritual existence by showing it exactly as it was. Here, too, the outer events of a life have been interpreted by seeking connections which are not merely those of cause and effect. To name these we can only find such words as value, purpose, significance and meaning. When we look more closely we see that interpretation only takes place through a special combination of these categories. Rousseau wanted, above all, to justify his individual existence. This contains a new conception of the infinite possibilities of giving value to life. From this point of view he formed the relationship between the categories in terms of which he understood life. And now for Goethe: In *Dichtung und Wahrheit* a man looks at his own existence from the standpoint of universal history. He sees himself in the context of the literary movement of his age and has a calm, proud consciousness of his position within it. So, to the old man looking back, every moment of his existence is doubly significant, as enjoyed fullness of life and as an effective force in the context of life. In Leipzig, Strasbourg or Frankfurt he experiences the present as always filled and determined by the past and stretching towards the shaping of the future; thus he feels it to be a development. Here we can see more deeply into the relations between the categories which are the tools for understanding life. The significance of life lies in its formation and development; because of this the meaning of the parts of life is determined in a special way; it is both the experienced, intrinsic, value of the moment and its effective power.

Every life has its own significance, determined by a context of meaning in which every remembered moment has an intrinsic value, and yet, in the perspectives of memory, is also related to the meaning of the whole. The significance of an individual existence is unique and cannot be fathomed by knowledge; yet, in its way, like one of Leibniz' monads, it reflects the historical universe.

(4) Autobiography

In autobiography we encounter the highest and most instructive form of the understanding of life. Here life is an external phenomenon from which understanding pentrates to what produced it within a particular environment. The person who understands it is the same as the one who created it. This results in a particular intimacy of understanding. The person who seeks the connecting threads in the history of his life has already, from different points of view, created connections which he is now putting into words. He has created them by experiencing values and realizing purposes, making plans for his life, seeing his past in terms of development and his future as the shaping of his life by its highest ideal. In his memory he has singled out and accentuated the moments which he experienced as significant; others he has allowed to sink into forgetfulness. The future has corrected his illusions about the significance of certain moments. So the primary problems of comprehending and presenting historical connections are already half-solved by life itself. The units are formed by the conceptions of experience in which present and past events are held together by a common meaning. Among these experiences those which have a special dignity, both in themselves and for the passage of his life, have been preserved by memory and lifted out of the endless stream of forgotten events. Constantly changing connections have been formed from different standpoints within life itself, so that the task of historical presentation is already half-performed by life. Units have been formed on the basis of experience; from an endless, countless multiplicity what is worth recording has been pre-selected. Between the parts we see a connection which neither is, nor is intended to be, the simple likeness of the passage of a life of so many years, but which, because understanding is involved, expresses what the individual knows about the continuity of his life.

Here we approach the roots of all historical comprehension. Autobiography is merely the literary expression of a man's reflection on his life. Every individual reflects, more or less, on his life. Such reflection is always present and expresses itself in ever new forms. It occurs in the verses of Solon as well as in the introspection of the Stoics, in the meditations of the saints and in the modern philosophy of life. It alone makes historical insight possible. The power and breadth of our own lives and the energy with which we reflect on them are the foundations of historical vision which enables us to give new life to the bloodless shadows of the past. Combined with an infinite desire to surrender to, and lose onself in, the existence of others, it makes the great historian.

What is it, then, which, in the contemplation of one's life, links the parts into a whole and thus makes it comprehensible? It is the fact that understanding involves, in addition to the general categories of thought, those of value, purpose and meaning. Comprehensive

concepts like the shaping and development of human life are subsumed under these. The differences between these categories are, in
the first place, determined by the point of view from which the passage
of a life is reviewed.

Looking back at the past in memory we see the connections between
the parts of life in terms of the category of meaning. In the present we
feel the positive or negative value of the realities which fill it and, as we
look towards the future, the category of purpose arises. We interpret
life as the achieving of over-riding purposes to which all individual
purposes are subordinated; that is, as the realizing of a supreme good.
None of these categories can be subordinated to the other because each
of them makes the whole of life accessible to the understanding from
different points of view. They are incommensurable.

And yet, there is a distinction in the way they are related to the
understanding of a life. The intrinsic values experienced in, and only
in, the living present, are directly accessible to experience but are not
connected with each other. Each of them arises in the relationship
between a subject and an object in front of him at the time. (In contrast,
when we set ourselves a purpose we relate ourselves to the idea of an
object which is to be achieved.) Thus the intrinsic values of the
experienced present stand unconnected beside each other; they can
only be compared with each other and evaluated. Anything else
described as valuable refers only to relationships to intrinsic values.
Ascribing an objective value to something only means that we can have
some value experience or other when it exists. If we ascribe an
instrumental value to it we mean that it is capable of bringing about
something valuable later. All these are purely logical relationships into
which a value, experienced in the present, can enter. Life, from the
point of view of value, thus appears as an infinite multiplicity of positive
and negative existential values. It is like a chaos of chords and discords.
Each is a structure of notes which fills a present but has no musical
relation to the others. The category of purpose, or of good, which
considers life as directed towards the future, presupposes that of value.
But the connectedness of life cannot be established from this category
either, for the relations of purposes to each other are only those of
possibility, choice and subordination. Only the category of meaning
overcomes mere co-existence of the subordinating of the parts of life to
each other. As history is memory and as the category of meaning
belongs to memory, this is the category which pertains most intimately
to historical thinking. We must now enlarge on its gradual development.

Construction of the Historical World

Supplement to (3): *the connectedness of life*

In connection with the categories of doing and suffering there arises the category of power. Doing and suffering are, as we saw, the basis of the principle of causality in the sciences (the strict development of it is mechanics). In the sciences power is a hypothetical concept. Where its validity is assumed it is determined by the principle of causality. In the human studies power is the expression, in the form of a category, of something that can be experienced. It originates when we turn towards the future and does so in different ways: in dreams of future happiness, in the way imagination plays with possibilities, in hesitation and in fear. But then we re-focus this idle expansion of our existence; surrounded by various possibilities we decide to realize one of them. The idea of a purpose which now emerges contains something new which must be brought into the circle or reality; here we have, quite independent of any theory of the will, a bracing of oneself (which the psychologist might interpret physiologically), a purposefulness, the emergence of an intention to realize something, the selection and definition of a special goal, the choice of the means for achieving it, as well as the achievement itself. The continuous process of life which produces all this we call power, a concept which is decisive for the human studies. However far they extend we are dealing with a coherent whole which contains circumstances that seem self-explanatory; but, in so far as history strives to understand and express change, it must operate with concepts which express energy, trends and regroupings of historical forces. The more historical concepts assume this character the better will they express the nature of their subject-matter. What gives the conceptualization of an object its timeless validity belongs to its logical form. This is why it is necessary to form concepts which express the freedom of life and history. Hobbes frequently says that life is constant movement. Leibniz and Wolff[26] assert that happiness, for both the individual and the community, lies in the consciousness of advance.

All these categories of life and history are forms of judgment which become generally applicable in the human studies (if not always in empirical statements then in their elaboration by additional thought-processes). They originate from experience itself. They are not types of formation added to it; the structural forms of temporal life are expressed in them because of the formal operations founded on the unity of consciousness. What, then, is the empirical subject-matter of these categories? It is primarily the passage of a life which takes place in a human body and which, as a self, with its intentions and their

[26] Christian Wolff, German rationalist philosopher, 1679–1754.

217

frustration by pressure from the outside world, is distinguished from what is outside, impossible to experience and strange. But it is more closely defined by the predications already explained; and so all our empirical judgments, in so far as they refer to a particular life and so express its predicates, are confined to that particular life. They achieve universality by having as their background the objective mind and as their constant counterpart insight into other people.

Understanding one's own life takes place through a final group of categories which differ significantly from the previous ones. The latter were related to those of the knowledge of nature. Those we face now have nothing in the sciences to compare them with.[27]

Comprehending and interpreting one's own life takes place in a long series of stages; the most complete presentation is the autobiography. Here the self comprehends its own life in such a way that it becomes conscious of the basis of human life, namely the historical relations in which it is interwoven. Therefore autobiography can, ultimately, widen out into a historical portrait; this is only limited but is also made meaningful by being based on experience, through which the self and its relations to the world are comprehended. The reflection of a person about himself remains the standard and basis for understanding history.

11. *The understanding of other people and their expressions*

Understanding and interpretation is the method used throughout the human studies. It unites all their functions and contains all their truths. Understanding opens up the world.

Understanding of other people and their expressions is developed on the basis of experience and self-understanding and the constant interaction between them. Here, too, it is not a matter of logical construction or psychological dissection but of an epistemological analysis. We must now establish what understanding can contribute to historical knowledge.

(1) *Expressions*

What is given always consists of expressions. Occurring in the world of the senses they are manifestations of mental content which they enable us to know. By expressions I mean not only signs and symbols but also manifestations of mental content which make it comprehensible without having that purpose.

---

[27] The discussion of the categories is taken up in 'The Categories of Life', pp. 231 ff.

Construction of the Historical World

The kind and amount of understanding differs according to the classes of expressions.

Concepts, judgments and larger thought-structures form the first of these classes. As constituent parts of knowledge, separated from the experience in which they occurred, what they have in common is conformity to logic. They retain their identity, therefore, independently of their position in the context of thought. Judgment asserts the validity of a thought independently of the varied situations in which it occurs, the difference of time and people involved. This is the meaning of the law of identity. Thus the judgment is the same for the man who makes it and the one who understands it; it passes, as if transported, from the speaker to the one who understands it. This determines how we understand any logically perfect system of thought. Understanding, focusing entirely on the content which remains identical in every context, is, here, more complete than in relation to any other expression. At the same time such an expression does not reveal to the one who understands it anything about its relation to the obscure and rich life of the mind. There is no hint of the particular life from which it arose; it follows from its nature that it does not require us to go back to its psychological context.

Actions form another class of expressions. An action does not spring from the intention to communicate; however, the purpose to which it is related is contained in it. There is a regular relation between an action and some mental content which allows us to make probable inferences. But it is necessary to distinguish the state of mind which produced the action by which it is expressed from the circumstances of life by which it is conditioned. Action, through the power of a decisive motive, steps from the plenitude of life into one-sidedness. However much it may have been considered it expresses only a part of our nature. It annihilates potentialities which lie in that nature. So action, too, separates itself from the background of the context of life and, unless accompanied by an explanation of how circumstances, purposes, means and context of life are linked together in it, allows no comprehensive account of the inner life from which it arose.

It is quite different with emotive expressions. They are related in a particular way to the living being who is their author and the understanding which they produce. For expressions can contain more of the psychological context than any introspection can discover. They lift it from depths which consciousness does not illuminate. But it is characteristic of emotive expressions that their relation to the mental content expressed in them can only provide a limited basis for understanding. They are not to be judged as true or false but as truthful or untruthful. For dissimulation, lie and deception can break the relation between the expression and the mental content which is expressed.

The important distinction which thus emerges is the basis for the highest significance which emotive expressions can achieve in the human studies. What springs from the life of the day is subject to the power of its interests. The interpretation of the ephemeral is also determined by the moment. It is terrible that in the struggle of practical interests every expression can be deceptive and its interpretation changed with the change in our situation. But in great works, because some mental content separates itself from its creator, the poet, artist or writer, we enter a sphere where deception ends. No truly great work of art can, according to the conditions which hold good and are to be developed later, wish to give the illusion of a mental content foreign to its author; indeed, it does not want to say anything about its author. Truthful in itself it stands – fixed, visible and permanent; this makes its methodical and certain understanding possible. Thus there arises in the confines between science and action an area in which life discloses itself at a depth inaccessible to observation, reflection and theory.

(2) *The elementary forms of understanding*

Understanding arises, first of all, in the interests of practical life where people are dependent on dealing with each other. They must communicate with each other. The one must know what the other wants. So first the elementary forms of understanding arise. They are like the letters of the alphabet which, joined together, make higher forms of understanding possible. By such an elementary form I mean the interpretation of a single expression. Logically it can be expressed as an argument from analogy, based on the congruence between the analogy and what it expresses. In each of the classes listed individual expressions can be interpreted in this way. A series of letters combined into words which form a sentence is the expression of an assertion. A facial expression signifies pleasure or pain. The elementary acts of which continuous activities are composed, such as picking up an object, letting a hammer drop, cutting wood with a saw, indicate the presence of certain purposes. In this elementary understanding we do not go back to the whole context of life which forms the permanent subject of expressions. Neither are we conscious of any inference from which this understanding could have arisen.

The fundamental relationship on which the process of elementary understanding rests is that of the expression to what is expressed.

Elementary understanding is not an inference from an effect to a cause. Nor must we, more cautiously, conceive it as a procedure which goes back from the given reality to some part of the context of life which made the effect possible. Certainly the latter relation is contained in the circumstances themselves and thus the transition from one to the other is, as it were, always at the door, but it need not enter.

What is thus related is linked in a unique way. The relation between expressions and the world of mind which governs all understanding, obtains here in its most elementary form; according to this, understanding tends to spell out mental content which becomes its goal; yet the expressions given to the senses are not submerged in this content. How, for instance, both the gesture and the terror are not two separate things but a unity, is based on the fundamental relation of expression to mental content. To this must be added the generic character of all elementary forms of understanding which is to be discussed next.

(3) *Objective mind and elementary understanding*

I have shown how significant the objective mind is for the possibility of knowledge in the human studies. By this I mean the manifold forms in which what individuals hold in common have objectified themselves in the world of the senses. In this objective mind the past is a permanently enduring present for us. Its realm extends from the style of life and the forms of social intercourse to the system of purposes which society has created for itself and to custom, law, state, religion, art, science and philosophy. For even the work of genius represents ideas, feelings and ideals commonly held in an age and environment. From this world of objective mind the self receives sustenance from earliest childhood. It is the medium in which the understanding of other people and their expressions takes place. For everything in which the mind has objectified itself contains something held in common by the I and the Thou. Every square planted with trees, every room in which seats are arranged, is intelligible to us from our infancy because human planning, arranging and valuing – common to all of us – have assigned a place to every square and every object in the room. The child grows up within the order and customs of the family which it shares with other members and its mother's orders are accepted in this context. Before it learns to talk it is already wholly immersed in that common medium. It learns to understand the gestures and facial expressions, movements and exclamations, words and sentences, only because it encounters them always in the same form and in the same relation to what they mean and express. Thus the individual orientates himself in the world of objective mind.

This has an important consequence for the process of understanding. Individuals do not usually apprehend expressions in isolation but against a background of knowledge about common features and a relation to some mental content.

This placing of individual expressions into a common context is facilitated by the articulated order in the objective mind. It embraces particular homogeneous systems like law or religion, which have a firm, regular structure. Thus, in civil law, the imperatives enunciated in legal clauses designed to secure the highest possible degree of perfection in the conduct of human affairs, are related to judicial procedures, law courts and the machinery for carrying out what they decide. Within such a context many kinds of typical differences exist. Thus, the individual expressions which confront the understanding subject can be considered as belonging to a common sphere, to a type. The resulting relationship between the expression and the world of mind not only places the expression into its context but also supplements its mental content. A sentence is intelligible because a language, the meaning of words and of inflections, as well as the significance of syntactical arrangements, is common to a community. The fixed order of behaviour within a culture makes it possible for greetings or bows to signify, by their nuances, a certain mental attitude to other people and to be understood as doing so. In different countries the crafts developed particular procedures and particular instruments for special purposes; when, therefore, the craftsman uses a hammer or saw, his purpose is intelligible to us. In this sphere the relation between expressions and mental content is always fixed by a common order. This explains why this relation is present in the apprehension of an individual expression and why – without conscious inference based on the relation between expression and what is expressed – both parts of the process are welded into a unity in the understanding.

In elementary understanding the connection between expression and what is expressed in a particular case is, logically speaking, inferred from the way the two are commonly connected; by means of this common connections we can say of the expression that it expresses some mental content. So we have an argument from analogy; a finite number of similar cases makes it probable that a subject has a particular attribute.

The doctrine of the difference between elementary and higher forms of understanding here put forward justifies the traditional distinction between pragmatic and historical interpretation by basing the difference on the relation – inherent in understanding – between its elementary and higher forms.

(4) *The higher forms of understanding*

The transition from elementary to higher forms of understanding is already prepared for in the former. The greater the inner distance between a particular, given expression and the person who tries to understand it, the more often uncertainties arise. An attempt is made to overcome them. A first transition to higher forms of understanding is made when understanding takes the normal context of an expression and the mental content expressed in it for its point of departure. When a person encounters, as a result of his understanding, an inner difficulty or a contradiction of what he already knows, he is forced to re-examine the matter. He recalls cases in which the normal relation between expression and inner content did not hold. Such a deviation occurs when we withdraw our inner states, ideas or intentions from observation, by an inscrutable attitude or by silence. Here the mere absence of a visible expression is misinterpreted by the observer. But, beyond this, we must frequently reckon on an intention to deceive. Facial expressions, gestures and words contradict the mental content. So, for different reasons, we must consider other expressions or go back to the whole context of life in order to still our doubts.

The interactions of practical life also require judgments about the character and capacities of individuals. We constantly take account of interpretations of individual gestures, facial expressions, actions or combinations of these; they take place in arguments from analogy but our understanding takes us further; trade and commerce, social life, profession and family point to the need to gain insight into the people surrounding us so that we can make sure how far we can count on them. Here the relation between expression and what is expressed becomes that between the multiplicity of expressions of another person and the inner context behind them. This leads us to take account of changing circumstances. Here we have an induction from individual expressions to the whole context of a life. Its presupposition is knowledge of mental life and its relation to environment and circumstances. As the series of available expressions is limited and the underlying context uncertain, only probable conclusions are possible. If we can infer how a person we have understood would act in new circumstances, the deduction from an inductively arrived insight into a mental context can only achieve expectations and possibilities. The transition from an, only probable, mental context to its reaction in new circumstances can be anticipated but not forecast with certainty. As we shall soon see, the presupposition can be infinitely elaborated but cannot be made certain.

But not all higher forms of understanding rest on the relations between product and producer. It is clear that such an assumption is not even true in the elementary forms of understanding; but a very important part of the higher ones is also based on the relation between expression and what is expressed. In many cases the understanding of a mental creation is merely directed to the context in which the individual, successively apprehended, parts form a whole. If understanding is to produce knowledge of the world of mind as efficiently as possible, it is most important that its independent forms should be appreciated. If a play is performed, it is not only the naive spectator who is wholly absorbed in the plot without thinking of the author; even the cognoscenti can be wholly captivated by the action. Their understanding is directed towards the plot, the characters and the fateful interplay of different factors. Only so will they enjoy the full reality of the cross-section of life presented and understand and relive the action as the poet intended. All this understanding of mental creations is dominated by the relation between expressions and the world of mind expressed in them. Only when the spectator notices that what he has just accepted as a piece of reality is the poet's artistically planned creation does understanding pass from being governed by the relation between expression and what is expressed to being dominated by that between creation and creator.

The common characteristic of the forms of higher understanding mentioned is that by means of an induction from the expressions given they make the whole context comprehensible. The basic relation determining the progress from outer manifestations to inner content is either, in the first instance, that of expression to what is expressed or, frequently, that of product to producer. The procedure rests on elementary understanding which, as it were, makes the elements for reconstruction available. But higher understanding is distinguishable from elementary by a further feature which completely reveals its character.

The subject-matter of understanding is always something individual. In its higher forms it draws its conclusions about the pattern within a work, a person or a situation, from what is given in the book or person and combined by induction. But analysis and understanding of our own experience show that the individual is an intrinsic value in the world of mind; indeed it is the only intrinsic value we can ascertain beyond doubt. Thus we are concerned with the individual not merely as an example of man in general but as himself. Quite independently of the practical interest which constantly forces us to reckon with other people, this concern, be it noble or wicked, vulgar or foolish, occupies a considerable place in our lives. The secret of personality lures us on to new attempts at deeper understanding for its own sake. In such understanding, the realm of individuals, embracing men and their creations, opens up. The unique contribution of understanding in the human studies lies in this; the objective mind and the power of the individual together determine the mind-constructed world. History rests on the understanding of these two.

But we understand individuals by virtue of their kinship, by the features they have in common. This process presupposes the connection between what is common to man and the differentiation of these common features into a variety of individual mental existences; through it we constantly accomplish the practical task of mentally living through, as it were, the unfolding of individuality. The material for accomplishing this task is formed by the facts combined by induction. Each fact has an individual character and is grasped as such; it, therefore, contains something which makes possible the comprehension of the individual features of the whole. But the presupposition on which this procedure is based assumes more and more developed forms as we become absorbed in the particular and the comparison of it with other things; thus the business of understanding takes us into ever greater depths of the mind-constructed world. Just as the objective mind contains a structural order of types, so does mankind, and this leads from the regularity and structure of general human nature to the types through which understanding grasps individuals. If we assume that these are not distinguished qualitatively, but, as it were, through emphasis on particular elements – however one may express this psychologically – then this represents the inner principle of the rise of individuality. And, if it were possible, in the act of understanding, both to grasp the changes brought about by circumstances in the life and state of the mind, as the outer principle of the rise of individuality, and the varied emphasis on the structural elements as the inner principle, then the understanding of human beings and of poetic and literary works would be a way of approaching the greatest mystery of life.[28] And this, in fact, is the case. To appreciate this we must focus on what cannot be represented by logical formulae (i.e. schematic and symbolic representations which alone are at issue here).

[28] See n. 11. p. 140.

(5) *Empathy, re-creating and re-living*

The approach of higher understanding to its object is determined by its task of discovering a vital connection in what is given. This is only possible if the context which exists in one's own experience and has been encountered in innumerable cases is always – and with all the potentialities contained in it – present and ready. This state of mind involved in the task of understanding we call empathy, be it with a man or a work. Thus every line of a poem is re-transformed into life through the inner context of experience from which the poem arose. Potentialities of the soul are evoked by the comprehension – by means of elementary understanding – of physically presented words. The soul follows the accustomed paths in which it enjoyed and suffered, desired and acted in similar situations. Innumerable roads are open, leading to the past and dreams of the future; innumerable lines of thought emerge from reading. Even by indicating the external situation the poem makes it easier for the poet's words to evoke the appropriate mood. Relevant here is what I have mentioned before, namely that expressions may contain more than the poet or artist is conscious of and, therefore, may recall more. If, therefore, under-standing requires the presence of one's own mental experience this can be described as a projection of the self into some given expression.

On the basis of this empathy or transposition there arises the highest form of understanding in which the totality of mental life is active – re-creating or re-living. Understanding as such moves in the reverse order to the sequence of events. But full empathy depends on understanding moving with the order of events so that it keeps step with the course of life. It is in this way that empathy or transposition expands. Re-experiencing follows the line of events. We progress with the history of a period, with an event abroad or with the mental processes of a person close to us. Re-experiencing is perfected when the event has been filtered through the consciousness of a poet, artist or historian and lies before us in a fixed and permanent work.

In a lyrical poem we can follow the pattern of experiences in the sequence of lines, not the real one which inspired the poet, but the one, which, on the basis of this inspiration, he places in the mouth of an ideal person. The sequence of scenes in a play allows us to re-live the fragments from the life of the person on the stage. The narrative of the novelist or historian, which follows the historical course of events, makes us re-experience it. It is the triumph of re-experiencing that it supplements the fragments of a course of events in such a way that we believe ourselves to be confronted by continuity.

Construction of the Historical World

But what does this re-experiencing consist of? We are only interested in what the process accomplishes; there is no question of giving a psychological explanation. So we shall not discuss the relation of this concept to those of sympathy and empathy, though their relevance is clear from the fact that sympathy strengthens the energy of re-living. We must focus on the significance of re-living for grasping the world of mind. It rests on two factors; envisaging an environment or situation vividly always stimulates re-experiencing; imagination can strengthen or diminish the emphasis on attitudes, powers, feelings, aspirations and ideas contained in our own lives and this enables us to re-produce the mental life of another person. The curtain goes up and Richard appears. A flexible mind, following his words, facial expressions and movements, can now experience something which lies outside any possibility in its real life. The fantastic forest of *As You Like It* transposes us into a mood which allows us to re-produce all eccentricities.

This re-living plays a significant part in the acquisition of mental facts, which we owe to the historian and the poet. Life progressively limits a man's inherent potentialities. The shaping of each man's nature determines his further development. In short, he always discovers, whether he considers what determines his situation or the acquired characteristics of his personality, that the range of new perspectives on life and inner turns of personal existence is limited. But understanding opens for him a wide realm of possibilities which do not exist within the limitations of his real life. The possibility of experiencing religious states in one's own life is narrowly limited for me as for most of my contemporaries. But, when I read through the letters and writings of Luther, the reports of his contemporaries, the records of religious disputes and councils, and those of his dealings with officials, I experience a religious process, in which life and death are at issue, of such eruptive power and energy as is beyond the possibility of direct experience for a man of our time. But I can re-live it. I transpose myself into the circumstances; everything in them makes for an extraordinary development of religious feelings. I observe in the monasteries a technique of dealing with the invisible world which directs the monk's soul constantly towards transcendental matters; theological controversies become matters of inner life. I observe how what is thus formed in the monasteries *is spread* through innumerable channels – sermons, confessions, teaching and writings – to the laiety: and then *I notice* how councils and religious movements *have spread* the doctrine of the invisible church and universal priesthood everywhere and how it comes to be related to the liberation of personality in the secular sphere. Finally I see that what has been achieved by such struggles in lonely cells can survive, in spite of the church's opposition. Christianity as a force for shaping family, professional and political life converges with the spirit of the Age in the cities and wherever sophisticated work is done as by Hans Sachs[29] or Dürer.[30] As Luther leads this movement we can understand his development through the links between common human features, the religious sphere, this historical setting and his personality. Thus this process reveals a religious world in him and his companions of the first period of the Reformation which widens our horizon of the possibilities of human existence. Only in this way do they become accessible to us. Thus the inner-directed man can experience many other existences in his imagination. Limited by circumstances he can yet glimpse alien beauty in the world and areas of life beyond his reach. Put generally: man, tied and limited by the reality of life is liberated not only by art – as has often been explained – but also by historical understanding. This effect of history, which its modern detractors have not noticed, is widened and deepened in the further stages of historical consciousness.

(6) *Exegesis or interpretation*

Re-creating and re-living what is alien and past shows clearly how understanding rests on special, personal inspiration. But, as this is a significant and permanent condition of historical science, personal inspiration becomes a technique which develops with the development of historical consciousness. It is dependent on permanently fixed expressions being available so that understanding can always return to them. The methodical understanding of permanently fixed expressions we call *exegesis*. As the life of the mind only finds its complete, exhaustive and, therefore, objectively comprehensible expression in language, exegesis culminates in the interpretation of the written records of human existence. This method is the basis of philology. The science of this method is hermeneutics.

Exegesis of surviving remnants is inwardly and necessarily linked to their critical examination. This arises from difficulties of exegesis and leads to the purification of texts, and the rejection of documents, works and traditions. Exegesis and critical examination have, in the course of history, developed new methodological tools, just as science has constantly refined experiment. Their transmission from one genera-

---

[29] German poet, 1494–1576.
[30] Albrecht Dürer, German painter, 1471–1528.

tion of philologists and historians to another rests predominantly on personal contact with the great virtuosi and the tradition of their achievements. Nothing in the sphere of scholarship appears so personally conditioned and tied to personal contact as this philological method. Its reduction to rules by hermeneutics was characteristic of a stage in history when attempts were made to introduce rules into every sphere; this hermeneutic systematization corresponded to theories of artistic creation which considered it as production governed by rules. In the great period when historical consciousness dawned in Germany, Friedrich Schlegel,[31] Schleiermacher and Böckh replaced this hermeneutic systematization by a doctrine of ideals which based the new deeper understanding on a conception of mental creation; Fichte had laid its foundations and Schlegel had intended to develop it in his sketch of a science of criticism. On this new conception of creation rests Schleiermacher's bold assertion that one has to understand an author better than he understood himself.[32] In this paradox there is an element of truth which can be psychologically explained.

Today hermeneutics enters a context in which the human studies acquire a new, important task. It has always defended the certainty of understanding against historical scepticism and wilful subjectivity; first when it contested allegorical exegesis, again when it justified the great Protestant doctrine of the intrinsic comprehensibility of the Bible against the scepticism of the Council of Trent, and then when, in the face of all doubts, it provided theoretical foundations for the confident progress of philology and history by Schlegel, Schleiermacher and Böckh. Now we must relate hermeneutics to the epistemological task of showing the possibility of historical knowledge and finding the means for acquiring it. The basic significance of understanding has been explained; we must now, starting from the logical forms of understanding, ascertain to what degree it can achieve validity.

We found the starting-point for ascertaining how far assertions in the human studies correspond to reality in the character of experience which is a becoming aware of reality.

When the elementary acts of thought direct conscious attention to experience, they only note relations contained in it. Discursive thought represents what is contained in experience. Understanding rests primarily on the relationship, contained in any experience which is characterized by understanding, of expression to what is expressed. This relation can be experienced in its uniqueness. As we can only

[31] 1772–1829.
[32] For this (and some of the following) see 'The development of Hermeneutics', pp. 247–63.

transcend the narrow sphere of experience by interpreting expressions, understanding achieves central significance for the construction of the human studies. But it was also clear that it could not be considered simply as an act of thought; transposition, re-creation, re-living – these facts pointed towards the totality of mental life which was active in it. In this respect it is connected with experience which, after all, is merely a becoming aware of the whole mental reality in a particular situation. So all understanding contains something irrational because life is irrational; it cannot be represented by a logical formula. The final, but quite subjective, certainty derived from this re-living cannot be replaced by an examination of the cognitive value of the inferences by which understanding can be represented. These are the limits set to the logical treatment of understanding by its own nature.

Though laws and forms of thought are clearly valid in every part of science and scholarship and even the methods of research are extensively inter-related, understanding introduces procedures which have no analogy in the methods of science. For they rest on the relation between expressions and the inner states expressed in them.

We must distinguish understanding from the preliminary grammatical and historical work which merely serves to place the student of a fixed expression originating in the past or far away and linguistically strange, in the position of a reader from the author's own time and environment.

In the elementary forms of understanding we infer from a number of cases in which a series of similar expressions reflects similar mental content that the same relation will hold in other similar cases. From the recurrence of the same meaning of a word, a gesture, an overt action, we infer their meaning in a fresh case. One notices immediately, however, how little this form of inference achieves. In fact, as we saw, expressions are also reflections of something general; we make inferences by assigning them to a type of gesture or action or range of usage. The reference from the particular to the particular contains a reference to the general which is always represented. The relation becomes even clearer when, instead of inferring the relation between a series of particular, similar, expressions and the mental life expressed, we argue from analogy about some composite, individual, facts. Thus from the regular connection between particular features in a composite character we infer that this combination will reveal an, as yet unobserved, trait in a new situation. By this kind of inference we assign a mystical writing which has been newly discovered, or has to be chronologically re-classified, to a particular circle of mystics at a particular time. Such an argument always tends to infer the structure of such products from individual cases and thus to justify the new case more profoundly. So, in fact, the argument from analogy when applied to a new case becomes an induction. These two forms of inference can only be relatively distinguished in understanding. As a result, our expectations of a successful inference in a new case are invariably limited – how much no general rule can determine but only an evaluation of the varying circumstances. A logic of the human studies would have to discover rules for such evaluation.

So understanding itself, because it is based on all this, has to be considered as induction. This induction is not of the type in which a general law is inferred from an incomplete series of cases; it is rather one which co-ordinates these cases into a structure or orderly system by treating them as parts of a whole. The sciences and the human studies share this type of induction. Kepler discovered the elliptical path of the planet Mars by such an induction. Just as he inferred a simple mathematical regularity from observations and calculations by means of a geometrical intuition, so understanding must try to link words into meaning and the meaning of the parts into the structure of the whole given in the sequence of words. Every word is both determined and undetermined. It contains a range of meanings. The means of syntactically relating these words are, also, within limits, ambiguous; meaning arises when the indeterminate is determined by a construction. In the same way the value of the whole, which is made up of sentences, is ambiguous within limits and must be determined from the whole. This determining of determinate–indeterminate particulars is characteristic of hermeneutics.

The categories of life

Life

Vol. VII, pp. 228–45

The human world is the poet's proper subject-matter. It is the scene of the events which he describes and of the features through which he gives them significance. The great enigma of the poet who conjures up a new reality above life which moves us as much as life and extends and elevates the soul, can only be solved if we can explain the relations between this human world and its basic features and poetry. Then we can find a theory which transforms the history of poetry into historical scholarship.

Life is the context of actual externally-conditioned interactions between people, considered independent of particular changes in time and locations. In the human studies I shall confine the term 'life' to the human world; its meaning is thus determined by the sphere in which it is used and thus not open to misunderstanding. Life consists of interactions between people; the finite course of a particular life is regarded by a spectator as belonging to one person because the body in which it occurs seems to remain the same; yet, this lifetime has the strange characteristic that every part of it is consciously linked to the others by some kind of experience of continuity, coherence and identity. In the human studies the expression interaction does not signify the relation which, in nature, is an aspect of causality (for causality presupposes that cause and effect are equal); it describes an experience and can be put into experiental terms by the relation between impulse and resistance, pressure, awareness of being helped, joy in other people etc. Impulse here does not, of course, refer to a power of spontaneity or causality assumed in some explanatory psychological theories, but only a fact which is somehow rooted in the person and which he experiences; so we experience the intention to execute movements in order to achieve a certain effect. This is the experience which is usually described as an interaction between different people.

Life is the context in which these interactions, conditioned by the causal order of physical objects including the psychological events in bodies, take place. This life is always and everywhere spatially and temporally determined – localized, as it were, in the spatio-temporal order of people's lives. But if we emphasize what is constant in the human world and makes spatially and temporally determined events possible – not by an abstraction from the latter but an intuition which leads from the whole with its unvarying characteristics to its spatially and temporally differentiated instances – then the concept of life arises which forms the basis for all its individual forms and systems, for our experience, understanding, expressions and comparative study of them.

Then, and only then, do we discover with surprise a general property of life, not experienced in nature or even the natural objects which we call living organisms.

Experience

I

Life is very closely related to the filling of time. Its whole character, its ephemeral nature and its continuity through the unity of the self is determined by time.

In time life exists in the relation of parts to a whole, that is, as a context.

Thus, too, understanding through re-living occurs.

Living and re-living contain a special relation of parts to the whole. It is that of the significance of the parts for the whole. This is clearest in the case of memory. Any reference to oneself, or relation to others contains the significance of parts for the whole. I look at, and take in, a landscape. As we must assume that this is a relationship in life and not a mere apprehension, we should not call this experience of a landscape a picture but rather an 'impression'. Basically I only have such impressions and not a self separated from them, nor something of which it is the impression. The latter I only add by a construction.

Note

I should like to emphasize that meaning is related to the totality of the knowing subject. We can generalize the expression so that it becomes identical with every relation which the subject discovers between parts and the whole, so that even the objects of thought, or, put more precisely, the relation of parts in thinking of an object or the setting of a purpose, is included. This would include even the general ideas under which individual images are subsumed. Then, meaning means nothing except belonging to a whole; this eliminates the enigma of life, how can an organic or psychic whole be real?

II

From the psychological point of view, the present is a temporal sequence integrated into a unity. What cannot be distinguished because of its continuity we call the present. What we can experience is a moment of life. Even when we can distinguish temporal parts in our experiencing we describe what is structurally connected by memory as one experience.

The principle of experience: everything which exists for us does so only as given in the present. Even when an experience is past, it only exists for us as given in a present experience. This principle is more general (more complete) than that of consciousness for it also embraces what is not real.

The next characteristic is this; experience is qualitative being (i.e. reality) which cannot be defined by awareness but reaches into what can be possessed without making distinctions (note: can one say possessed?). The experience of an external world exists for me in a similar way: what is not apprehended can be inferred. (I can say: my experience contains even what cannot be seen and I can elucidate it.)

Dilthey's Epistemology and Methodology

The fact is that part of what my intuition (in the widest sense of the word) embraces, is focused upon and apperceived through its meaning and is distinguished from mental processes which are not apperceived. This is what we call 'I', and there is a double relation: I am and I have.

The next proof is that experience also contains the structure of life (i.e. a temporal-spatial localization stretching from the present) in which an inherent purpose is dynamically active.

When we remember experiences we can distinguish those which have a continued, dynamic, effect on the present from those which are wholly past. In the first case the feeling as such recurs; in the second an idea of feelings which in the present produces only a feeling about the idea of feelings.

Experiencing and experience are not separate; they are merely different terms for the same thing.

The presence of judgments distinguishes apperception from experience; I am sad, I observe or know about a death. This contains the double direction of statements expressing the given reality.

Duration apprehended in understanding

If we give our attention to the process of experiencing we cannot apprehend the forward movement of mental life: for every act of focusing halts the process and gives some duration to what is focused on. But here, too, the relation between experience, expression and understanding makes a solution possible. We apprehend the expression of activity and re-live it.

The advance of time leaves more and more of the past behind and moves into the future. The great problem about whether mental events are merely a happening or an activity is solved if we seek the expression which articulates the tendency of what is happening. Movement forward in time and the mental adding up of the past are not sufficient. I must seek an expression which can occur in time and is not disturbed from outside. Instrumental music is a case in point. However it may have originated it is an occurrence which the creator sees continuing from one phrase to the next. Here we have a direction, an activity, stretching towards a realization, a movement forwards of mental activity itself, conditioned by the past and yet containing different possibilities, a presentation which is at the same time creation.

Construction of the Historical World

Meaning

There is a further aspect of life which is conditioned by time but adds something new. Understanding the nature of life involves categories which have nothing to do with nature. The decisive point is that these categories are not applied to life *a priori* as something strange but lie in its nature. The approach which they express abstractly is the exclusive starting-point for understanding life, for it only exists in this particular kind of relationship of a whole to its parts. The fact that we abstract these relationships as categories implies that we cannot delimit the number of these categories or formalize their relationship logically. Meaning, value, purpose, development and ideal are such categories. But the totality of a life, or any section of the life of mankind, can only be grasped in terms of the category of the meaning which the individual parts have for the understanding of the whole. All the other categories depend on this. Meaning is the comprehensive category through which life can be understood.

The objects of scientific knowledge are as changeable as conscious life, but only in life does the present include memory pictures of the past and pictures of the future in which possibilities are imagined and selected as purposes. So the present is filled with past events and contains the future. This is the meaning of the word 'development' in the human studies. It does not mean that we can apply the concept of an unfolding purpose to the life of an individual, a nation or mankind; this would be a way of looking beyond the subject-matter and could be rejected. The concept only describes a relationship inherent in life and includes the principle of organization which is a general characteristic of life. A deeper look reveals organization even in the poorest soul. We see it most clearly where great men have a historical destiny; but no life is so poor that its course does not contain some organization. Wherever an innate and, based on it, an acquired, mental structure form the constant feature of a life within which change and decay occur, temporal life becomes organization. But this concept can only occur because we consider life under the category of meaning.

The category of meaning designates the relationship, inherent in life, of parts of a life to the whole. The connections are only established by memory, through which we can survey our past. Here meaning takes the form of comprehending life. We grasp the meaning of a past moment. It is significant for the individual because in it an action or an external event committed him for the future. Or, perhaps, the plan for the future conduct of life was conceived then. It is significant for communal life because the individual intervened in the shaping of mankind and contributed to it with his essential being. In all these and other cases the particular moment gains meaning from its relationship with the whole, from the connection between past and future, between individual and mankind. But in what does the particular kind of relationship of parts to a whole in a life consist of?

It is a relationship which is never quite complete. One would have to wait for the end of a life, for only at the hour of death could one survey the whole from which the relationship between the parts could be ascertained. One would have to wait for the end of history to have all the material necessary to determine its meaning. On the other hand, the whole is only there for us when it becomes comprehensible through its parts. Understanding always hovers between these two points of view. Our view of the meaning of life changes constantly. Every plan for your life expresses a view of the meaning of life. The purposes we set for the future are determined by the meaning we give to the past. The actual formation of life is judged in terms of the meaning we give to what we remember.

Just as words have meaning through which they designate something, or sentences a significance which we can construe, so can the pattern of a life be construed from the determined–undetermined meaning of its parts.

Meaning is the special relationship which the parts have to the whole in a life. We recognize this meaning as we do that of words in a sentence, through memory and future potentialities. The nature of the meaning-relationships lies in the pattern of life formed in time by the interaction between a living structure and its environment.

What is it, then, which, in the contemplation of one's life, constitutes the pattern which links the parts into a whole and makes the life comprehensible? An experience is a unit made up of parts linked by a common meaning. The narrator achieves his effect by emphasizing the significant elements of a course of events. The historian describes certain human beings as significant and certain turning-points in life as meaningful; he recognizes the meaning of a work or a man by its special effect on the common destiny. The parts of a life have a certain meaning for the whole; put briefly, the category of meaning has obviously a particularly close *connection with understanding*; this we must now try to comprehend.

Every expression has a meaning in so far as it is a sign which signifies or points to something that is part of life. Life does not mean anything other than itself. There is nothing in it which points to a meaning outside it.

If we single out something in life by means of concepts this serves above all to describe its unique quality. These general concepts serve, therefore, to express an understanding of life. Here there is only a loose progression from the presupposition to what follows from it; what is new does not follow formally from the presupposition; it is rather that understanding passes from something already grasped to something new which can be understood through it. The inner relationship between them lies in the possibility of re-creating and re-living. This is the general method that must be used as soon as understanding leaves the sphere of words and their meaning and seeks, not the meaning of signs, but the much deeper meaning of expressions. Fichte had the first inkling of this method. Life is like a melody the notes of which are not the expressions of hidden realities within. Like notes in a melody, life expresses nothing but itself.

1. The simplest case in which meaning occurs is the understanding of a sentence. Each word has a meaning and, by joining them, we arrive at the meaning of a sentence. Here understanding of the sentence results from the meaning of the individual words. But there is an interaction between the whole and the parts through which ambiguities of meaning are eliminated and the meaning of individual words determined.

2. The same relation holds between the parts and the whole of a life and here, too, the understanding of the whole, the significance of life, is derived from the meaning of the parts.

3. This relationship of meaning and significance holds, therefore, for the course of a life; individual events in the external world which form it have, like the words in a sentence, a relation to something which they signify. Through this every experience is significantly connected up into a whole. Just as the words of a sentence are joined to give it meaning so experiences are connected to give us the meaning of a life. It is the same with history.

4. Thus the concept of meaning arises, first of all, in relation to the process of understanding. It contains the relationship of something outward, something given to the senses, to something inward of which it is the expression. But this relationship is essentially different from the grammatical one. The expression of mental content in the parts of a life is different from the expression of meaning by a word.

5. Hence such words as meaning, comprehension, significance (of a life or of history) are only points to the relationship between events and an inner pattern, contained in understanding and required by it.

6. We are looking for the kind of connection which is inherent in life itself, and we are looking for it in the individual events. In each of these which contributes to the pattern something of the meaning of life must be contained; otherwise it could not arise from their inter-connection. The paradigm of science is the concept of a causal order in the physical world and its particular methodology consists of the procedures for discovering it; in an analogous way we can approach the categories of life, their relations to each other, the paradigm they constitute and the methods for apprehending them. In the one case we are dealing with abstract connections which, in their essence, are logically transparent. In the other we aim at understanding the connectedness of life itself which can never be known entirely.

We can only reach an approximate understanding of life; it lies in the nature of both understanding and life that the latter reveals quite different sides to us according to the point of view from which we consider its course in time. In the act of recollection the category of meaning is first disclosed. Every present is filled with reality and we attribute a positive or negative value to it. As we turn to the future the categories of purpose, ideal and giving shape to a life originate. It is the secret of life that a supreme purpose, to which all individual purposes are subordinated, is realized in it. It realizes a supreme value, and must be determined by ideals. It achieves a shape. Each of these concepts, from its own point of view, embraces the whole of life; so it has the character of a category through which life is understood. None of these categories can be subordinated to the others because each of them makes the whole of life comprehensible from a different point of view. They are thus incommensurable. Yet there is a difference in their roles. The intrinsic values of the experienced present stand separately side by side. One can only compare them. From the point of view of value life appears as an infinite wealth of existential, negative or positive intrinsic values. It is a chaos of harmonies and dissonances – where the dissonances do not dissolve into harmonies. No arrangement of sounds which fills a present has a musical relationship to an earlier or later one. Even the relationship between intrinsic and instrumental values only presupposes causal relations which because they are mechanical in character do not reach into the depth of life.

The categories which consider life while taking account of the future presuppose the category of value; they dissolve into the different possibilities for penetrating the future.

The connectedness of life is only adequately represented in the relation which the meaning of the events of life has to the understanding and significance of the whole. Only in this category is mere co-existence or subordination overcome. Thus the categories of value and purpose, which are individual aspects of the understanding of life, become part of the comprehensive context of this understanding.

Construction of the Historical World

Meaning and structure

1. Experience in its concrete reality is made coherent by the category of meaning. This is the unity which, through memory, joins together what has been experienced directly or through empathy. Its meaning does not lie in some focal point outside our experience but is contained in them and constitutes the connections between them.

This system of connections is, thus, the peculiar form of relatedness, or category, found in all that can be experienced.

Where the meaning of the life of an individual, of myself, of another, or of a nation, lies, is not clearly determined by the fact that there is such a meaning. That it is there is always certain to the person remembering it as a series of related experiences. But only in the last moment of a life can the balance of its meaning be struck, so it can be done only for a moment, or by another who retraces that life.

Thus Luther's life receives its meaning from the pattern presented by all the concrete events in which he embraced and established the new attitude to religion. This, in its turn, forms part of a more comprehensive context of actual events which precede and follow it. Here meaning is seen historically. But one can also seek this meaning in the positive values of life. There it stands in relation to subjective feelings.

2. Meaning, evidently, does not coincide with values nor with their connections in a life.

3. Meaning is the category for the whole context of life; the category of structure originates from the analysis of life's recurring features. Analysis, in this sense, seeks only what is contained in these recurrences and finds nothing except this content. This is an abstraction and its concept is only valid when it is linked to the consciousness of the context of life in which it is contained.

How far can this analysis go? Scientific, atomistic psychology was followed by the psychological scholasticism of Brentano's school which creates abstract entities like conduct, object, content, in order to reconstruct life from them. Husserl represents this tendency at its most extreme.

In contrast we must treat life as a whole, integrated structure, conditioned by its real relationships to the external world, and consider conduct as one of these relationships. Feeling and will are only concepts which indicate how we are to reconstruct the corresponding parts of life.

Dilthey's Epistemology and Methodology

Meaning, significance, value

1. The whole objectification of life consists of expressions, i.e. pieces of the objective world relevant for an interpretation of life. Each of them is a whole with parts and a part of a whole because it belongs to a system of reality which is sub-divided into parts and, at the same time, belongs to a larger system of reality. It is significant, through this double relationship, as a link in the greater whole. This is the hallmark which life impresses on all experience whether directly or through empathy. For experience contains an active attitude towards all the particular, economic, personal or religious circumstances occurring within it. It is a system of interactions conditioned by this attitude. Life is related to anything to which it has taken up an attitude; such attitudes are: strangeness, withdrawal, selection, love, isolation, longing, opposition, need, requirement, esteem, form, formlessness, conflict of life with objective facts and impotence in the face of them, the will to remove what is intolerable and restore enjoyment, ideal, remembrance, separation and unification.

Life itself contains the grief over its finitude and the desire to overcome it, striving for realization and objectification, denial or removal of existing limits, separation and combination.

Unholiness, grace, beauty, freedom, style, connectedness, development, inner logic and inner dialectic are all attributes of life, so are the opposites here and beyond, transcendence and immanence and reconciliation.

2. The relationships which originate in this way determine the significance of the individual parts of life. Significance is the meaning, defined by the system of interactions, which a part has for a whole. In the conduct of life it adds a relationship between the links in the system of interactions which goes beyond the experience of effective activity and so arranges them in an independent order. Effective activity constitutes everything which comes to the fore in life. Only the effects of this activity can be observed, for the activity of the self remains unknown. But conduct, or attitude, is something more profound and determines the way life produces its effects; all the concepts developed above are *concepts of life* contained in life. In every person, or period, they receive a new context. They give its colour to whatever presents itself to life. Even spatial relationships like broad, wide, high, low, receive additional meaning from conduct; it is the same with time.

3. According to this relationship anthropological reflection produces a context in art, history and philosophy in which only what is contained in life is made conscious.

Anthropological reflection comes first. It rests on such systems of interaction as passion etc: it sketches their various types and expresses their significance in the whole of life.

Contemplating, experiencing and understanding oneself as well as others and thus gaining knowledge of human nature, produces generalizations which give new expression to value, meaning and the purpose of life. They form a separate layer between life and art or historical representation. Autobiography is a literature of almost infinite extent. The question is how the historical categories facilitate understanding in it.

The historical development of the study of man is misrepresented if we confine the study to psychology as it has developed today. It has been approached from different directions. The greatest contrast, however, lies between what I once described as content psychology and what could also be called concrete psychology or anthropology and the proper science of psychology. This anthropology is still close to questions about the meaning and value of life because it is so close to concrete life. That is why it tries to distinguish types of life and stages of realizing types of significance of life.

One may think of the Neo-Platonic type, the Mysticism of the Middle Ages or the stages in Spinoza. A realization of the meaning of life takes place in these schemata.

The basic of poetry is the system of interactions, i.e. events. Every poem is somehow related to an event which has either been experienced or requires understanding. It shapes the event by making its parts significant through the free play of imagination. Poetry is made up of assertions about life which it expresses vigorously. Everything is coloured by this relationship and is seen as wide, high or remote. Past and present are not mere facts; through his empathy the poet restores the relationship to life which receded in the course of intellectual development and practical interests.

4. The significance which a fact receives as a determinate link in the meaning of a whole is based on a vital relationship and not an intellectual one; it is not a question of imposing reason and thought on part of an event. We draw significance from life itself. If we call the connections which arise from the meaning of its parts the meaning of life, then a poem expresses that meaning by a free creation of meaningful connections. The event depicted in the poem becomes a symbol of life.

Starting with anthropological reflection everything, including poetry, is explanation and explication of life itself. What is contained, inaccessible to observation and reasoning, in the depth of life, is drawn forth. Thus the poet feels himself to be inspired.

The limitation of poetry is that it has no method for understanding life. Its manifestations are not systematically ordered. Its strength is the direct relationship of the event depicted to life, through which the event and the free creation which expresses its significance become an unmediated expression of life.

The realm of life, treated as a temporal and causal construction objectified in time, is history. It is a whole which can never be completed. The historian shapes the course of the system of interactions from the events contained in his sources. He is committed to making us aware of its reality.

The meaning of the part is here determined by its relation to the whole, but this whole is treated as an objectification of life and understood through this relationship.

Values

The life of the mind contains an extensive realm of values. The value we attribute to objects reflects our personal relationship to them. So value is not, primarily, a product of conceptualization in the service of thought about objects. (It can become this when the result, on the one hand, represents an attitude and, on the other, enters into objective relationships.) It is the same with assessing values. This, too, is independent of the apprehension of objects. In this sense we must re-interpret the expression 'the sense of values'. Value is the abstract expression for the attitude described. It is common to explain values psychologically. This corresponds to the general procedure of psychological explanation. But this method is questionable because it makes what counts as a value and how values are related to each other, dependent on the psychological starting-point. A transcendental explanation, which contrasts unconditional and conditional values, is equally mistaken. We must use the reverse procedure. We must start from a complete survey of the expressions, in which all valuations are contained. Only then can we enquire into the attitude itself.

We colour the panorama of life with positive and negative attitudes – pleasure, liking, approval or satisfaction; objects conceived as permanent come to sustain memories of feelings which they evoke and these make varied states of mind possible. Thought distinguishes these states of mind from the object and then applies them to it; this is the origin of the idea and concept of value. As value has this special relationship to a person whom it can affect, it is clearly distinguished from the qualities which make up the reality of an object. The ways in which an object can affect the mind multiply with life itself. What affects us in the present is increasingly overlaid by memory. Thus value becomes less affected by when an object begins and ceases to attract us. Even when objects continue to exist the concept of their value can contain nothing but the idea of past possibilities. Because, in practice, evaluations are necessary when we determine the goals for our will, we compare values and so value comes to be related to the future as a good or goal. Thus value gains a new independence as a concept; elementary acts of valuing are combined into a total, organized evaluation. Values, then, continue to exist independently even when divorced from the will. This is how experience gradually develops the concept of value. Let me repeat that we are dealing with an analytical distinction, not a temporal stage.

When we reflect, turning the 'I' upon itself, the 'I' can become an object to itself; it becomes capable of enjoying itself and being an object of enjoyment to others. In the last resort it is not different from other objects which can be enjoyed though we cannot say that they can enjoy what they are or can achieve. But when we, as sensitive beings, become objects to ourselves and thus aware of ourselves, our actions and the enjoyment we derive from them, the unique concept of the intrinsic value of the person arises – distinguishing him from everything which, as far as we know, does not enjoy itself. In this sense the Renaissance formed the idea of the monad in which 'thinghood', enjoyment, value and perfection were united. Leibniz enriched German philosophy and literature with this concept and the strong emotion contained in it.

Understanding makes a different kind of contribution to the development of the concept of value. Here the primary experience in one's own life is the power with which another individual affects us. When understanding reconstructs the individuality of another, the idea and conception of value are further divorced from the experience of being affected. For they are not only reconstructed, they are also referred to another person. As a consequence the relation between the power to affect others and the self-awareness of the subject, who has this power, can be grasped much more clearly. The intrinsic value of the person becomes entirely objective and is objectively revealed in all his relations to his environment. One limitation remains which only historical distance can remove. Understanding is confused by comparing others with ourselves, conceit, envy, jealousy and suffering from an other's power; the yardstick for evaluation which we get when surveying the past, is missing.

Value is objective description by means of a concept. It has no life but it has not lost its relation to life.

Once the concept of value is formed it becomes, through its relation to life, a *power*, because it pulls together what is separated, dark and transitory in life. When we find in history values, and valuations expressed in documents, we can, by empathy, put back into them the relationship to life they once contained.

The whole and its parts

Temporal and spatial life is differentiated according to the category of the whole and its parts. History as the successive or simultaneous unfolding of life is categorially a further spelling out of this relationship of the parts to the whole. Here things belong together only because they refer to a person, to a life of which they are part. The course of history is not arranged like pieces of furniture in a room which can be observed by any one who enters, or removed because they are unrelated to each other. Viewed scientifically every configuration is the meaningless result of moving masses, but movement and mass and the laws of their relationships are not subject to time. Life, in any one of its forms, has an inner relationship of part to whole so the configuration is never meaningless.

This belonging-together appears in quite different, vital relationships and is different in each of them.

Development, essence and other categories

Here two further categories emerge. Life and its course form a pattern which develops through the constant absorption of new experiences on the basis of the older ones: I call this the acquired mental structure. The way this process takes place allows for the structure continuing even while change is going on. This fact, which can be demonstrated in all mental life, I refer to in terms of the category of essence. But essence has for its other side constant change. This means that the change which absorbs external influences is, at the same time, determined by the uniform pattern of life itself. This makes up the character of every life, and we must try to grasp it without prejudices. All theories about stages of progressive development must be abandoned.

What, then, is the universal course of events? The definiteness of every individual existence and every one of its states includes its limitations. This concept has a distinct meaning in the mental sphere and is unlike a spatial frontier. The existence of a person constitutes his individuality. Its limitations cause suffering and a desire to overcome them. Finitude is tragic and we feel impelled to transcend it. Limitation expresses itself externally as the pressure of the world on the subject. Through the power of circumstances and the character of the mind this can become so strong that it impedes progress. But in most cases finitude makes man try to overcome the pressure of new circumstances and new human relationships. As every state is equally finite it produces the same will to power which springs from being conditioned, the same will to inner freedom which results from inner limitations. But all is held together by the inner power and inner limitation resulting from the definiteness of the individual existence and the persistence of the acquired structure deriving from it. So, the same essence affects the whole course of events. In everything there is the same limitation of possibilities and yet freedom to chose between them, and the beautiful feeling of being able to move forward and to realize new potentialities in one's own existence. This inwardly-determined pattern of life, which promotes the restless progress of change, I call development.

This concept is quite different from the speculative fantasies about progress to ever higher stages. It means that the subject becomes clearer and more differentiated. But the life of an individual, like the lower forms of life, can lack the realization of a higher meaning and remain tied to the natural basis of plant-like growth, of rise and decline between birth and death. It can decline early or move upwards until the end.

The Development of Hermeneutics

EDITOR'S INTRODUCTION

This essay, first published in a Commemoration volume for C. Sigwart[1] in 1900, is based on a lecture given at the Prussian Academy of Science in 1896. In the historical portions of the essay Dilthey used material from an early work of his own – a competition essay on Schleiermacher's hermeneutics submitted in 1860.

When the essay was reprinted V. G. Misch, the editor of Vol. v, added a selection of passages from Dilthey's alternative ms drafts. As these contain some very incisive formulations and definitions I have included some of them but I have been selective and excluded obscure sentences and casual cross-references to particular authors.

The historical part of the article is designed to show that hermeneutics has as long and respectable a history as experimental science. We see from what needs it arose and what pressures shaped its methodology. Special emphasis is placed on the way in which the conception of its nature and function came to be enlarged. Some of the details may only be of interest to specialists but they have been retained to illustrate the thoroughness and width of Dilthey's scholarship.

The real importance of this essay lies in the fact that it is one of the clearest expressions of Dilthey's most distinctive and fruitful hypothesis. Understanding man and society is more like interpreting a text than acquiring knowledge of the physical world by using the methods of physics or chemistry. Therefore the traditional skills of literary critics, jurists, linguistics or Biblical scholars must be systematized and transformed into a methodology of the human studies.

[1] German philosopher, 1830–1904.

The Development of Hermeneutics

Vol. v, pp. 317–37

In a previous work I have considered how to describe the process by which individual works of art, in particular of poetry, are produced. Now we must ask if it is possible to study individual human beings and particular forms of human existence scientifically and how this can be done.

This is a question of the greatest significance, for our actions always presuppose the understanding of other people and a great deal of human happiness springs from empathy with the mental life of others. Indeed, philology and history rest on the assumption that the understanding of the unique can be made objective. The historical sense based on this assumption enables man to recapture the whole of his past; he can look across all the barriers of his own age at past cultures and increase his happiness by drawing strength from them and enjoying their charm. While the systematic human studies derive general laws and comprehensive patterns from the objective apprehension of the unique they still rest on understanding and interpretation. These disciplines, therefore, like history, depend for their certainty on the possibility of giving general validity to the understanding of the unique. So, from the beginning, we are facing a problem which distinguishes the human studies from the physical sciences.

No doubt the human studies have the advantage over the physical sciences because their subject is not merely an appearance given to the senses, a mere reflection in the mind of some outer reality, but inner reality directly experienced in all its complexity. Here we are not considering what difficulties, arising from the way in which this reality is experienced, obstruct objective apprehension but a further problem that inner experience of my own states can never, by itself, make me aware of my own individuality. Only by comparing myself to others and becoming conscious of how I differ from them can I experience my own individuality. However Goethe is, unfortunately, right when he notes how difficult it is to gain this most important of our experiences, and how imperfect our insight into the extent, nature and limit of our powers always remains. We are mainly aware of the inner life of others only through the impact of their gestures, sounds and acts on our senses. We have to reconstruct the inner source of the signs which strike our senses. Everything: material, structure, even the most individual features of this reconstruction, have to be supplied by

247

transferring them from our own lives. How, then, can an individually structured consciousness reconstruct – and thereby know objectively – the distinct individuality of another? What kind of process is this which steps so strangely into the midst of the other cognitive processes?

We call the process by which we recognize some inner content from signs received by the senses *understanding*. This is how the word is used and a much-needed, fixed psychological terminology can only be established when every firmly coined, clearly and usefully circumscribed expression is used by writers consistently. Understanding of nature – *interpretatio naturae* – is a figurative expression. Even awareness of our own state of mind cannot properly be called understanding. It is true I may say: I can't understand how I could do that; I don't understand myself any longer. But then I mean that an expression of my nature which has been externalized confronts me as something alien that I cannot interpret, or else that I have got into a state at which I gaze astonished as if it were foreign to me. Understanding is the process of recognizing a mental state from a sense-given sign by which it is expressed.

Understanding ranges from the apprehension of childish patter to understanding *Hamlet* or the *Critique of Pure Reason*. The same human spirit speaks to us from stone, marble, musical compositions, gestures, words and writings, from actions, economic arrangements and constitutions, and has to be interpreted. This process of understanding must always have common characteristics because it is determined by common conditions and means of its own, and remains the same in its basic features. If, for example, I want to understand Leonardo[1] I must interpret actions, pictures and writings in one homogeneous process.

Understanding shows different degrees which are, to start with, determined by interest. If the interest is limited so is the understanding. We listen impatiently to some explanations if all we want to know about is one point of practical importance and are not interested in the inner life of the speaker. In other cases we strain to get inside a speaker through every facial expression or word. But even the most strenuous attention can only give rise to a systematic process with a controllable degree of objectivity if the expression has been given permanent form so that we can repeatedly return to it. *Such systematic understanding of recorded expressions we call exegesis or interpretation.* In this sense there is also an art of interpreting sculptures or pictures. F. A. Wolf called for a hermeneutic and critique in archaeology. Welcker[2]

[1] Leonardo da Vinci, 1452–1519.
[2] F. G. Welcker, German classical scholar, 1784–1868.

advocated it and Preller[3] tried to develop it. But Preller emphasized that such interpretations of non-verbal works depended on explanations from literature.

Because it is in language alone human inwardness finds its complete, exhaustive and objectively comprehensible expression that literature is immeasurably significant for our understanding of intellectual life and history. The art of understanding therefore centres on the *interpretation of written records of human existence.*

Therefore, the exegesis – and the critical treatment inseparably linked with it – of these records formed the starting-point of philology. This is essentially a personal skill and virtuosity in the treatment of written records; any interpretation of monuments or historically transmitted actions can only flourish in relation to this skill and its products. We can make mistakes about the motives of historical agents, indeed these agents may themselves mislead us about their motives; but the work of a great poet or explorer, of a religious genius or genuine philosopher can only be the true expression of his mental life; in human society, full of lies, such work is always true and can therefore – in contrast to other permanent expressions – be interpreted with complete objectivity. Indeed it throws light on the other artistic records of an age and on the historical actions of contemporaries.

This art of interpretation has developed just as slowly, gradually and in as orderly a way as, for example, the questioning of nature by experiment. It originated and survives in the personal, inspired virtuosity of philologists. Naturally it is mainly transmitted through personal contact with the great masters of interpretation or their work. But every skill also proceeds according to rules which teach us to overcome difficulties and embody what can be transmitted of a personal skill. So the art of interpretation gives rise to the formulation of rules. The conflict between such rules and the struggle between different schools about the interpretation of vital works produces a need to justify the rules and this gives rise to hermeneutics, which is *the methodology of the interpretation of written records.*

Because it determines the possibility of valid interpretation by means of an analysis of understanding, it penetrates to the solution of the whole general problem with which this exposition started. Understanding takes its place beside the analysis of inner experience and both together demonstrate the possibility and limits of general knowledge in the human studies in so far as it is determined by the way in which we are originally presented with mental facts.

I shall document this orderly progress from the history of her-

[3] L. Preller, German philologist, 1809–61.

meneutics, by showing how philological virtuosity arose from the need for deep and valid understanding. This gave rise to rules which were purposefully organized and systematized according to the state of scholarship in a given period, and finally an assured starting-point for making these rules was found in the analysis of understanding.

I

Systematic interpretation of poets developed as a required part of education in Greece. Clever play with interpretations and criticism of Homer and other poets was popular wherever Greek was spoken during the age of Greek Enlightenment. A more firm foundation was laid when the interpretations of the Sophists and rhetorical schools was related to rhetoric. For this contained – applied to eloquence – a more general theory of literary composition. Aristotle, the great classifier and analyst of the organic world, of states and literary works, taught in his *Rhetoric* how to dissect the whole of a literary work into its parts, distinguish literary forms and recognize the effects of rhythm, period and metaphor. The definitions of the elements of effective speech such as example, enthymeme, sentence, irony, metaphor and antithesis, are assembled even more simply in the *Rhetoric for Alexander*.[4] Aristotle's Poetics deals quite specifically with the way the nature and purpose of poetry and its different types determine their inner and outer form.

The art of interpretation and its systematization took a second important step in Alexandrian philology. The literary heritage of Greece was collected in libraries; textual revisions were made and the results of critical work were recorded by means of a refined system of signs. Spurious writings were eliminated and complete inventories made. Philology as an art of textual revision based on intimate linguistic understanding, higher criticism, interpretation and evaluation had come into existence as one of the last and most characteristic creations of the Greek spirit which was powerfully motivated, from Homer onwards, by joy in human speech. The great Alexandrian scholars also began to be conscious of the rules contained in their inspired technique. Aristarch[5] worked on the consciously formulated principle of establishing Homeric usage strictly and comprehensively, and of basing explanation and textual emendation on it. Hipparch[6] deliberately based his factual interpretation on a literary-historical investigation when he pointed to the sources for the *Phenomena*[7] of

---

[4] *Rhetorica ad Alexandrum*, formerly ascribed to Aristotle, now considered spurious.
[5] Alexandrian grammarian of the third century B.C.
[6] Hipparchus, Greek astronomer of the second century B.C.
[7] A poem by Aratos who was a Greek astronomer and poet of the third century B.C.

The Development of Hermeneutics

Aratos and interpreted the poems accordingly. It was the ingenious handling of the principle of analogy, according to which a canon of usage, a range of ideas, the inner consistency and aesthetic value of a poem was ascertained (and what contradicted it eliminated) which made it possible to recognize spurious poems in the transmitted body of Hesiod's poems, to eliminate many lines from Homer's epics and to judge the last section of the Iliad and part of the penultimate and the whole of the last section of the Odyssey as of more recent origin. The application of moral-aesthetic canons by Zenodot[8] and Aristarch emerges clearly from the following argument by Atethesen,[9] i.e. *si quid heroum vel deorum gravitatem minus decere videbatur*.[10] Aristarch also relied on Aristotle.

Methodological consciousness about the right procedures of interpretation was strengthened by the reaction of the Alexandrian school against the philology of Pergamon. This conflict of hermeneutic trends proved of significance for world history because it re-emerged – in a new situation – in Christian theology. Two great historical views about poets and religious writers are conditioned by it.

From the Stoics, Krates of Malos[11] imported allegorical interpretation into the philology of Pergamon. This form of interpretation was influential for a long time because it eliminated the conflict between religious texts and an enlightened world view. This is why it was almost indispensable for the interpretation of the Vedas, Homer, the Bible and the Koran – a skill as necessary as it is pernicious. But it was also based on a deeper view of poetic and religious creation. Homer is a visionary and the contradiction between deep insights and sensuously coarse ideas in his work can only be explained by treating the latter simply as a poetic means of presentation. So allegorical interpretation originated when this relation was understood as a deliberate enfolding of a spiritual meaning in images.

2

If I am not mistaken, this conflict recurs under altered circumstances in the struggle between the theological schools of Alexandria and Antioch. Their common assumption was, of course, that an inner connection between prophecy and fulfilment linked the Old and New Testaments because this was implied by the use of prophecies and examples in the New Testament. Starting from this presupposition the

[8] Zenodotus of Ephesus. Head of the library at Alexandria, fourth century B.C.
[9] Fourth century B.C.
[10] 'If anything pertaining to heroes or gods seems less befitting to their dignity.'
[11] Greek philologist of Pergamon, second century A.D.

Dilthey's Epistemology and Methodology

Christian church found itself in a complicated position *vis-à-vis* its opponents as regards the interpretation of its Holy Writ. If the logos-theology was to be applied to the Old Testament the Church had to maintain an allegorical interpretation where the Jews were concerned but where the Gnostics[12] were involved it had to limit the allegorical method. Following in the footsteps of Philo,[13] Justin[14] and Irenäos[15] tried to establish rules for limiting and managing the allegorical method. In this same struggle with Jews and Gnostics, Tertullian[16] takes up the procedure of Justin and Irenäos but, on the other hand, develops fruitful rules for better interpretation which, alas, he does not always follow himself. The contrast found fundamental expression in the Greek church. The school of Antioch explained its texts strictly accordingly to grammatical-historical principles. The Antiochian Theodorus[17] saw the Song of Songs simply as a wedding song. Job was for him merely the poetic rendering of a historical tradition. He rejected the titles of the psalms and refuted the direct reference to Christ of a sizeable part of Messianic prophecies. He did not assume a double meaning of the texts but only a higher connection between the events. In contrast to this Philo, Clemens[18] and Origen[19] distinguished a literary and spiritual meaning of the texts.

From this struggle the first worked out hermeneutic theories we know of originated. This is a further step in the development of interpretation into hermeneutic through which it became scientific. According to Philo κανόνες[20] and νόμοι τῆς ἀλληγορίας[21] are already applied in the Old Testament and have to be assumed as underlying his interpretation. On this Origenes in the fourth book of his work Περὶ ἀρχῶν[22] and Augustine in the third book of *De Doctrine Christiana* based a coherently presented hermeneutic theory. These were opposed by two, unfortunately, lost hermeneutic works of the Antiochian school: Diodoros' Τίς διαφορὰ θεωρίας καί ἀλληγορίας[23] and Theodoros' *De Allegoria et Historia Contra Originem*.

[12] A religious school of the first century A.D.
[13] Philo the Jew, Alexandrian philosopher, 20 B.C.–A.D. 40.
[14] Religious writer and martyr of the second century A.D.
[15] Religious writer, A.D. 140–200.
[16] Christian apologist, A.D. 165–220.
[17] Ecclesiastical historian, A.D. 393–458.
[18] Clement of Alexandria, religious writer, second to third century A.D.
[19] Father of Christian theology, A.D. 185–254.
[20] 'rules', 'criteria'.
[21] 'laws of allegory'.
[22] '*On principles.*'
[23] '*What is the difference between theory and allegory?*'

The Development of Hermeneutics

3

Interpretation and its systematization have entered a new stage since the Renaissance. Language, conditions of life and nationality separated it from classical and Christian antiquity. In contrast to what it was once in Rome, interpretation thus became transposition by means of grammatical, factual and historical studies into an alien mentality. This new philology, polymathy and critique had frequently to deal with mere reports and fragments. So it had to be creative and constructive in a new way. Philology, hermeneutic and critique therefore entered a higher stage. We have voluminous hermeneutic literature from the next four centuries. There were two strands because classical and Biblical writings were powerful influences to be absorbed. The classical-philological systematization described itself as *ars critica*. Its works – eminent among them those of Scioppius[24] and Clericus[25] and the incomplete one of Valesius[26] – contained a methodology in their first part. Innumerable essays and prefaces were *de interpretatione*. But the final putting together of hermeneutics we owe to Biblical interpretation. The first significant and perhaps most profound of these writings was the *clavis*[27] of Flacius.[28]

Here, for the first time, the essence of the rules of interpretation discovered so far was linked into a system of teaching, based on the postulate that valid understanding was possible through the systematic use of these rules. Flacius became conscious of this fundamental point of view, which, in fact, dominates hermeneutics, through the struggles of the sixteenth century because he had to fight on two fronts. Both the Anabaptists and the Catholicism of the Counter-Reformation maintained that the holy scriptures were obscure. In opposing this, Flacius learned especially from Calvin's[29] exegesis which frequently referred from interpretation back to its principles. The most urgent business of a Lutheran of the period was to refute the then newly-formulated Catholic doctrine of tradition. The right of tradition to determine interpretation could in the quarrel with the Protestant principle of interpretation only be justified by the assumption that no sufficient and valid interpretation could be elicited from the Biblical writings themselves. The Council of Trent, in session from 1545 to 1563, dealt with this question from its fourth session onwards; in 1564 the first authentic edition of its decrees appeared. Later, some time after

---

[24] K. Scioppius (or Schoppe), religious controversialist from Prague, 1576–1649.
[25] J. Leclerc, Arminian theologian, 1657–1736.
[26] H. Valesius, French ecclesiastical theologian, 1603–76.
[27] 'The Key.'   [28] M. Flacius, Lutheran theologian, 1520–75.
[29] J. Calvin, 1509–64.

Flacius, Bellarmine,[30] the exponent of Tridentine Catholicism, attacked the comprehensibility of the Bible most incisively in a pamphlet of 1581 and tried to prove the need for tradition to supplement Holy Writ. In the context of these controversies, Flacius embarked on proving the possibility of valid interpretation hermeneutically. In his struggle to accomplish this task he became conscious of methods and rules which earlier hermeneutics had not elicited.

If the interpreter encounters difficulties in his text there is a sublime aid for overcoming them at hand – to place them into the context of vital Christian religious experience. As we would say, rather than expressed as dogma, the hermeneutic value of religious experience is only one example of the principle that every interpretation contains as one of its factors reference to the factual context. Beside this religious principle of interpretation there are also rational ones. The first of these is grammatical interpretation. It was Flacius who was also the first to grasp the significance of the psychological or technical principle of interpretation according to which an individual passage must be interpreted in terms of the aim and composition of the whole work. He was the first to use methodically the insights of rhetoric about the inner units of a literary product, its composition and effective elements for technical interpretation. Melanchthon's[31] transformation of Aristotle's rhetoric had prepared the ground for him. Flacius himself is conscious of having been the first to use methodically the help to be gained from context, aim, proportion and the consistency of individual parts or links in determining the definite meaning of passages. He sees the hermeneutic value of these aids in the general perspective of a methodology. 'Everywhere else too the individual parts of a whole become comprehensible through their relation to the whole and the other parts.' He traces the inner forms of a work back to its style and the factors by which its impact is achieved and subtly characterizes the styles of Paul and John. It was a great step forward though confined by the limits of the rhetorical point of view. For Melanchthon and Flacius every literary work is created and can be understood according to rules. It is like a logical automaton dressed in style, images and tropes.

The formal deficiencies of his work were overcome in Baumgarten's[32] hermeneutic. A second, great theological-hermeneutic movement emerges in this. Through Baumgarten's *News from a Library in Halle* not only Dutch interpreters but English free-thinkers and anthropological interpreters of the Old Testament

---

[30] R. Bellarmine, theologian and controversialist, 1542–1621.
[31] 1497–1560.
[32] A. Baumgarten, German philosopher, 1714–62.

became known in Germany. Semler[33] and Michaelis[34] developed their ideas through personal contact with him and through participation in his work. Michaelis was the first to apply a consistent, historical view of language, history, nature and law to the interpretation of the Old Testament. Semler, the forerunner of the great Christian Baur, shattered the unity of the New-Testament canon, set the correct task of understanding every individual work against its background, and then linked these writings into a new unity based on the lively historical apprehension of the original Christian conflicts between Judeo-Christianity and the more loosely organized Christians. In preparing for a theological hermeneutic he based the whole discipline with down-to-earth decisiveness on two points, interpretation from linguistic usage and interpretation from historical circumstances. With this exegesis was liberated from dogma and the grammatical-historical school founded. Ernesti's[35] subtle and careful spirit produced in his *Interpres* the classical work of this new hermeneutic. Schleiermacher still read it and developed his own hermeneutic from it. But even this step forward occurred within fixed limits. In the hands of these interpreters the composition and thought structure of every work of an age dissolves into the same threads; the locally and temporally conditioned circle of ideas. According to this pragmatic view of history human nature is uniform in its response to religion and morality and only *externally* limited by local and temporal factors. Human nature is unhistorical.

Until then classical and Biblical hermeneutics developed independently. But should they not be considered as applications of a general hermeneutic? The Wolfian Meier[36] took this step in his attempt at a general hermeneutic. He conceived the idea of his discipline in the most general terms – he wanted to draft the rules which are to be observed in every interpretation of signs. But the book shows once more that one cannot invent new disciplines from the standpoint of architectonics and symmetry. This only produces blind windows through which no one can look. An effective hermeneutics could only emerge in a mind which combined virtuosity of philological interpretation with genuine philosophic capacity. A man with such a mind was Schleiermacher.

[33] S. Semler, German philosopher, 1725–62.
[34] J. D. Michaelis, German Protestant theologian, 1717–91.
[35] J. A. Ernesti, German Lutheran theologian, 1707–91.
[36] G. F. Meier, German philosopher, 1718–77.

4

The background for his work was provided by Winkelmann's interpretation of works of art, Herder's congenial empathy into the spirit of ages and people and the philology, orientated towards the new aesthetic, of Heyne,[37] Friedrich August Wolf[38] and his disciples. One of these, Heindorf,[39] was closely linked to Schleiermacher by their common interest in Platonic studies. All this combined in Schleiermacher with the procedure of German transcendental philosophy which reaches behind what is given in consciousness to the creative capacity which, working harmoniously and unconscious of itself, produces the whole form of the world in us. From the combination of these elements his own particular art of interpretation and the definitive founding of a scientific hermeneutic originated.

Until then, hermeneutics had at best been an edifice of rules, the parts of which – the individual rules – were held together by the aim to achieve a valid interpretation. It had separated the functions which combine in this process into grammatical, historical, aesthetic-rhetorical and factual exegesis. From the philological virtuosity of many centuries it had crystallized the rules according to which these must function. Now Schleiermacher went behind these rules to the analysis of understanding, i.e. to the comprehension of the purposive act itself and from this comprehension he deduced the possibility of valid interpretation, its aids, limits and rules. But he could only analyse understanding which is a reshaping or reconstruction on the basis of its relationship to the process of literary creation. He recognized the imaginative consideration of the creative process through which a vital literary work originates as the basis for appreciating the process by which we understand the whole of a work from its written signs and from this the purpose and mentality of its author.

But to solve the problem set he needed a new psychological-historical view. We have traced the relation in question from the connection between Greek interpretation and rhetoric as a methodology of a special kind of literary production. But the conception of both processes always remained a logical-rhetorical one. The categories according to which this methodology proceeded were always: production, logical connection, logical order and then a clothing of this logical product with style, tropes and images. Now quite new concepts for the understanding of a literary product came into use. It assumes the existence of a unitary and creatively active capacity which, unconscious

[37] C. G. Heyne, German classical scholar, 1729–1812.
[38] F. A. Wolf, German classical scholar, 1759–1824.
[39] L. F. Heindorf, German philologist, 1774–1816.

of its doing and shaping, receives the first stimulus for its work and then develops it. Receptivity and creativity cannot be separated. Individuality is all-pervasive right to the fingertips and individual words. Its highest expression is the outer and inner form of a literary work. Such a work meets with the insatiable desire (of the reader) to supplement his own individuality through contemplation of that of others. Understanding and interpretation therefore are constantly alive and active in life itself, but they are perfected by the systematic interpretation of vital works and the unity they were given in the author's mind. This was the .new conception in the special form it assumed in Schleiermacher.

One of the further conditions for this great enterprise – a general hermeneutic – was the development of a *philological* hermeneutic in terms of the new psychological-historical views by Schleiermacher and his friends. German intellectual life, in the persons of Schiller, Wilhelm von Humboldt, and the brothers Schlegel had just turned from poetic production to the understanding of the historical world. It was a powerful movement and Böckh, Dissen,[40] Welcker, Hegel, Ranke and Savigny were influenced by it. Friedrich Schlegel became Schleiermacher's guide in the art of philology. The concepts which guided him in his brillient works on Greek poetry, Goethe and Boccaccio were: the inner form of the work, the development of the author and the articulated whole of literature. Behind his individual achievements of philological reconstruction lay the plan for a science of criticism, for an *ars critica* which was to be based on a theory of literary creativity. How close this plan was to Schleiermacher's *Hermeneutic* and *Critique*!

Schlegel also initiated the plan of a Plato-translation. In it he developed the new technique of interpretation which Böckh and Dissen then applied to Pindar.[41] Plato must be understood as a philosophic artist. The goal of interpretation is the unity between the character of Platonic philosophizing and the artistic form of the Platonic works. Here philosophy is still alive, rooted in conversation; its literary presentation is only an aid to memory. So it must be dialogue, and so stylized in form that it forces us to recreate the living context of thought. At the same time the strict unity of Plato's thought requires that each dialogue should continue earlier, and prepare later, themes, thus spinning together the threads of the different parts of the philosophy. If one follows the relation between the dialogues their connection, which discloses Plato's central intention, emerges. According to Schleiermacher only by grasping this methodically-developed

[40] G. L. Dissen, German philologist, 1784–1837.
[41] 521–441 B.C.

257

context does a real understanding of Plato emerge. Compared with this ascertaining the chronological sequence of his works is unimportant, though the order may coincide. Böckh could say in his famous review that this masterpiece made Plato accessible to philology for the first time.

But in Schleirmacher's intellect philological virtuosity was combined for the first time with a philosophic capacity of genius. He was specifically trained in transcendental philosophy which was the first to provide adequate means for stating the problem of hermeneutics in general terms and solving it. This was the origin of a general discipline and methodology of interpretation.

Schleiermacher sketched the first draft of it, based on his reading of Ernesti's *Interpres,* in the autumn of 1804 because he wanted to use it as the start of his course of exegetic lectures in Halle. We have the hermeneutic which thus resulted only in a very ineffective form. It was strengthened by a disciple of Schleiermacher from the Halle period, Böckh, in the magnificent section of his lectures on philosophic encyclopedia.

I select from Schleiermacher's hermeneutic the statements on which further development seems to depend.

All interpretation of literary works is merely the methodical development of the process of understanding, which extends over the whole of life and relates to any kind of speech or writing. The analysis of understanding is, therefore, the basis for making interpretation systematic. But this can only be done in the analysis of literary productions. The system of rules which determines the means and limits of interpretation can only be based on the relation between understanding and creation.

The possibility of valid interpretation can be deduced from the nature of understanding. There the personalities of the interpreter and his author do not confront each other as two facts which cannot be compared: both have been formed by a common human nature and this makes common speech and understanding among men possible. Here Schleiermacher's formal expressions can be further explained psychologically. All individual differences are, in the last resort, conditioned not by qualitative differences between people but by differences of degree in their mental processes. By transposing his own being experimentally, as it were, into a historical setting the interpreter can momentarily emphasize and strengthen some mental processes and allow others to fade into the background and thus reproduce an alien life in himself.

On the logical side this process is one of coming to know a whole context from only partially defined signs by making use of existing grammatical, logical and historical knowledge. Expressed in logical terminology this aspect of understanding consists of the combination of induction, application or general truth to a particular case and comparison. It would also be necessary to ascertain the precise nature of the above logical operations and how they combine.

Here we encounter the general difficulty of all interpretation. The whole of a work must be understood from individual words and their combination but full understanding of an individual part presupposes understanding of the whole. This circle is repeated in the relation of an individual work to the mentality and development of its author, and it recurs again in the relation of such an individual work to its literary genre. In practice Schleiermacher solved this problem most beautifully in his introduction to Plato's *Republic*; in the postscripts to his exegetic lectures there are other examples of this procedure. He started with a survey of the structure, comparable to a superficial reading, tentatively grasped the whole context, illuminated the difficulties and halted thoughtfully at all those passages which afforded insight into the composition. Only then did interpretation proper begin. Theoretically we are here at the limits of all interpretation; it can only fulfil its task to a degree; so all understanding always remains relative and can never be completed. *Individuum est ineffabile.*[42]

Schleiermacher rejected the division of the exegetic process into grammatical, historical aesthetic and factual interpretation which he found established. These distinctions merely indicate that grammatical, historical, factual and aesthetic knowledge must be present at the beginning of interpretation and can influence every one of its procedures. In the process of interpretation itself we can only distinguish two aspects to grasping an intellectual creation through linguistic signs. Grammatical interpretation proceeds from link to link to the highest combinations in the whole of the work. The psychological interpretation starts with penetrating the inner creative process and proceeds to the outer and inner form of the work and from there to a further grasp of the unity of all his works in the mentality and development of their author.

Here we have reached the point from which Schleiermacher developed the rules of interpretation in a masterly fashion. His theory of inner and outer form is fundamental and his drafts for a general theory of literary creation which was to form the methodology of literary history were particularly profound.

The final goal of the hermeneutic procedure is to understand the

---

[42] The individual is not definable.

author better than he understood himself; a statement which is the necessary conclusion of the doctrine of unconscious creation.

To summarize, understanding only becomes interpretation which achieves validity when confronted with linguistic records. When we consider the philological procedures of hermeneutics and the justification for it we may – rightly – not think very highly of the practical value of such a discipline compared with the living practice of Fr. A. Wolf. But it seems to me that it has, beyond its use in the business of interpretation, a second task which is indeed its main one: it is to counteract the constant irruption of romantic whim and sceptical subjectivity into the realm of history by laying the historical foundations of valid interpretation on which all certainty in history rests. Absorbed into the context of the epistemology, logic and methodology of the human studies the theory of interpretation becomes a vital link between philosophy and the historical disciplines, an essential part of the foundations of the studies of man.

Additions from the Manuscripts

Vol. v, pp. 332–7

Understanding comes under the general concept of cognition taken in its widest sense and meaning any process which aims at valid knowledge.

(Proposition 1) *By understanding I mean the process in which we use expressions given to the senses to gain knowledge of mental life.*

(Proposition 2) *All acts of understanding the expressions of mental life, however different these may be physically, must have common characteristics which are determined by the specific way they are known.*

(Proposition 3) *By exegesis or interpretation I mean methodical understanding of recorded expressions.*

Exegesis is a matter of personal skill and complete success depends on the genius of the interpreters; it is based on kinship intensified by close and constant study of the author. [References to a number of authors omitted.] Inspired guesswork in interpretation depends on this.

Because interpretation is so difficult and important it has taken mankind immense labour. All philology and history is concerned with it and one can hardly imagine the immeasurable amount of scholarly work put into it. *Man's power of understanding* grows in as gradual, orderly, slow and laborious a way as the power to know and control nature.

The Development of Hermeneutics

But because genius is rare and interpretation has to be practised and learned by the less gifted it is necessary that (Proposition 4a) *the art of inspired interpreters must be spelled out in rules implied by their method or consciously formulated by them.* For every human skill is refined and increased when the achievements of the expert can, in some form, be passed on to his successors. Methods of understanding only develop when language provides a firm foundation and permanent, valuable, creations exist which are controversial because they can be interpreted in various ways; *then attempts must be made by means of valid rules to settle the conflict between interpreters of genius.* Undoubtedly, contact with an interpreter of genius or his work stimulates one's own interpretative skill. But the brevity of life requires a short cut – formulation of the methods which have been discovered and the rules implied by them. *I call this methodology of the understanding of recorded expressions hermeneutics* (Proposition 4b).

So we can define the nature of hermeneutics and, to some extent, justify its use. At present it does not seem to attract the attention its exponents desire. The reason appears to be that it is not concerned with the problems which interest today's scholars. Hermeneutics has had a strange fate. It only gains recognition when there is a movement among historians which considers understanding individual historical manifestations on urgent matter for scholarship; at other times it vanishes again into obscurity...[Some references to nineteenth-century scholarship omitted.]

(Proposition 5) *Understanding taken in a wide sense – which will be explained – is the fundamental procedure for all further operations of the human studies.*...All knowledge of scientific laws depends on measurable, countable and regular aspects of experience; similarly, every abstract proposition of the human studies can only be justified by reference to mental life which has been experienced and understood.

(Proposition 6) It follows from the fundamental role of understanding in the human studies that *the epistemological, logical and methodological analysis of understanding is one of the main tasks involved in establishing the foundations of the human studies.* The significance of the task emerges when one considers what difficulties the nature of understanding raises for the practice of valid scholarship.

Everyone is enclosed within his own consciousness which is unique and makes all apprehension subjective. The sophist, Gorgias,[43] formulated this problem as follows: 'Even if there were knowledge he who has it could not communicate it to anyone else.' For him thinking

---

[43] Greek sophist, 483–375 B.C.

comes to an end with this problem. We must solve it. The possibility of apprehending something alien is one of the most difficult problems of epistemology. How can an individual understand another person's expressions objectively and validly? It is possible only on the condition that the other person's expression contains nothing which is not also part of the observer. The same functions and elements are present in all individuals and their degree of strength accounts for the variety in the make-up of different people. The same external world is mirrored in every one's ideas...[Two lines consisting of incomplete sentences omitted.]

Second Aporia.[44] The whole must be understood in terms of its individual parts, individual parts in terms of the whole. To understand the whole of a work we must refer to its author and to related literature. Such a comparative procedure allows one to understand every individual work, indeed, every individual sentence, more profoundly than we did before. So understanding of the whole and of the individual parts are interdependent.

Third Aporia. Even particular mental states can only be understood in terms of the external stimulations which produced them. I can understand hatred in terms of the injury to life which caused it. Without this relationship I could have no idea of the passions. The environment is indispensable for understanding, which, at its most extreme, is indistinguishable from explanation (as far as we can explain mental states). Explanation, in turn, presupposes complete understanding.

So the epistemological problem is always the same – how to transform experience into valid knowledge. But in the human studies this problem is conditioned by the character of the experiences they deal with. In mental life the structural context needed for understanding is active within us and so familiar.

So the first, important, epistemological problem which confronts us in the human studies is the analysis of understanding. *Hermeneutics, by starting from this problem and seeking its solution, becomes relevant to the questions about the nature and foundation of the human studies which occupy present-day scholars.* So its problems and propositions have become a living issue.

The solution of the epistemological questions leads on to the logical problem of hermeneutics.

This, too, is the same everywhere. The elementary logical operations which occur in the sciences and the human studies are, of course, the same...[A bracketed aside omitted.] These are induction, analysis,

[44] *Aporia* = philosophic problem without a solution.

The Development of Hermeneutics

construction and comparison. What matters is how they are used in the empirical sphere of the human studies. Here, too, induction, using observable processes for its data, is based on knowledge of a context. In physics and chemistry this is the mathematical knowledge of quantitative relationships; in biology it is fitness for survival; in the human studies the structure of mental life. This basis is not a logical abstraction but a real, experienced, connection; it is, however, particular to individuals and, therefore, subjective. This determines the aim and form of this type of induction. A more specific form is imposed on the logical operations of induction by the characteristics of language. So, within the linguistic sphere, the theory of induction is given specific form by grammar, the theory of language. This induction, therefore, involves, specifically, recognition of familiar grammatical constructions and the more or less determinate meaning of words and syntactical arrangements. Inductive understanding of a particular whole is supplemented by the comparative method which clarifies it and makes it more objectively known by relating it to other particular wholes.

p. 335
Existing methodology which is indispensable for achieving validity must be supplemented by the description of the creative methods of inspired interpreters in many spheres.

p. 337
Because particular entities can only be comprehended in their whole context we must ask if it is possible to make a distinction between *understanding and explanation.* [A few lines omitted.] *When general knowledge is consciously and methodically used to make the particular fully known, it is appropriate to call this knowledge of the particular explanation.* But it is only justified as long as we remember that there is no question of dissolving the particular in the general.

This settles the controversial question about whether reflective knowledge of mental experiences or the science of psychology is the general basis of understanding. Psychology takes its place among all the other human studies as the basis for the successful explanation of particular entities.

Bibliography

Dilthey's writings

A chronological bibliography is available in *Bibliographie Wilhelm Dilthey* by V. Herrmann (Berlin/Basel, 1969). Here I have given a translation of the table of contents of the *Collected Works* (*Gesammelte Schriften*, Leipzig etc., 1914) which are thematically arranged, and added a few notes [in brackets].

Vol. I. *Introduction to the Human Studies*

[The first part discusses the relationship between individual human studies; the second gives a historical account of the origin and development of the sciences from the dawn of history to the Renaissance with special reference to the influence and eventual decline of Metaphysics.]

Vol. II. *The World-view and Analysis of Man During the Renaissance and Reformation*

'Conception and Analysis of Man in the Fifteenth and Sixteenth Centuries' (1891–92).
'The Natural System of the Human Studies in the Seventeenth Century' (1892–93).
'The Autonomy of Thought, Constructive Rationalism and Pantheistic Monism in the Seventeenth Century' (1893).
'Giordano Bruno' (1893).
'Developmental Pantheism and its Historical Links with older Pantheistic Systems' (1900).
'When Goethe Studied Spinoza' (*Aus der Zeit der Spinoza-Studien Goethes*) (1894).
'The Function of Anthropology in Sixteenth and Seventeenth Century Culture'.

Vol. III. *Contributions to the History of the German Spirit*

'Leibniz and his Age' (1900).
'Frederick the Great and the German Enlightenment' (1901).
'The Eighteenth Century and the Historical World' (1901).
'The Beginnings of Niebuhr's Historical World-view' (1911).

Vol. IV. *The History of the Young Hegel* (1905)

[The volume also contains other, short treatises on the history of German Idealism, mostly from about 1900.]

Bibliography

Vol. v. *The World of Mind. Introduction to the Philosophy
of Life*, Part I, *Autobiographical Material*

'Preface' [Dilthey's introduction to the subsequent articles] 1911.
'Speech on his Seventieth Birthday' (1903).
'Inaugural Lecture at the Academy of Sciences' (1887).
'The Poetical and Philosophical Movement in Germany 1770–1800'
(Inaugural Lecture at Basel, 1867).

Essays and Treatises

'Study of the History of the Disciplines concerned with Man, Society and the
State'.
'Experience and Thought; A Study of Nineteenth Century epistemological
Logic' (1892).
'The Origins of our Belief in the Reality of the External World' (1890).
'Ideas about a Descriptive and Analytical Psychology' (1894).
'The Study of Individuality' (1895/6).
'The Origin of Hermeneutics' (1900).
'The Nature of Philosophy' (1907).

Vol. vi. *The World of Mind. Introduction to the Philosophy
of Life*, Part II.

'Attempts at an Analysis of Moral Consciousness' (1864).
'The Possibility of a Universal Science of Education' (1888).
'School Reform and the Schoolroom' (1890).
'Poetical Imagination and Madness' (1886).
'The Poet's Imagination' (1887).
'The Three Stages of Modern Aesthetics and its Present-day Task' (1892).
'The Problem of Religion' (1911).

Vol. vii. *The Construction of the Historical World in the
Human Studies*

[Consists of the work of that title (1910) together with earlier studies and later
revisions and additions.]

Vol. viii. *The Theory of World-views*

'The types of World-views and their Development in Metaphysical Systems'
(1911).
'Drafts and articles on the Doctrine of World-views' (1870–1904).

Vol. ix. *Theory of Education.* History and Outline of the
System

[Based on lectures between 1874 and 1894.]

Bibliography

Vol. x. *Systems of Ethics*

[Based on lectures of 1890.]

Vol. xi. *The Origin of Historical Consciousness*

[Early articles and recollections.]

Vol. xii. *Contributions to Prussian History*

'Schleiermacher's Political Outlook and Activities' (1862).
'The Re-organization of the Prussian State (1807–1813)' (1872).
'The Legal Code' [*Das Allgemeine Landrecht*] (1900).

Vol. xiii/1 and Vol. xiii/2.

[First and second halves of the first volume of the Life of Schleiermacher.]

Vol. xiv/1 and Vol. xiv/2.

[First and second halves of the second volume of the Life of Schleiermacher. 'Schleiermacher's System as Philosophy', and 'Schleiermacher's System as Theology'.]

Vols. xv, xvi and xvii. *Contributions to the History of Ideas of the Nineteenth Century*

Vol. xv.

[Contains portraits, biographical sketches and book reviews of poets (for example, Goethe, Tieck, H. Heine and Hölderlin), philosophers (Schopenhauer and Mill) and historians such as Gibbon.]

Vols. xvi and xvii.

[Contain historical, literary and philosophic articles and reviews from news-papers and periodicals.]

Some of Dilthey's most important essays on literature and art were published separately in the following collections:
  Das Erlebnis und die Dichtung (Leipzig and Berlin, 1929).
  Die Grosse Phatansie Dichtung (Göttingen, 1954).
  Von Deutscher Dichtung und Musik (Stuttgart, 1957).

Bibliography

Dilthey's work in translation (listed chronologically)

H. A. Hodges: *W. Dilthey, An Introduction* (London, 1944). Contains fifty pages of translations comprising 29 separate passages from Dilthey's work.

S. A. & W. T. Emery: *The Essence of Philosophy* (North Carolina, 1955). Translation of *Das Wesen der Philosophie* (Vol. v, pp. 339–416).

W. Kluback & M. Weinbaum: *Philosophy of Existence: Introduction to Weltanschauungslehre* (London/Toronto, 1959). Translation of *The Types of World-view and their Development in the Metaphysical Systems* (Vol. viii, pp. 75–118).

W. Kluback: *W. Dilthey's Philosophy of History* (New York, 1956). Contains translation of 'Der Traum' (Vol. viii, pp. 218–24).

P. Gardiner (ed.): *Theories of History* (New York, 1959). Contains 'The Understanding of Other Persons and their Life-expressions' (translation by J. Knehl from Vol. vii, pp. 205–20).

H. P. Rickman: *Meaning in History* (London, 1961). Contains about 100 pages of translations (selected passages from Vol. vii).

Secondary literature

A very full bibliography, including the literally hundreds of works on Dilthey in German may be found in V. Herrmann's *Bibliographie Wilhelm Dilthey*, mentioned above. Here I have concentrated on works in English about Dilthey or containing extensive reference to him, on particularly important German works and works of distinguished authors influenced by him.

Antoni, C. *From History to Sociology* (translated from the Italian by H. V. White), London, 1962.

Aron, R. *German Sociology* (New York, 1964).

Betti, E. *Zur Grundlegung einer allgemeinen Auslegungslehre* (Tübingen, 1954).
  Die Hermeneutik als allgemeine Methode der Geisteswissenschaften (Tübingen, 1962).

Bollnow, O. F. *Dilthey* (Leipzig, 1936).
  Das Verstehen (Mainz, 1949).
  Die Methode der Geisteswissenschaften (Mainz, 1950).
  Die Lebensphilosophie (Berlin, 1958).

Brock, W. *An Introduction to Contemporary German Philosophy* (Cambridge, 1935).

Diwald, H. *W. Dilthey, Epistemologie und Philosophie der Geschichte* (Göttingen, 1963).

Gadamer, H. *Wahrheit & Methode* (Tübingen, 1960).

Gardiner, P. (ed.). *Theories of History* (New York, 1959).

Habermas, J. *Zur Logik der Sozialwissenschaften* (Tübingen, 1967).
  Knowledge and Human Interests (London, 1971) (Translated by J. J. Shapiro).

Bibliography

Hodges, H. A. *W. Dilthey. An Introduction* (London, 1944).
  The Philosophy of W. Dilthey (London, 1952).
Hughes, H. S. *Consciousness and History* (London, 1959).
Krausser, P. *Kritik der endlichen Vernunft (Dilthey's Revolution der allgemeinen Wissenschafts- und Handlungstheorie)* (Frankfurt, 1968).
Mandelbaum, M. *The Problem of Historical Knowledge* (New York, 1938).
Merz, J. T. *A History of European Thought in the Nineteenth Century* (Edinburgh and London, 1896–1914).
Misch, Clara. *Der Junge Dilthey* (Göttingen, 1933).
Misch, G. Hundred page introduction to Vol. v, *Collected Works. Lebensphilosophie and Phenomenologie* (Stuttgart, 1967).
Palmer, R. E. *Hermeneutics: Interpretation theory in Schleiermacher, Dilthey, Heidegger and Gadamar* (Evanston, Ill., 1969).
Rickman, H. P. *Meaning in History. W. Dilthey's Thoughts on History and Society* (London, 1961).
  Understanding and the Human Studies (London, 1967).
Rothacker, E. (ed.). *Briefwechsel zwischen W. Dilthey und Graf Paul York von Wartenburg* (Halle, 1932).
Schutz, A. 'Concept and Theory Formation in the Social Sciences', in *The Problem of Social Reality* (M. Natanson, ed., The Hague, 1962).
Spranger, E. *Lebensformen, geisteswissenschaftliche Psychologie und Ethik der Persönlichkeit* (Halle, 1914).
  Zur Theorie des Verstehens und zur geisteswissenschaftlichen Psychologie (München, 1918).
Weber, M. *The Methodology of the Social Sciences*, ed. E. Shils & H. A. Finch (New York, 1949).
  Essays in Sociology, ed. H. H. Garth & C. W. Wills (New York, 1946).
  The Theory of Economic and Social Organizations, ed. Talcott Parsons (New York, 1947).

Index

acquired structure of mental life, 93, 95, 96, 170, 240-1, 244
anthropology, 23-4, 240-1
autobiography, 213

categories, 15-17, 18, 208-17, 231-45; of development *see* development; of essence, 244; of inner and outer, 173, 192; of meaning, 215, 216 *see also* meaning; of part and whole, 190, 211, 213, 233, 235-6, 244; of power, 217; of purpose 215, 216, 238; of value 215, 216, 238, 242-4
cultural system, 130, 181, 191, 197

development, 92, 96, 135, 205, 214, 235, 244-5

empathy, 181, 226-8
empiricism, 21, 160-1
epistemological point of view, 161
epistemology, 91, 125, 161-2
exegesis, 228, 248, 260
experience, 170, 182, 184-6, 210-2
expressions, 8, 175-6, 218-20

Fichte, 47, 149, 200

Geist 128-9 *see also* mind
'Geisteswissenschaften', 29, 163, 175
Goethe, 54-67, 74, 76, 77, 99-103, 213-14

Hegel, 59, 97, 146, 151, 193-5
hermeneutics, 10-11, 228-31, 246-63
hermeneutic circle, 10, 203, 259, 262
historical approach, 162-3
historical consciousness, 121, 123, 134, 135-6, 145, 194
historical school, 157, 159-60
history, 84, 93, 146, 188-90, 192, 194, 195, 202-60; and biography, 184
human studies, 29, 157-63; methods of, 171, 187-90, 202, 205; philosophic basis of, 157-63; relation of sciences to, *see* sciences; subject matter of, 89, 91, 93, 170, 173-5, 227

idealism of freedom, 149-51
imagination, 82, 227; Goethe's imagination, 98-103; literature of, 78-83
individuals, 176, 181, 197, 201-2, 224-5
individuality, 247, 257; rise of, 195, 225
interpretation, 248-63
intuition, 53-4, 58, 60, 67, 146, 153

Kant, 50-1, 53, 60, 113, 127, 151, 153, 161

Leibniz, 38, 51-2, 153, 243
Lessing, 47-52, 55
life, 136, 145-6, 177-8, 183, 231-2, 236-7, 240; knowledge of, 126-7, 178-80; meaning of, 115; objectifications of, 191-5; philosophy of, 125, 128, 143

meaning, 215, 233, 235-42, *see also* category of meaning; meaning of the world, 131
metaphysics, 122-4, 141-54, 157
mind, 18, 190-5, 221; mind-constructed world, 181, 186, 190, 195-7, 207; objective mind, 191-5, 221-2, 224
Mill, J. S., 113, 129, 160-1

naturalism, 147-8
Nietzsche, 112, 114, 116-18, 129

objective idealism, 151-4

philosophy, 20-3, 105-54; scientific philosophy, 125
poetry, 54, 241
positivism, 113, 129
power, *see* category of power
psychology, 87-97, 174, 239, 241, 263

relativity, 112, 121, 135
Rousseau, 120, 231-2